Northwest Historical Series
XIV

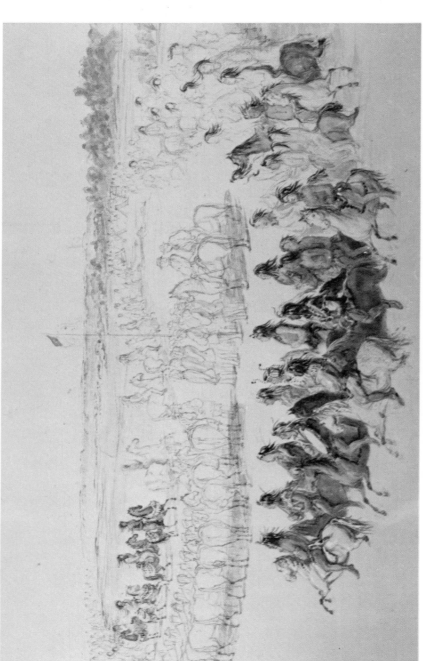

ARRIVAL OF THE NEZ PERCES AT THE WALLA WALLA COUNCIL, MAY 24, 1855
About 5,000 Indians were present, of whom 2,500 per Nez Perces, headed by
Chief Lawyer. The largest Indian Council ever held west of the Rockies.
From a drawing by Gustavus Sohon, courtesy of the Smithsonian Institution.

CHIEF LAWYER
of the
Nez Perce Indians
1796-1876

by
CLIFFORD M. DRURY

THE ARTHUR H. CLARK COMPANY
Glendale, California
1979

Contents

Illustrations

A TRIBUTE TO CHIEF LAWYER

Following receipt of the news of the death of Chief Lawyer at Kamiah on January 3, 1876, Milton Kelly, then editor of the Idaho *Tri-weekly Statesman,* Boise, wrote the following tribute to Chief Lawyer which appeared in the February 3, 1876, issue. Since Kelly had served as an Associate Justice of the Idaho Supreme Court and also as District Judge at Lewiston, he was able to write from his personal knowledge of Lawyer.

We never had much affection for Indian character, but we venture to say if there ever was one whose true life and character is worthy of the pen of the historian, it is Lawyer, the Chief of the Nez Perces.

Sources and Abbreviations

Information used in the writing of this, the first full-length biography of Chief Lawyer, has been gathered from sources scattered from the National Archives in Washington, D.C., to the Oregon Historical Society in Portland.

A major source was the files of the Old Indian Bureau, National Archives, which included the proceedings of the Indian Councils held at Walla Walla, 1855, and at Lapwai, 1863, together with the correspondence and official reports of the several Indian Agents appointed by the Government to serve the Nez Perces, beginning with Dr. Elijah White, 1842, and concluding with John B. Monteith, 1871-77. One of the most important documents used was the obituary of Lawyer written by Monteith and included as Appendix I in this volume.

I have also used an unpublished diary of Robert Newell, who visited Washington, D.C., with Lawyer and three other Nez Perce chiefs in the summer of 1868. Permission to quote from this document has been granted by Chester A. Wiggin of Lewiston, Idaho, a descendant of Robert Newell. Also consulted were the official records of the Presbyterian Church, U.S.A., which included the record book of the First Presbyterian Church of Oregon, organized at the Whitman Mission, August 18, 1838.

Much information was gleaned from the files of such historical periodicals as *Idaho Yesterdays, Oregon Historical Quarterly, Pacific Northwest Quarterly, Portland Oregonian,* and *Washington Historical Quarterly.* Lawyer's name appears many times in each of the eleven volumes I have had published on the history of the Oregon Mission of the American Board, between 1936-1976.

The following abbreviations will be used in footnotes to designate several of my books from which quotations or relevant information will be taken:

F.W.W. — *First White Women Over the Rockies, 3 vols.*, Glendale, Ca., 1963-6.

M. & N.W. — *Marcus and Narcissa Whitman and the Opening of Old Oregon,* 2 vols., Glendale, Ca., 1973.

Spalding — *Henry Harmon Spalding, Pioneer of Old Oregon,* Caldwell, Id., 1936.

S. & S. — *Diaries and Letters of Spalding and Smith,* Glendale, Ca., 1958.

Tepee — *A Tepee in His Front Yard, a Biography of Henry T. Cowley,* Portland, Or., 1949.

Walker — *Nine Years with the Spokane Indians, The Diary of Elkanah Walker, 1838-1848,* Glendale, Ca., 1976.

Other abbreviations used include:

O.I.B. — Old Indian Bureau, National Archives, Washington, D.C.

O.H.Q. — *Oregon Historical Quarterly.*

O.H.S. — Oregon Historical Society, Portland.

H.B.C. — Hudson's Bay Company.

Some titles listed in the Bibliography which are frequently mentioned in footnotes will be abbreviated, for instance — Josephy, *The Nez Perces* for Alvin M. Josephy, Jr., *The Nez Perce Indians and the Opening of the Northwest.*

In order to make it more convenient for those who wish to have a fuller documentation than can be given in this volume, the author has often referred to his earlier writings in the footnotes since these volumes will also be more accessible than the scattered locations of original sources.

In Appreciation

I wish to express my deep appreciation to the following individuals and institutions for help received in the writing of this book:

To the library staffs of the following institutions: Huntington Library and Art Gallery, San Marino, California; Idaho State Historical Society, Boise, Idaho, Dr. Merle W. Wells, State Archivist; National Archives and Records Service, Washington, D.C.; Oregon Historical Society, Portland, Oregon; and the Graduate Theological Union, Berkeley, California.

To those who have supplied pictures used as illustrations in this book: Mrs. Gordon Alcorn, Tacoma, Washington; Smithsonian Institution, Washington, D.C.; Washington State Historical Society, Tacoma, Washington; Whitman College, Walla Walla, Washington; and the Spokane Public Library, Spokane, Washington. And to Andy Dagosta for his map showing the reservation boundaries of 1855 and 1863.

To the following members of the National Park Service: Erwin Thompson, Historian, Denver, Colorado; Robert L. Morris, Superintendent, and Douglas J. Riley, Historian, Nez Perce National Historical Park, Spalding, Idaho; Larry Waldron, Historian, formerly with the Whitman National Historic Site, Walla Walla, Washington; and to the British Museum, London, for two believed-to-be hitherto unpublished photographs of Lawyer.

To those who have supplied other needed information: Carroll E. Brock, Orofino, Idaho; Father Edward J. Kowrach, Verndale, Washington; David and Beatrice Miles (Nez Perces), Spalding, Idaho; and Angus Wilson (Nez Perce), Kamiah, Idaho.

And to those who have read my manuscript in whole or in part and who have made corrections and suggestions: Rev. E. Paul Hovey, Portland, Oregon; Dr. D. G. Stewart, Pasadena, California; Drs. Robert

H. Ruby and John A. Brown, Moses Lake, Washington. Some acknowl-
edgments will be given in footnotes or in the captions under the
illustrations.

Without their individual and combined help, this book could not
have been written. I thank you.

CLIFFORD M. DRURY
Pasadena, California

Chronology of Lawyer's Life
and Some Pertinent Contemporary Events

1796 — Lawyer born. Son of Twisted Hair, Nez Perce Chief who welcomed Lewis and Clark, and a Flathead mother. Thus, Lawyer was bilingual, speaking both Nez Perce and Flathead.

1831 — Lawyer inspires four Nez Perces to go to St. Louis in search of Christian teachers.

1832 — Lawyer wounded in left hip at Battle of Pierre's Hole. Wound never healed.

1836 — Whitmans arrive in Oregon and settle at Waiilatpu, and the Spaldings found a mission at Lapwai.

1838 — Four more couples arrive to reenforce the American Board's Mission — the Eellses, Grays, Smiths, and Walkers. Lawyer becomes Smith's teacher at Kamiah and learns English.

1838 — Chiefs Joseph and Timothy baptized and join the Mission Church.

1840 — Missionary efforts to settle and "civilize" the Indians precipitate a clash of cultures. Big Thunder, a Nez Perce te-wat or medicine man, causes trouble for Spalding. Ute-sin-male-cum and Looking Glass force the Smiths to leave Kamiah in 1841.

1842 — Whitman leaves for Boston. Dr. Elijah White persuades the Nez Perces to adopt a code of laws and appoints Ellis as Head Chief.

1847 — The Whitmans and twelve others are killed at Waiilatpu in November.

1848 — Cayuse War. Ellis dies and Lawyer begins his service as Head Chief.

1855 — Gov. I. I. Stevens calls Walla Walla Council; 5,000 Indians, including about 2,500 Nez Perces, attended. Lawyer protects

Stevens. The Nez Perce Reservation containing about 23,666 square miles established.

1855 — Hostilities against Americans started by Yakima Chiefs — Kam-i-ah-kan, Owhi, and Qualchan. Again Lawyer protects Stevens.

1857 — Col. E. J. Steptoe defeated in May. Lawyer sends aid.

1858 — Col. George Wright defeats the rebellious Indians at Spokane; hangs fourteen ringleaders; captures and slaughters 700 Indian horses.

1861 — Lawyer accepts amendments to 1855 Treaty.

1863 — Lapwai Council. The area size of the 1855 Reservation reduced by 95%. Lawyer and 51 other Chiefs sign; Old Joseph and four others refuse.

1865 — Lawyer writes to President Lincoln protesting the Government's broken promises.

1868 — Lawyer and three other Nez Perce Chiefs go to Washington. They agree to amend the 1863 Treaty.

1871 — Lawyer baptized by Spalding; becomes first elder of Kamiah Church.

1875 — Lawyer ends his service as Head Chief after about twenty-five years.

1876 — Lawyer dies on January 3 at age 80. Eulogized as "The noblest man in the Nez Perce tribe."

Introduction

"Lawyer" was the nickname bestowed on Hol-lol-sote-tote,[1] a Nez Perce warrior, when he was about thirty-five years old by some Rocky Mountain trappers during the early 1830s. The nickname carried a compliment. Frances Fuller Victor, author of H. H. Bancroft's *History of Oregon*, met Lawyer in the summer of 1873 at Lapwai, Idaho. She wrote that his name was a "sobriquet applied to him by the mountain men on account of his argumentative powers and general shrewdness by which he obtained great influence with his people and with white people."[2]

The earliest discovered reference to the name Lawyer is found in *The Rocky Mountain Journal of William Marshall Anderson and the West in 1834.*[3] Anderson, who spent some time during the summer of 1834 traveling in the Rockies, became acquainted with many of the mountain men and some of the Nez Perces. In the ethnological notes at the end of his Journal, he wrote: "Ol-lot-coat-sum, the talker — The Whites knew him by the name of Lawyer."[4]

These early evaluations of Lawyer's astuteness and eloquence were confirmed by his white contemporaries of later years. Hazard Stevens, in his life of his father, Governor Isaac I. Stevens who presided over the great Indian Council held at Walla Walla in June 1855, called Lawyer, "an Indian Solon."[5] And Judge George C. Hough, who sat in council with Lawyer at Lapwai in June 1867, wrote that Lawyer was a "consummate diplomat."[6]

---

[1] This spelling of Lawyer's Indian name is taken from the Lawyer monument on the campus of Whitman College, Walla Walla, Wash. There are other variations in spelling.   [2] Bancroft, *History of Oregon*, I, p. 135.

[3] Dale L. Morgan and Eleanor Towles, eds., Huntington Lby., San Marino, Ca., 1967.   [4] *Op. cit.*, p. 233.   [5] Stevens, *Stevens*, II, p. 35.

[6] Hough to Indian Commissioner Taylor, June 27, 1867. O.I.B. (*see* Abbreviations).

The life of Lawyer during the years 1830-1876, is so closely inter-twined with the political, historical, and cultural history of the Nez Perce tribe that one could say that his life story reflects the history of his tribe during these years.

According to the testimony of his descendants, Lawyer was the son of Twisted Hair, the friendly Nez Perce chief who welcomed and be-friended Lewis and Clark in the fall of 1805. According to the best available evidence, Lawyer was born in 1796. Thus he would have been eight or nine years old when the explorers arrived in the Nez Perce country. The feeling of friendliness toward the Whites, exemplified by his father, was deeply ingrained in Lawyer. Throughout his life, he was firmly convinced that the destiny of his people could best be served through friendship with the Whites.

Lawyer's interest in Christianity, the white man's religion, began in the spring of 1830. While in the Spokane country, he heard one of the native youths, known as Spokane Garry, read from the Bible. Since Lawyer had knowledge of the Spokane or Flathead language from his mother, he was able to understand Garry. Garry had spent four years in an Anglican Mission school at Red River, on the site of present-day Winnipeg. There he had been baptized and had learned to read, write, and speak English.

Lawyer was envious. He, too, wanted the Bible. When he returned to his people in the Kamiah Valley, in what is now northern Idaho, he so aroused their interest that they sent a delegation of four to St. Louis, in the summer of 1831, to get Christian missionaries and the Bible. The wide publicity given in the religious press of the East to this incident sparked the thrust of the Protestant missionary movement into the Pacific Northwest, then known as Oregon.

Lawyer was one of those who welcomed the five members of the Whitman-Spalding party at the American Fur Company's Rendezvous held on the Green River in the Rockies in the summer of 1836. The members of this mission party had been sent to Oregon by the Amer-ican Board of Commissioners for Foreign Missions,[7] which had its headquarters in Boston.

The coming of the missionaries made a deep and lasting impression on Lawyer. While he helped them to learn the Nez Perce language,

---

[7] Throughout most of the 19th century, both the Congregational and Presbyterian denominations classified missionary work for non-English speaking groups within the United States as "foreign missions."

they in turn taught him English and even to read and write in his native tongue. John B. Monteith, who served as Indian Agent at Lapwai in the 1870s, wrote: "Lawyer was among the first to read and write the Nez Perce language, and, in fact, was the only one who could do so with any degree of correctness." [8]

The missionaries were the advance agents of the white man's civilization. Had they never gone to Oregon, still, with the arrival of the great Oregon immigrations of 1843 and following years, there would have come the inevitable clash of cultures. The Indians were doomed to have the white man's civilization forced upon them. The pioneer efforts of the missionaries to educate and civilize the Nez Perces made it easier for them to make the necessary adjustments when the white men arrived in overwhelming numbers. Lawyer was in full sympathy with the policies pursued by the missionaries.

Another important change imposed on the Nez Perce nation was the appointment of a Head Chief and the imposition of a code of eleven laws by Indian Agent Dr. Elijah White in 1842. White was the first U.S. Agent to be appointed for Oregon. With the approval of the other chiefs, White appointed Ellis to be the first Head Chief of the tribe. Ellis, like Spokane Garry, had spent several years at the Red River school and had, therefore, a fair knowledge of English. Up to this date, each of the approximately fifty bands of Nez Perces had had its own headman. There was no central tribal organization with a Head Chief as its supreme leader. Such an office was the white man's innovation, made necessary by the need of having someone who could represent the entire nation in its dealings with government officials.

Following the death of Ellis in the fall of 1847, Lawyer gradually assumed leadership of the tribe and was recognized as being Head Chief by the Whites, even though there is no record of a Nez Perce council being held to elect him. The first recorded meeting of the Nez Perce chiefs held when Lawyer was designated as Head Chief was during the Walla Walla Council of June 1855.

Lawyer led his people in the negotiations with the U.S. Government of four treaties, two major — 1855 and 1863 — and two of lesser importance — 1861 and 1868. Each time Lawyer signed first as Head Chief.

The Nez Perces were sharply divided by the Lapwai Treaty of 1863 which, by the government's insistance, reduced the size of the 1855

---

[8] From Monteith's obituary of Lawyer. *See* Appendix i.

Reservation by about 95% or to an area containing 1,187 square miles. This treaty was signed by Lawyer and fifty-one other chiefs, all of whom were unaffected by the boundary changes, except Chief Timothy, who also signed.

Chief Joseph (sometimes referred to as Old Joseph to distinguish him from his better known son, also called Joseph), and four other chiefs refused to sign the 1863 Treaty since Joseph's beloved Wallowa Valley and some areas along the Snake and Salmon Rivers had been excluded from the boundaries of the reduced reservation. Old Joseph refused to leave his homelands and move onto the new reservation.

Old Joseph died in 1871 and was succeeded in the chieftainship of his band by his eldest son who followed his father's policies of noncooperation with the government. This led to the Chief Joseph uprising of 1877, the centennial of which was marked by extensive ceremonies in northern Idaho and western Montana in 1977. An understanding of the events connected with the negotiations of the treaties of 1855 and 1863, as experienced by Chief Lawyer, is needed for an understanding of the reasons which led to the Chief Joseph uprising of 1877.

Young Joseph has often been eulogized as a military genius and has frequently been referred to as a War Chief. Indeed one of the best known biographies of Joseph, which has sold over 25,000 copies, was called *War Chief Joseph*.[9] The consensus of recent scholarship is that Joseph was more of a Camp Chief than a War Chief. In contrast to the extensive attention which has been given to Chief Joseph, Chief Lawyer has almost been forgotten. Indeed, he is remembered more by his critics than by his friends. Prior to the publication of this, his first full-length biography, only a few short articles about Lawyer have appeared in either historical magazines or in the public press.[10]

---

[9] This work by Helen Addison Howard and Dan L. McGrath was first published by Caxton Printers, Caldwell, Idaho, in 1941. It was reprinted in 1942, 1952, and 1958, making a total of over 6,200 copies. The University of Nebraska's Bison Book paperback edition reprint of the 1958 edition sold over 25,000 copies up to January 1978. The text was rewritten by Howard and a new edition called *Saga of Chief Joseph* was brought out by Caxton with hard covers in 1965. According to the author, the total number of copies of this biography sold between 1941-77 was over 35,000. The large sale of the first title of this biography did much to magnify Joseph's reputation as a War Chief.

[10] An article by J. F. Santee appeared in the *Washington Hist. Qtly.*, Vol. 25

If Joseph is known as the War Chief of the Nez Perces, Lawyer, because of his consistent policy of cooperation with the Government, should be remembered as the Peace Chief. Although Lawyer died a little more than a year before the Chief Joseph uprising began, his influence upon his tribe was so enduring that about three-fourths of the Nez Perces refrained from going on the war path. This fact in itself is an eloquent tribute to Lawyer's consistent advocacy of the necessity of the Nez Perces to cooperate with the government and to obey the white man's laws.

Lawyer served as Head Chief for about twenty-five years, or until he was seventy-nine years old. He served during the critical years when the Nez Perces were making the transition from a semi-nomadic way of life to becoming an agrarian culture. The story of his life becomes a commentary on the history of the Nez Perces. By virtue of his intelligence, his wise leadership, and his many years of distinguished service, Chief Lawyer towers above all of his Nez Perce contemporaries. His story deserves to be told and remembered.

CLIFFORD M. DRURY
Pasadena, California

(Jan. 1934), pp. 37 ff.; C. M. Drury's, "I, the Lawyer," in the *New York Westerners,* Vol. 7, No. 1 (May 1960); and an article by Mylie Lawyer, a great-granddaughter of Chief Lawyer, "Chief Termed Noblest Man," in the Lewiston, Idaho, *Tribune,* June 12, 1935.

CHAPTER ONE

Birth, Ancestry, and Early Life

When was Lawyer born? The exact date is unknown as the Nez Perces had no calendar before the white man came. The inscription on Lawyer's tombstone at Kamiah states that he died on "January 3, 1876, about 74 yrs. of age." This would place his birth in 1802. Indian Agent John B. Monteith, who knew Lawyer intimately during the last four years of his life, wrote in his obituary of Lawyer that the chief was the "last of the tribe who remembers Lewis and Clark and their journey through this section of country." [1] If Lawyer had been born in 1802, he would have been too young to remember the arrival of the explorers in 1805 or their departure the next spring.

When J. F. Santee was gathering information for his article on Chief Lawyer, which appeared in the January 1934, issue of the *Washington Historical Quarterly*, he interviewed Miss Mylie Lawyer, who is living at the time of this writing at Lapwai, Idaho. Miss Lawyer is a third generation descendant of Chief Lawyer, being the daughter of Corbett Lawyer, the son of Archie, the son of Chief Lawyer. According to Mylie, her great-grandfather was born about 1800.

The most reliable witness to Lawyer's age is John B. Monteith, who served as Indian Agent at Lapwai from February 6, 1871, to March 3, 1879. Writing from Lapwai on February 17, 1872, to the Commissioner of Indian Affairs, Washington, D.C., Monteith stated: "Lawyer is now about 78 years old. . . He has several times told me of the first appearance of Whites among them when he was about 12 years of age." [2] According to this, Lawyer would have been born in 1793. In another letter to the Commissioner, dated March 14, 1874, Monteith

---

[1] *See* Monteith's obituary of Lawyer, App. I.   [2] Original letter in O.I.B. files.

referred to Lawyer as being "nearly 80 years old." This would have put his birth in 1794. And finally, in the excellent biographical sketch in Lawyer's obituary, Monteith states that the Chief was eighty years old at the time of his death.

Therefore, according to this last date given by Monteith, Lawyer was born in 1796. This is the date I have accepted. Monteith also noted that Lawyer "must have been eight to nine years old when Lewis and Clark passed through the Kamiah country, and that "the impression made upon his mind remained until the day of his death."

Frances F. Victor, writing in Bancroft's *History of Oregon*, confirms the family tradition and Monteith's account, by stating: "He [Lawyer], was the son of the chief who took charge of the horses of Lewis and Clark while these explorers visited the Lower Columbia." [3] Since Victor interviewed Lawyer at Lapwai in 1873, we may assume that she had reported what he had told her.

The Journals of Lewis and Clark contain several references to Twisted Hair, the Nez Perce chief who cared for the white men's horses during the winter of 1805-06 and who rendered assistance in other ways.[4] Additional evidence supporting the claim that Lawyer was the son of Chief Twisted Hair, is found in Thomas Donaldson's *Idaho of Yesterday*. Donaldson, referring to Lawyer, wrote: "The old Indian was a son of the Nez Perce [chief] with whom Lewis and Clark left their horses when they started toward the coast." [5]

According to Monteith, Lawyer was born "on the south fork of the Clearwater River." This stream branches off of the Middle Fork at present-day Kooskia, Idaho. Lawyer had at least one younger brother. Some critics of Lawyer have referred in a disparaging way to the fact that he was not of "royal blood," since his mother was a Flathead. Lucullus V. McWhorter, in his *Hear Me, My Chiefs*, advances the theory that Lawyer's father was a Flathead and his mother a Nez Perce.[6] Such a theory denies that Twisted Hair was Lawyer's father. All reliable evidence contradicts this theory.

The Nez Perces belong to the Sahaptin language family while the Flatheads spoke Salish as did the Spokane Indians. As a child, Lawyer grew up learning both Indian languages, as previously mentioned.

[3] *Op. cit.*, I, p. 133.

[4] Bernard DeVoto, *The Journals of Lewis and Clark* (Boston, 1953), pp. 240 ff.

[5] *Op. cit.*, Caxton Press, 1941, p. 23.   [6] *Op. cit.*, p. 101.

What did Lawyer's Indian name, Hol-lol-sote-tote, mean? According to an unverified statement in *Idaho Yesterdays*, it meant "Shadow of the Mountains." [7] A more reasonable explanation is that given by Monteith in his obituary of Lawyer. He stated that the name meant "The bat that flies in the daytime." Nez Perce friends have told me that they do not know the meaning of the first two syllables of Lawyer's Indian name but that the last two refer to the Nez Perce word for bat, "hu-tsoots." This is similar to the way that Santee spelled the last two syllables of the Indian name, "hu-tsot." [8]

The strange references to a bat that flies in the daytime may be a reference to the Nez Perce belief in the existence of a guardian spirit for each individual, called Wy-ya-kin. Kate McBeth, who spent some thirty-six years as a Presbyterian missionary to the Nez Perces, beginning in 1880, wrote:

> When a child was seven, eight, or ten years old, he or she was sent off to the mountains alone, to get his or her "Wy-ya-kin," and with it a new name. The child was to remain there night as well as day — having nothing to eat — until some animal or bird would come and speak to the child. Then he was free to return. A feather of that species of bird, or a tail of the kind of animal that talked to him, was to be kept and worn throughout life as a symbol of his attending spirit.[9]

Possibly Lawyer, as a small boy, had this experience, and when he returned was asked what he had seen. He could have replied: "I saw a bat that flies by daytime." Therefore his name — Hol-lol-sote-tote. For the sake of clarity and uniformity, I will be using the name "Lawyer" rather than his Indian name, except when the latter is used in quotations.

LAWYER AND THE NEZ PERCE DELEGATION OF 1831

George Simpson, acting as Governor of the great Hudson's Bay Company's commercial empire which then included what is now western Canada and the Old Oregon country,[10] made a tour of the Pacific

---

[7] *Op. cit.*, Vol. IV, 3 (Fall 1960), p. 6. No reason for this interpretation was given. [8] Santee in *Washington Hist. Qtly.*, Vol. 25 (Jan. 1934), p. 37.

[9] McBeth, *Nez Perces*, p. 266.

[10] The term "Old Oregon" is commonly used to indicate the area which lies west of the Continental Divide and north of the present-day California-Oregon border.

Northwest, in 1824-25. He was under orders from the Governing Committee of the H.B.C. in London to select some Indian boys and send them to the Anglican Mission school at Red River, in central Canada.

On his way back to Red River, Simpson stopped at Spokane House [11] where he persuaded a chief of the Kootenai tribe and a chief of the Spokanes to let him take their twelve-year-old sons with him to the Red River school. Each lad was named after his tribe and then after a member of the Governing Committee of the H.B.C. in London — Kootenai Pelly and Spokane Garry. The latter was destined to play a prominent role in the history of his tribe. Both lads were baptized at the school on June 24, 1827, being the first natives from the Pacific Slope of the United States to have received baptism from a Protestant minister.

In the fall of 1829, Simpson returned to the Oregon country, taking with him the two Indian boys who by that time had learned to read, write, and speak English to a somewhat limited degree. The archives of the H.B.C. contain only a few fragments of what was once an extensive series of journals of each of the Company's forts in the Old Oregon country. Among the extant records is a part of the Fort Colville Journal which covers the period April 12, 1830, to April 3, 1831.[12] During this time, Francis Heron was Chief Trader.

Heron's entry for April 14, 1830, carries the following reference to Spokane Garry: "Last evening all the Indian Chiefs about the place were admitted into the Gentlemen's Mess Hall and a speech was made to them, repeated by Spokane Garry in a satisfactory manner." Heron then listed seven tribes which were represented, including the Nez Perces. All spoke the Flathead tongue except the Nez Perces.

In all probability Lawyer was present at this meeting, although Heron did not mention his name nor that of any of the other chiefs.

Following the settlement of the border question with Great Britain in 1846, the states of Washington, Oregon, Idaho, and the western parts of Montana and Wyoming were carved out of Old Oregon. Prior to 1846, therefore, Oregon or Old Oregon refers to the whole Pacific Northwest.

[11] Spokane House was located on the Spokane River about ten miles to the northwest of the present city of Spokane. The post was established in 1810 and closed in 1821 when Fort Colville, further to the north, was established on the Columbia River.

[12] I had the privilege of going through the H.B.C. records in London in the summer of 1966, at which time I located the item quoted. The H.B.C. records have since been moved to its headquarters in Winnipeg.

Confirmation of such a visit to Spokane by Lawyer at this time is found in a letter which the Rev. Asa B. Smith wrote to the American Board on August 27, 1839, from Kamiah. Smith, who was a member of the 1838 reenforcement sent out to Oregon by the American Board, spent the winter with his wife at the Whitman station at Waiilatpu. They then opened a station at Kamiah in the spring of 1839. Smith enlisted the help of Lawyer, whose home was at Kamiah, to tutor him in the Nez Perce language.

In this letter of August 1839, Smith wrote:

I have recently been making inquiries of the natives concerning the origin of their notions concerning the Christian religion & the object of those who went to the States, as it was said, in search of Christian teachers. . . About ten years ago a young Spokan, who goes by the name of Spokane Garry, who had been at the Red River School, returned. My teacher, the Lawyer,[13] saw him & learned from him respecting the Sabbath & some other things which he had heard at the school. . . He returned & communicated what he had heard to his people. Soon after which, six individuals set out for the States, in search as he says of Christian teachers. Two of this number turned back in the mountains, & the other four went on & arrived at St. Louis.[14]

Smith failed to explain that since Lawyer spoke both the Nez Perce and Spokane languages, he was able to understand Spokane Garry. Lawyer's statement that Garry had returned from the Red River school "about ten years ago" harmonizes with the fact that Garry had returned in the fall of 1829.

While gathering material for my biography of Henry Harmon Spalding in 1934, I interviewed the late Corbett Lawyer, grandson of Chief Lawyer, who told me that his grandfather's report of what Garry had said about the white man's religion had been received too late in the spring of 1830 for action to be taken that year. The Nez Perces knew that if any of their number were to travel to St. Louis, they would have to go with the caravan of the American Fur Company on its return trip from the Rocky Mountain Rendezvous. Since the Rendezvous was usually held during the first weeks of July, and since it would take the

---

[13] Even as Lawyer usually referred to himself as "I, the Lawyer," so his white contemporaries often called him "the Lawyer."

[14] Drury, S. & S., p. 107. Drury, M. & N.W. Vol. I: pp. 28 ff., gives a detailed account of the Nez Perce delegation to St. Louis in 1831.

Nez Perces about a month to travel from their country to the Rendez-vous, time was too short. However, Lawyer's report was discussed around their campfires, especially when the Nez Perces met their allies, the Flatheads, in the buffalo country of western Montana, during the following months.

By the spring of 1831, it was agreed that a delegation from the two tribes should attend the Rendezvous and then travel with the caravan on its return trip to St. Louis. Six Indians started out on this journey but two turned back. The other four reached St. Louis in the fall of 1831 where they called on General William Clark, then Superintendent of Indian Affairs for the territory lying west of the Mississippi River. This was the same Clark who, with Meriwether Lewis, had passed through the Nez Perce country in the fall of 1805 and the spring of 1806. Although handicapped by the lack of a good interpreter, the Nez Perces in a round-about way made known their wishes to Clark. They wanted Christian teachers and the white man's Bible.

RESPONSE OF THE PROTESTANT CHURCHES

It so happened that during the time the Nez Perces were in St. Louis, an educated half-Wyandot Indian from Sandusky, Ohio, William Walker, called on General Clark to make arrangements for the removal of members of his tribe to some reservation west of the Missouri River. Walker's call on General Clark came a few days after the death of one of the Nez Perces, called Speaking Eagle, who was buried from the Roman Catholic cathedral in St. Louis on October 31, 1831, and before the death of a second Nez Perce, Ka-ou-pu,[15] who was buried on November 17.

Clark told Walker about the arrival of the four Indians from west of the "Stony Mountains," and that one had died. The other three were then in Clark's home, one of whom was seriously ill. Moved by curios-ity, Walker entered the room where the sick Indian lay. He was at-tracted by the deformed skull of the man, which had been caused by pressure applied to the forehead in infancy when the bones were pliable, thus depressing the forehead and making the head wedge-

---

[15] Buried from the Catholic Cathedral on Nov. 17, 1831, where he is listed as a Flathead. McBeth, *Nez Perces*, p. 30, states that his mother was a Flathead; his father, Nez Perce.

shaped. This was a custom followed in that day by some of the natives who lived along the Columbia River. Walker made a sketch of the head, later acknowledging that his drawing was somewhat exaggerated.

After returning to his home in Sandusky, Walker, for some unknown reason, waited more than a year before writing on January 19, 1833, to his friend Gabriel P. Disosway, a Methodist merchant in New York City, telling him what he had heard and seen in St. Louis regarding the mission of the Nez Perce Indians. Walker enclosed with his letter his drawing of the deformed head of the sick Indian.

Disosway, who was much interested in the Methodist Missionary Society, was so stirred by Walker's account that he sent the letter and the sketch to the editor of the New York *Christian Advocate and Journal and Zion's Herald.* The editor was likewise impressed, so much so that he devoted nearly one-half of the front page of his issue of March 1, 1833, to printing Walker's letter and reproducing the sketch. The paper's pages were the size of most modern metropolitan dailies.

The publication of this "Macedonian Appeal" [16] of the Nez Perces created a sensation in Protestant missionary circles throughout the East. The story was copied in an abbreviated form in other religious periodicals. Never before in the history of American Christianity had a delegation arrived from a foreign land or from a non-Christian group within this country petitioning for Christian missionaries and the Bible. The response of the churches was as quick and as generous as circumstances then permitted.

So great was the impact of the Walker-Disosway article that within seven years, from 1834 to and including 1840, the Methodist Missionary Society and the American Board of Commissioners for Foreign Missions sent ninety-one men, women, and children to Old Oregon. When the five couples, who went out to Oregon on an independent basis in 1839 and 1840, were added to this number, the total came to 101.[17]

Dr. Ray Billington, a well-known authority on the history of America's western frontier, has written: "In all American history no single letter accomplished such impossible wonders as that penned on January

---

[16] Refers to Paul's vision, *Acts 16, 9:* "Come over into Macedonia and help us."

[17] By a curious coincidence, this number almost equalled the passenger list of the *Mayflower* which carried 102 Pilgrims to Cape Cod in 1620. Some contemporary religious writers, noting this, sometimes referred to the missionaries as being the "Pilgrim colony" in Oregon.

19, 1833, by an educated Wyandote Indian named William Walker to his friend Gabriel P. Disosway. . . For that letter set off a chain reaction which added the Pacific Northwest to the United States." [18]

The facts indicate that Lawyer was the connecting link between Spokane Garry and the Nez Perce delegation to St. Louis of 1831. What if Lawyer had not gone to Spokane in the spring of 1830 where he heard Spokane Garry read from the Bible? What if there had been no Nez Perce delegation to St. Louis in 1831? If there had been a failure in either case, there would have been no westward thrust of Protestant missionaries in 1834-40 and the history of the Pacific Northwest would have been much different from what it proved to be.

THE BATTLE OF PIERRE'S HOLE, 1832

In his earlier years, Lawyer frequently accompanied Nez Perce hunting parties in their excursions after buffalo in what is now western Montana. On these occasions the Nez Perces would often clash with their hereditary enemies, the Blackfeet Indians. According to his great-granddaughter, Mylie Lawyer, Lawyer was wounded several times in these encounters.[19] None of these skirmishes was as serious as that which took place at Pierre's Hole, in what is now called the Teton Basin of Idaho, on July 18, 1832.

It appears that a party of about forty American trappers with their Nez Perce and Flathead allies had just left a rendezvous, which was held that year near what is now Driggs, Idaho, when they unexpectedly met a band of Blackfeet Indians. The Blackfeet took refuge in a swamp along Trail Creek and quickly threw up a rude barricade of logs. The trappers, with their Indian allies, attacked. In the fight that followed, six white men, one half-breed, seven Nez Perce or Flathead Indians, and nine Blackfeet were killed. The conflict broke off before dark on th 18th when the Americans withdrew. During the night, the Blackfeet fled.[20]

Several were wounded on both sides during the engagement, including Lawyer who received either an iron arrowhead or a musket ball in

---

[18] From "A Letter to the Editor that Got Unexpected Results," *Together,* a Methodist publication, Chicago, Nov. 1959.

[19] Mylie Lawyer's article in Lewiston, Id., *Tribune,* June 12, 1955.

[20] Willard C. Harden's article in *Idaho Yesterdays,* Vol. 16, No. 2 (Summer 1972), pp. 2 ff., gives a fine account of this battle.

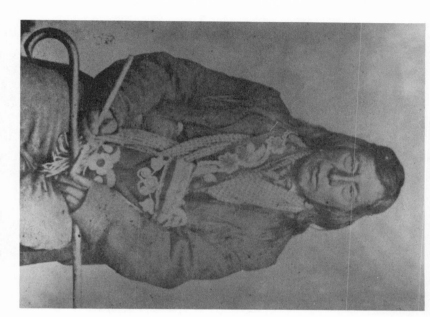

Lawyer with his Cane and Peace Pipe
Possibly in the early 1860s. His 1832 hip wound
received in battle with the Blackfeet
obliged him to use a cane.
From the original at Whitman College

Chief Lawyer
A photograph taken in Washington, D.C., in 1868.
From the original, believed to be unpublished.
Courtesy of the Blackmore Collection, British Museum.

JUNE 3, 1855   JUNE 3, 1930

HOL-LOL-SOTE-TOTE

HERE WERE ENCAMPED FROM MAY 24 TO JUNE 12, 1855, TWO THOUSAND
INDIANS OF THE NEZ PERCE TRIBE, WITH THEIR FAMOUS CHIEF HOL-LOL-SOTE-TOTE,
LAWYER, ATTENDING THE GREAT COUNCIL CALLED BY GOVERNOR STEVENS.
DISCOVERING A PLOT OF THE OTHER INDIAN TRIBES TO KILL THE AMERICANS,
CHIEF LAWYER MOVED HIS LODGE AND FAMILY BEFORE DAWN ON JUNE 9 TO THE
WHITE MEN'S CAMP, THEREBY PROTECTING THEM FROM ATTACK.
THE CLASS OF 1930 PRESENTS THIS TABLET IN HONOR OF CHIEF LAWYER,
THE WISE, MAGNANIMOUS AND BRAVE LEADER OF A NOBLE PEOPLE.

Lawyer Plaque at Walla Walla
On the Whitman College campus.
To commemorate Laywer's moving
his lodge to the vicinity of the
tent of Governor I. I. Stevens.

An Early Portrait of Chief Lawyer
From the original presented to
the Spokane Public Library by the
Rev. E. J. Connor, Nez Perce preacher.

his left hip.[21] Not being able to extract the foreign object, Lawyer was afflicted with an open wound for the remainder of his life. As will be noted, several of his white contemporaries refer to the unhealed wound in his side. He was obliged to use a cane when walking.

Another Nez Perce wounded in this battle was Tack-en-sua-tis, who was wounded in the abdomen. Because of the long festering nature of this wound, he was nicknamed "Rotten Belly" by the mountain men. In time his wound healed but the nickname persisted. As will be noted, he figures in the Lawyer story.

According to Mylie Lawyer's account of her great-grandfather, he was unusually proud of one item that reminded him of his warrior days. That was a scalp "with long glossy black hair" which he had taken from one of his Blackfoot victims. Perhaps this trophy had been secured at the battle of Pierre's Hole.

Miss Lawyer also stated in her article in the *Lewiston Tribune* that Lawyer was once wounded in a battle with the Shoshone Indians at what is now known as Thousand Springs in southern Idaho, but no date is indicated. Another experience was related by Miss Lawyer: "On a trip to the Montana country, Lawyer encountered a large grizzly bear on the trail, and in the hand-to-hand fight, had his arm muscles torn by its sharp claws. The wound was slow in healing and caused no little pain and discomfort."

21 A rather obscure photograph in the files of the Nez Perce National Historical Park, Spalding, Id., shows Lawyer carrying a cane in his right hand which indicates that he had been wounded in his left hip.

CHAPTER TWO

The Early Mission Period, 1834-1841

The life of Chief Lawyer was so closely intertwined with the activities and policies of the Protestant missionaries who settled in the Oregon country that a knowledge of their history is essential to an understanding of his.

THE COMING OF THE METHODISTS, 1834

The first to respond to the Macedonian appeal of the Nez Perces were the Methodists who, in 1834, sent the Rev. Jason Lee and his nephew, the Rev. Daniel Lee, and three laymen overland to Oregon. They were the first Protestant missionaries to cross the Rockies. They traveled across the country as far west as a site on the Snake River, near present-day Pocatello, Idaho, with Captain Nathaniel Wyeth, an independent fur trader. There Captain Wyeth established Fort Hall which, two years later, became an outpost of the Hudson's Bay Company.

According to J. F. Santee, who interviewed Lawyer's grandson, Corbett Lawyer, in 1933, a party of Nez Perces including Lawyer met the Lee party at Fort Hall.[1] However, Jason Lee, in his diary, states that he first met the Nez Perces at the Rendezvous. Here for the first time the Nez Perces were seeing some tangible results of the appeal made by the delegation that went to St. Louis in 1831.

Lee's diary, covering the events of the days spent at the Rendezvous, contains the following entries:[2]

June 21, 1834. Have had a visit from some 10 or 12 Pierced Nose

---

[1] *Washington Hist. Qtly.*, Vol. 25 (Jan. 1934), p. 39. Also, Carey, *Oregon*, Vol. I, p. 287.   [2] *O.H.Q.*, Vol. XVII (1916), pp. 139-40.

[i.e., Nez Perces] and 1 or 2 Flat Heads to-day and conversed a little with them through an interpreter.

Sunday, June 22 . . . as many Indians as could enter our tent, came to see us and we told them our object in coming, showed them the Bible, told them some of the commandments and how they were given, to all of which they listened with the utmost attention and then replied that it was all good.

On this particular Sunday, some of the men of Wyeth's party wanted to purchase some meat from the Indians, but they refused to sell because it was Sunday. Lee noted in his diary: "Thus while the whites who have been educated in a Christian land pay no regard to the Sabbath, these poor savages who have at most only some vague idea of the Christian religion respect the Sabbath of the Lord, our God."

The strictness with which the Nez Perces observed Sunday by refraining from trading or traveling on that day reflects a common Protestant emphasis of that time. According to the report given by Lawyer to Smith in 1839, Spokane Garry had stressed the importance of observing the Sabbath, as Sunday was then called.[3] This Garry had learned from his teachers at the Red River Mission school, where the Anglican ministers on duty represented the evangelical branch of that denomination. As far as the Protestant missionaries who went to Old Oregon were concerned, "remembering the Sabbath day" was an outward sign of being a Christian.

On Monday, June 23, still at the Rendezvous, Lee wrote in his diary: "Heard the Indians in one lodge praying and singing, went to listen to them but they were just closing as we approached. How encouraging to see these red men thus religiously inclined."

Although the Nez Perces were eager to have the Lees settled with them, Jason Lee decided that it would be best to consult with Dr. John McLoughlin, then Chief Factor of the Hudson's Bay Company's Oregon headquarters at Fort Vancouver, located on the Columbia River, opposite present-day Portland. This was done and McLoughlin advised the Lees to settle in the Willamette Valley, to the great disappointment of the Nez Perces. About seventy additional Methodist missionaries, including men, women, and children, arrived in Oregon in 1837 and 1840, all going by sea around South America. The Methodist Mission in Oregon lasted only ten years, being closed in 1844.

---

[3] Strictly speaking, Saturday is the Sabbath, but the term was generally used to refer to Sunday by American Protestants during these years under review.

THE EXPLORING TOUR OF WHITMAN AND PARKER, 1835

In 1835, the American Board, also responding to the Nez Perce appeal, sent Dr. Marcus Whitman and the Rev. Samuel Parker, both Presbyterians, on an exploratory tour of the Rockies and the country beyond, to investigate the possibilities of establishing missions among the natives there. The two men traveled to the Rendezvous that year under the protection of the American Fur Company's caravan. The caravan left Liberty, Missouri, on May 14, but because of some unforeseen delays, did not arrive at the Rendezvous until August 12. That year the Rendezvous was held on the Green River, a branch of the Colorado.

The 1835 Rendezvous was one of the largest in the history of the Rocky Mountain Fur trade. In addition to the fifty or sixty men of the caravan, there were some 200 trappers in attendance and about 2,000 Indians. Whitman reported that there were "forty lodges of Flatheads & Napiersas [Nez Perces]." [4]

Whitman, writing in his Journal on August 16, stated: "We had a talk with the chiefs of the Flathead and Napiersas tribes, in which they expressed great pleasure in seeing us and strong desires to be taught." [5] And Parker wrote in his Journal: "The first chief of the Nez Perces, Tai-quin-su-watish [Tack-en-sua-tis or Rotten Belly] arose and said, 'He had heard from white men a little about God, which had only gone into his ears; he wished to know enough to have it go down into his heart.' " [6]

Although neither Whitman nor Parker mentioned Lawyer as being at the 1835 Rendezvous, there is reason to believe that he was. Mylie Lawyer, in her reminiscences of her great-grandfather, stated that Lawyer was with Parker when he traveled through the Nez Perce country in the late summer and fall of 1835. [7]

The Nez Perces showed such enthusiasm at the prospect of having missionaries settle among them and made so many promises of cooperation that Whitman and Parker decided to separate. Whitman would go back to the States for reenforcements and then return to the Rendezvous the following year, while Parker would travel with the Nez Perces

---

[4] Drury, *Marcus Whitman, M.D.*, p. 100.   [5] Drury, *M. & N.W.*, Vol. i, p. 135.

[6] Samuel Parker, *Journal of an Exploring Tour Beyond the Rocky Mountains*, 4th ed. (Ithaca, N.Y.), 1844, p. 82. This book went through five American editions and two European.   [7] Lewiston, Id., *Tribune*, June 12, 1855.

to their homelands, select possible sites for mission stations, and also return to the 1836 Rendezvous. This plan appealed to Whitman as he was then engaged to Miss Narcissa Prentiss and had discovered that it was entirely feasible to take women over the Rockies. Whitman and Parker separated on August 21, never to see each other again, for Parker failed to return to the 1836 Rendezvous.

On Friday, August 21, the Nez Perces with the fifty-six year old missionary started back to their country. Their trail led over some rugged mountain terrain. Traveling at a leisurely pace, they averaged about thirteen miles a day. Parker, with his Nez Perce escort, arrived at the junction of the Snake and Clearwater Rivers, where present-day Lewiston, Idaho, is located on October 1. This was an amazing journey for Parker to make at his age, especially when we remember Whitman's description of him as being ill-adapted to roughing it.

After spending some time with the Nez Perces and Cayuses, Parker went to Fort Vancouver where he spent the winter of 1835-36. He returned to the upper Columbia River country in the spring of 1836. His description of a meeting with the Spokane Indians held sometime during the latter part of May follows:

> They brought with them a good interpreter, a young man of their nation, who had been in the school at the Red River settlement, [Spokane Garry], . . . and who had obtained a good knowledge of English. We had public worship that evening in the Spokein and Nez Perce languages. One of the Nez Perces, a chief who understood the Spokein language, collected his people, a little to the left of the Spokeins, and translated the discourse as it was delivered, into the language of his people, without an interruption in the service.[8]

The reference very clearly is to Lawyer, for there was no other prominent Nez Perce chief who knew both of these Indian languages at that time.

When Parker thought of the long overland journey back to the States, and remembered all of the hardships which he had endured on his westward journey, his heart failed him. He entrusted a letter addressed to Whitman to a Nez Perce who was planning to attend the 1836 Rendezvous, in which he stated that he would return to the States by sea. Parker gave no recommendations as to where the members of the

---

[8] Parker, *Journal*, 4th ed., p. 301.

Whitman party might settle, a great disappointment to Whitman. Parker sailed from Fort Vancouver on June 18, 1836, going first to Hawaii, where he had to wait several months for a ship to take him to the Atlantic coast. He did not arrive in New London, Connecticut, until May 18, 1837.

THE ARRIVAL OF THE WHITMAN-SPALDING PARTY, 1836

Whitman was back in his home in Rushville, New York, by December 17, 1835. In his report to the American Board, he stressed his belief that it was feasible for women to cross the Rockies. He urged the Board to appoint at least one other married couple to accompany him and his bride to Oregon in the spring of 1836. After many disappointments, Whitman finally secured the consent of the Rev. Henry H. Spalding and his wife, Eliza, to go with him to Oregon. Marcus and Narcissa Prentiss were married on February 18, 1836, and left the next day for the Missouri frontier. They overtook the Spaldings at Cincinnati. On April 19, an unmarried man, William Henry Gray, having obtained a belated appointment from the American Board, joined the party at Liberty, Missouri. All five were Presbyterians.

The mission party traveled to the Rendezvous under the protection of the American Fur Company's caravan. They crossed the Continental Divide through South Pass on July 4, an epoch-making event in that it proved that women could cross the Rockies. The feat accomplished by Narcissa Whitman and Eliza Spalding is all the more remarkable when we remember that they had ridden the 1,300 miles from the Missouri frontier side-saddle on horseback.

According to the custom of the time, the captain of the caravan sent a messenger ahead to the Rendezvous to inform the trappers and the Indians, who were impatiently awaiting its arrival, of the caravan's approach. The messenger carried the exciting news that there were two white women in the party.

William H. Gray, who in 1870 published his *History of Oregon*, tells the story of how four or five mountain men and some ten Indians, including Lawyer, rode out from the Rendezvous to give the incoming caravan, and especially the missionaries, a boisterous welcome. The welcoming committee met the caravan late on the afternoon of July 4, just after it had gone through South Pass and just before it was to stop and make camp. "As they came in sight over the hills," wrote Gray, "they all gave a yell, such as hunters and Indians only can give; whiz,

whiz, came their balls over our heads." For a time, the missionaries were alarmed, thinking that they were being attacked. Their fears, however, were soon quieted when they saw a white flag flying from a raised gun.[9]

That evening, the missionaries invited Tack-en-sua-tis and Lawyer to take supper with them. In Gray's account of the incident, he spelled Lawyer's name as Ish-hol-hol-hoats-hoats. Since Whitman had met both of these Nez Perces the previous year, a bond of friendship had already been established. Gray and Lawyer happened to meet in 1863 at which time they recalled their first meeting. Gray referred to this reunion in his *History of Oregon* by writing: "The Lawyer, twenty-seven years after spoke of it as the time when his heart became one with the . . . Americans." [10]

When the caravan, with the mission party, arrived at the Rendezvous on the 6th, they were given another boisterous welcome. Special attention was paid to the women. White women at the Rendezvous! This had never happened before. Contemporary accounts of the arrival of the mission party at the 1836 Rendezvous gave no hint that anyone, not even the missionaries themselves, realized the dramatic significance of what had been accomplished. White women had crossed the Rockies! The Rocky Mountain doorway to the Pacific Northwest had been burst open! Soon entire families, men, women and children, would follow.

Fortunately for the missionaries, a small party of Hudson's Bay men, under the command of John L. McLeod, arrived at the Rendezvous. McLeod offered to escort the missionaries as far west as Fort Boise. He and his enlarged party left the Rendezvous on July 16. Traveling with them as far as Fort Hall were the Nez Perces.

Shortly before the caravan arrived at Fort Hall, Gray became ill and had to drop out of the line of march for a short time. Narcissa Whitman, writing in her diary for July 29, explained what happened: "I had overtaken an Indian & told him how sick he [Gray] was, who went back, met husband, and both returned to Mr. Gray. The Indian helped him on his horse, got on behind him, supported him in his arms & in this manner rode slowly into camp." [11] Gray refers to this experience in his *History of Oregon* and identified the Indian as Lawyer.[12]

On reaching Fort Hall on August 3, the main body of the Nez Perces

[9] Gray, *op. cit.*, p. 120.   [10] *Ibid.*
[11] Drury, *F.W.W.*, Vol. i, p. 76.   [12] Gray, *Oregon*, p. 130.

left the Snake River trail and turned to the north. Only a few of the Indians, including Tack-en-sua-tis, remained with the mission party. Since no mention is made of Lawyer remaining with the missionaries, it may be assumed that he left them at Fort Hall. Lawyer's name disappears from the contemporary writings of the missionaries for about two years. He enters our story again after the arrival of the American Board's reenforcement in 1838.

Mission Stations Located

Even though no record remains as to Lawyer's activities during these two years, 1836-1838, yet it is well to summarize the events of these years as they give the background for Lawyer's experiences after 1838.

The Whitman-Spalding party, with their Hudson's Bay escort, arrived at Fort Boise on August 19. Since the country between Fort Boise and Fort Walla Walla was considered to be relatively safe, the missionaries traveled it without escort except for a few friendly Nez Perces including Tack-en-sua-tis. The Whitmans and Gray arrived at Fort Walla Walla on September 1; the Spaldings on the 3rd. Their long 1900-mile horseback journey from Liberty, Missouri, was over.

Before making decisions as to where they should establish their mission stations, they decided that it was best for all five to make the 300-mile trip down the Columbia River to Fort Vancouver to consult with Dr. McLoughlin. They arrived at Vancouver on September 12. While there, the decision was made that the Whitmans would settle among the Cayuses, a relatively small tribe numbering about 300, who lived along the Walla Walla River, while the Spaldings would go to the Nez Perces in the Clearwater River Valley. They numbered about 3,000. Gray would be free to work at either station as need arose. Leaving the women at Fort Vancouver, the three men returned to Walla Walla on October 2.

On Tuesday, October 4, the three men, with Pierre Pambrun, the H.B.C. Trader in charge of Fort Walla Walla, set out to explore the Walla Walla River Valley in search of a suitable site for a mission. The next day they selected what they considered to be a suitable site. It lay in a triangular area between Walla Walla River and its tributary, Mill Creek. This was about twenty-five miles to the east of Fort Walla Walla. The Indians called the general area Wy-ee-lat-poo, "the place of the rye grass." This tall coarse grass still grows in clumps on the former mission site.

According to previous arrangements, Tack-en-sua-tis with a party of from twenty to thirty Nez Perces arrived at Fort Walla Walla early in October to escort Whitman and Spalding into the Clearwater Valley. Gray, in the meantime, was to begin the erection of an adobe house at Waiilatpu. The Nez Perces were disappointed when they learned that the Whitmans were to settle among the Cayuses and warned the doctor of possible trouble. Writing in her diary on October 18, 1836, Narcissa, evidently quoting information passed on to her by her husband, noted: "The Nez Perces are exceedingly anxious for the location. Make many promises to work & listen to instruction. They do not like to have us stop with the Cayuses. They do not like the Cayuses. Say they do not have difficulty with the white people as the Cayuses do, & that we shall find it so." [13] Prophetic words!

Whitman and Spalding with their Nez Perce escort left Walla Walla on October 8 for the Clearwater Valley and, on the 11th, camped at the confluence of the Snake and Clearwater Rivers. The next day they rode into the Lapwai Valley, about ten miles up from the mouth of the Clearwater. As the missionaries rode up the Clearwater Canyon, Spalding's heart sank within him as he saw the barren bluffs, rising on either side to an elevation of about 2,700 feet, crowding in on the river. The area did not look promising.

Tack-en-sua-tis, seeing Spalding's dejection, comforted him by saying: "We are now near the place where there is good land, if anywhere in the Nez Perce country. Perhaps it will not answer, but if it does I am happy. This is my country, and where he [meaning Spalding] settles, I shall settle. And he need not think he will work by himself; only let us know what he wants done, and it shall be done." [14]

Upon their arrival at Lapwai Creek, both Whitman and Spalding were impressed with the possibilities of the site. The valley was about one-half mile wide at the mouth of the creek with an even wider valley up stream. The two men found three springs of water about two miles up the creek and Spalding selected that place for the location of his cabin. Two years later, Spalding found it necessary to relocate at the mouth of the creek on the bank of the Clearwater.

Since Lawyer's home was at Kamiah, some sixty miles up the Clearwater River, he evidently was too far away to be involved in these events.

---

[13] Drury, *F.W.W.*, Vol. I, p. 108.   [14] Drury, *Spalding*, p. 159.

THE REENFORCEMENT OF 1838

W. H. Gray returned to the States in the summer of 1837 to get married and to induce the Board to send out a reenforcement for its Oregon Mission in 1838. Previous to Gray's return with his enthusiastic report regarding the eagerness of the Nez Perces to have missionaries, Spalding had sent a number of long letters to the Board in which he gave glowing accounts of the response of the natives. The October 1837 issue of the *Missionary Herald,* the official publication of the Board, carried 6,000 words from one of Spalding's letters and the December issue of the same periodical devoted five pages to another of Spalding's optimistic reports. For the time being, the Board promoted its Oregon Mission as being the most promising of all the fields it then occupied.

Moved by the reports given by Gray and Spalding, the American Board appointed three couples, all newlyweds, to go out to Oregon in the spring of 1838 with Gray and his bride, Mary. They were the Rev. Cushing and Myra Eells, the Rev. Elkanah and Mary Walker, and the Rev. Asa and Sarah Smith. The Grays left for the Missouri frontier on February 19. The other three couples left New York on March 20 on a cross-country journey which took them more than five months. While passing through Cincinnati, they were joined by Cornelius Rogers, unmarried and in his twenty-third year. This brought the total members of the Oregon Mission to thirteen. It was never any larger. The Whitmans, Spaldings, Grays, and Rogers were Presbyterians. The others were Congregationalists.

The 1838 Rendezvous was held east of the Rockies, at the confluence of the Wind and Popo Agie Rivers in what is now western Wyoming. The trade in beaver pelts had been dealt a death blow when the style in men's hats changed from the beaver skin top hat to one made of silk. The 1838 gathering of trappers was small. There is no evidence that any Nez Perces were present. The Rocky Mountain fur trade was coming to an end.

The mission party, escorted by a small company of Hudson's Bay men under the command of Francis Ermatinger, rode through South Pass on July 15. This Rocky Mountain doorway to Oregon and California, first opened for Oregon-bound emigrant families by Narcissa Whitman and Eliza Spalding in 1836, was pushed open a little wider by the accomplishments of the four women of the 1838 reenforcement.

Several years had to pass before the full impact of the achievements of these six white women who had ventured to cross the Rockies was felt in the States.[15] Where these women could go, covered wagons with families could follow. In 1841 the first trickle of Oregon-bound emigrants, numbering twenty-four, made the westward crossing. The next year there were over 100. Both of these parties left their wagons at Fort Hall and completed the journey on horseback. Then in 1843, the first great Oregon emigration took place when about 1,000 men, women, and children moved through South Pass with their wagons on their way to the Willamette Valley.[16]

As will be noted, this ever-increasing incoming tide of white people into the Pacific Northwest posed a serious threat to the Oregon Indians, including the Cayuses and Nez Perces. By the early 1850s, white settlers were intruding on lands long claimed by the Cayuse, Walla Walla, and Nez Perce Indians. Here is the basic reason for the Indian councils called by the U.S. Government which met in 1855 at Walla Walla and in 1863 at Lapwai, in each of which Lawyer was destined to play a prominent role.

By August 27, all members of the 1838 reenforcement had arrived at Waiilatpu. The Spaldings happened to be present. They and the Whitmans had organized the First Presbyterian Church of Oregon on August 18, 1838. This was the first Protestant church to be established on the Pacific Slope of what is now the United States. At first the Whitmans and the Spaldings were overjoyed with the arrival of new missionaries but this feeling soon vanished when they became aware of deep antipathies which had been engendered among the members of the reenforcement during their overland travels.

In the business meeting which followed the arrival of the reenforcement, Walker and Eells were selected to open a new station among the Spokane Indians; Gray was to live with the Spaldings at Lapwai; Smith was to stay with the Whitmans; while Rogers was free to move from station to station as he wished.

---

[15] Drury's 3-vol. work on *F.W.W.* contains the diaries of five of these six women written during their overland travels; and one, that of Mary Gray, after her arrival in Oregon.

[16] Time-Life Books, *The Pioneers*, 1974, p. 25, states that before the transcontinental railroad was completed in 1869, at least 350,000 emigrants traveled through South Pass after the way had been opened by the missionary women in 1836 and 1838.

Walker and Eells made an exploratory tour of the Spokane country in the fall of 1838 and selected a site, called Tshimakain, for their station. This was located on the trail that connected Fort Walla Walla with Fort Colville, about seven miles north of the Spokane River crossing. The season was too far advanced to permit the men to complete the erection of their cabins and to move their families that fall. Hence they and the Smiths had to spend the winter with the Whitmans at Waiilatpu.

Cushing Eells, in his unpublished reminiscences,[17] noted that he and Walker began their study of the Flathead language under the tutelage of Lawyer during the winter of 1838-39. Of this Eells wrote:

> One of the [Nez Perce] tribe was distinguished for intellectual discrimination. For that reason he was called Lawyer. He not only was familiar with his mother tongue, but he also had acquired a knowledge of the Flathead language. This is said to be identical with the language of the Spokane Indians. The services of Lawyer were secured to aid Mr. Walker and myself in obtaining knowledge of the language of the people among whom we have been appointed to labor. Consequently, Lawyer and his family [18] dwelt near Waiilatpu.

Writing during a temporary absence from Waiilatpu on January 29, 1839, Whitman in a letter addressed to Walker requested that a supply of potatoes and corn be paid to Lawyer, evidently for the services he was rendering.[19]

JOSEPH AND TIMOTHY CONVERTED

By December 1838, Spalding at Lapwai had mastered the Nez Perce language sufficiently well to use it in his preaching. He therefore began about the first of December a series of what he called "protracted meetings" which continued into January. Hundreds of natives were encamped about the Mission and attended these services. By this time Gray had succeeded in erecting a log schoolhouse which measured 20 x 40 feet. When the congregation overflowed this building, the meetings were moved into the open air. During the weeks of these meetings, Spalding induced the Indians to help him dig a millrace for

---

[17] Original manuscript in Whitman College, Walla Walla, Wash.

[18] Lawyer had two sons, James and Archie.

[19] Original in Beinecke Manuscript Lby., Yale Univ., New Haven, Conn.

the grist mill he planned to build. He had harvested that fall a bumper crop of potatoes, about 1,500 bushels, and thus was able to pay the Indian workers with potatoes.

The names of two Nez Perce chiefs, who figure prominently in the history of that tribe and also in the life of Lawyer, appear for the first time in Spalding's diary during December 1838. On December 2, Spalding wrote: "Joseph speaks most affectingly, urging all present to give their hearts to Jesus Christ without delay." [20] This Joseph is also known as Old Joseph to distinguish him from his better-known son, also called Joseph, who became famous in the Nez Perce uprising of 1877. Old Joseph's home was in the Wallowa Valley of what is now northeastern Oregon.

The second important Nez Perce to be mentioned in Spalding's diary was Timothy, whose Indian name was Timosa. Timothy's wife was a sister of Joseph. On December 23, Spalding wrote: "Before the sermon closed, Timothy was before the stand in tears." The meeting became charged with emotion. A former mountain man, then working for Spalding, James Conner, who had a Nez Perce wife and who had a good command of that language, followed Timothy to the stand. Of this, Spalding commented in his diary: "Conner gives a brief history of his wicked life & concludes by saying he hates what he once loved & is determined to serve & love no one but Jesus Christ in the future." Others arose to confess their sins. "Before we closed," wrote Spalding, "many more were before the stand, men & women & the scene, the most awful & interesting I have ever witnessed, continued, many waiting for the speakers to close, many deeply affected, till I rose and said those before the stand were all that could speak till evening."

Since Lawyer was at Waiilatpu during these days, where he was tutoring Walker and Eells in the Spokane language, he was not present for this emotional service. On February 15, 1839, Spalding noted in his diary that Lawyer had returned from Waiilatpu.

A reaction to the revival and even open opposition on the part of several important chiefs came a few weeks later. On April 22, 1839, Spalding wrote in his diary: "Last evening had some talk with Meiway . . . and Rotten Belly. Today they leave. I do not know that I ever felt discouraged in the least before in relation to this people. . .

---

[20] Drury, S. & S., p. 248. Other quotations from this diary are from this volume under the dates indicated in the text.

Surely many of them appear like another race of beings from what they did when we first came among them."

Here we meet for the first time in our story the name of Meiway,[21] also known as Apash Wyakaikt, but better known as Looking Glass because he sometimes wore a small round mirror around his neck. Perhaps this mirror had been received as a trade item from some white man. Just as Old Joseph had a son who took his name, so Looking Glass' son took his father's name. This son was one of the chief strategists in the Chief Joseph uprising of 1877. Since neither the younger Joseph nor the younger Looking Glass figures in this story of Lawyer, all references to these names will be to the fathers.

Monteith in his sketch of Lawyer wrote: "Looking Glass was not a chief, but a 'te-wat,' or medicine man, and by his jugglery performances made the Indians believe that he could cause their death by merely wishing it, hence the Indians on the Ashotin [22] where he lived made him their chief." [23] Alvin Josephy, in his book *The Nez Perce Indians,* commented: "He was not a man for the untutored missionaries to trifle with." [24]

Spalding's confrontation with Looking Glass in April 1839 was but the beginning of a series of clashes which both he and A. B. Smith had with the te-wat. Looking Glass was quick to note the irreconcilable differences between Christian teachings and the medicine men's practices. Therefore he, and other te-wats, who found their beliefs, and possibly their livelihood threatened, became anti-Christian, even as the missionaries became anti-te-wat.

Spalding's discouraging diary entry for April 22, 1839, mentions his confrontation with both Looking Glass and Tack-en-sua-tis (or Rotten Belly). No one of the Nez Perces had been more enthusiastic in welcoming the missionaries in 1836 than Tack-en-sua-tis. It was he who had provided a company of Nez Perces to escort the Spaldings to Lapwai in November 1836. Writing on February 16, 1837, Spalding had the following to say in praise about this chief: "Tack-en-sua-tis, our favorite chief . . . came into the school this morning and ap-

---

[21] Also spelled Meoway, an Indian term for a strong chief. Josephy, *Nez Perces,* p. 211.

[22] *I.e.,* Asotin, on the Washington side of the Snake River, about eight miles up from its confluence with the Clearwater River.

[23] *See* Appendix I. Hereafter all references to Monteith's sketch or obituary of Lawyer, will be to this Appendix and will be referred to as "Monteith, Obituary."

[24] *Op. cit.,* p. 111.

peared to be delighted with the exercises. . . After the singing was closed, I observed Tack-en-sua-tis was bathed in tears, apparently deeply affected by something." [25] Yet by the time of the December 1838 revival, this chief had lost his enthusiasm both for Spalding and for Christianity. This explains Spalding's lament: "Surely many of them appear like another race of beings from what they did when we first came among them."

It appears that Tack-en-sua-tis had come under the domineering influence of Looking Glass and had turned on Spalding. Writing from Kamiah to Secretary Greene of the American Board on February 6, 1840, Asa Smith stated: "First, I will refer you to the *Herald* for 1837 . . . the account of the promising Nez Perce chief, Tackensuatis. People at home may think from what was written of him that he is a Christian, but he is far from it. Instead of having settled with Mr. S., he has become his enemy & proves to be a very wicked man." [26]

Some mystery surrounds the name of Tack-en-sua-tis, for it disappears from the contemporary writings of the missionaries and even of later Government reports. His name does not appear as one of the signers of the 1855 or 1863 Treaties, when presumably one of his importance would have been included. It is possible that this chief was known by another Indian name and was, therefore, present at both of these councils. As will be told, Tack-en-sua-tis had a change of heart in his old age and was baptized with Lawyer by Spalding on November 12, 1871.

With the passing of the months following the revival, Spalding and Whitman felt that both Joseph and Timothy should be baptized and received into the membership of the Mission church. This took place on November 17, 1839, at which time Spalding noted in the church's record book: "Joseph Tuitakas, the principal Nez Perce chief, some 37 years old. Timothy Timosa, a native of considerable influence, some 31 years of age." [27]

On Sunday, April 12, 1840, Spalding wrote in his diary that he had on that day baptized a son of Chief Joseph whom he named Ephraim. Since Young Joseph was born in 1840, we may assume that he was this child. If so, his baptismal name of Ephraim does not seem to have been used.

---

[25] Drury, *Spalding*, p. 175.   [26] Drury, S. & S., p. 129.

[27] The original record book is in the Presbyterian Hist. Soc., Phila., Pa.

LAWYER AND ASA B. SMITH

Of all the thirteen members of the Oregon Mission, there was no one so ill-adapted to be a missionary to the Indians as Asa Bowen Smith. He joined the 1838 reenforcement on an impulse of the moment, being frustrated and impatient because of the long delay of the Board in sending him to some foreign field. The mission party had not been more than two weeks on the trail after leaving the Missouri frontier when Smith regretted his decision. But then it was too late for him to turn back.[28] By the time the reenforcement had arrived at Waiilatpu, Smith was so unhappy and disagreeable that no couple of that party was willing to live in the same station with him. The Mission at its September 1838 meeting voted that the Smiths should stay with the Whitmans but, as will be seen, Smith was soon discontented with this arrangement.

When Lawyer was at Waiilatpu during the winter of 1838-39, he suggested to Smith that he and his wife should move to Kamiah where, Lawyer claimed, the purest Nez Perce was spoken. Smith seized the idea with enthusiasm. When a special meeting of the Mission was held at Lapwai in February 1839, Smith emphatically declared that he would leave the Mission rather than live with the Whitmans any longer.[29] Smith asked permission to open a new station at Kamiah, but this request was denied. Finally, a compromise was worked out. The Smiths would be permitted to move to Kamiah for the purpose of studying the language.

Asa and Sarah arrived at Kamiah on May 10, 1839. Gray accompanied them in order to help erect a small cabin. This was a rude structure with no floor except the earth and no windows. Sarah wrote in her diary that they really did not need windows as "the many cracks furnish us with sufficient light." [30] None of the other couples in the Oregon Mission lived in such an isolated place or under such primitive conditions as the Smiths at Lapwai. And none of the other five women of the Mission suffered so much from ill health as Sarah Smith.

In his lonely cabin at Kamiah, Smith had plenty of time to write long letters. Fortunately, many of these have been preserved and some have been published.[31] These give excellent descriptions of Indian life, na-

---

28 Drury, *F.W.W.*, Vol. II, p. 77.   29 Drury, *Spalding*, p. 217.
30 Drury, *F.W.W.*, Vol. II, p. 120.
31 Drury, *S. & S.*, pp. 145 ff. Hereafter quotations from Smith's letters or diary will be from this volume under the dates indicated.

tive religious beliefs, the Nez Perce language, and missionary problems. Smith was much more of an objective observer of Nez Perce life and customs than was any of his contemporaries.

Smith's first letter from Kamiah to Greene was dated August 27, 1839. In this letter we find the following comment about Lawyer:

> I have enjoyed the instruction of the best teacher that could be obtained in the country. He exhibits more mind than I have witnessed in any other Indian. He is one who has been much in the mountains with the American Fur Co. & on account of his knowledge of different languages & his talent at public speaking, he was called by them Lawyer, by which name he is generally known. He has stood by me during the summer & has been faithful in giving me instruction, for which I have fed him & in part his family & promised him some clothing. This is necessary for Indians always live from hand to mouth.

While at Kamiah, Smith with Lawyer's help compiled a dictionary and grammar of the Nez Perce language, the first to be written.[32] In his letter to the Board of August 29, 1839, Smith gave a long description of the complexities of the Nez Perce language, again drawing upon information given him by Lawyer.

This letter of August 1839 contains the account of Lawyer's previously reported visit to Spokane, when he heard Spokane Garry read from the Bible, and of the subsequent sending of the Nez Perce delegation to St. Louis in 1831 to get the Bible and Christian teachers.

Smith, in his diary-letter to Greene, begun on November 11, 1839, gave the following favorable account of Lawyer's understanding of Christianity:

> [Sunday, Nov. 24] Met the people today in a grass meeting house, or rather lodge which they completed yesterday. A little more than 200 were present including all the young children. This will probably be the usual number during the winter. Had an interesting conversation with my teacher [Lawyer] this evening. He seemed to have some sense of his situation as being without hope. He understands more truth than any other individual & it seems to take some effect. His hopes of salvation from his own works seem to be cut off, & now he is in darkness & knows not what to do. I have endeavored to tell him but it is only the Spirit of God that can make him understand what it is to yield himself up to the Savior.

---

[32] Original documents in American Board Archives, Harvard Univ. Lby., Boston.

During the eleven-year mission period, 1836-47, only twenty-one natives joined the Mission church. All but one of these were Nez Perces, mostly from the Lapwai area. The one exception was Five Crows, whose father was a Cayuse and whose mother was a Nez Perce. Lawyer never joined during these years, although he probably had a better understanding of Christian doctrine than any of those who had been instructed by Spalding.

Writing to Secretary Greene on February 25, 1840, Smith condemned what he called the "supreme selfishness" of the Nez Perces. "They are self righteous to the extreme," he wrote, "& labor hard to convince us of their goodness, but their hearts are enmity against God. They love not the truth when it condemns them. They have considerable knowledge of the Bible, its historical parts which they remember extremely well, but they know very little of the doctrines of Christianity.

> I have not seen one who has any clear idea of the atonement. This I think arises from the fact that they have no idea of law, penalty, or justice. This has for months been my principal topic of instruction, the atonement as connected with the transgression of the divine law, . . . I have seen but one individual since I have been at this station who has seemed to be at all affected by the truth. This is my teacher [Lawyer], who has more knowledge of the truths of the gospel than any one of the natives with whom I have conversed. . . His heart is full of pride & he is evidently resting on his own good works.

Perhaps Smith was more Calvinistic in his theology than any of the other members of the Mission. All of the missionaries had difficulty in explaining the deeper doctrines of Christianity, such as that of the atonement, when the native languages had no words which could express such concepts. It may be that much of Spalding's success in winning converts was due to the fact that he was not as strict in requiring the natives to give intellectual answers to doctrinal questions as were his co-workers.

LAWYER AND THE ROMAN CATHOLICS

The first Roman Catholic missionaries to arrive in the Oregon country came from Canada. They were Fathers Francois Norbert Blanchet and Modeste Demers who were given free passage by the Hudson's Bay Company in the spring and summer of 1838. Father Blanchet confined his ministry largely to the French Canadians who were employed by the Company at Fort Vancouver or with their retired "servants" then living in the Willamette Valley. Father Demers made itinerating trips into the upper Columbia River Valley going as far north as Fort Colville. He did not, however, visit the Clearwater Valley.

The second Roman Catholic thrust into the Pacific Northwest was spearheaded by the Belgian Jesuit, Father Pierre Jean de Smet, working overland out of St. Louis. De Smet visited the Flathead country in the summer of 1840 where he met a number of Nez Perces including Lawyer. Of this meeting, Smith wrote to Elkanah Walker on October 12, 1840, saying:

> A Catholic Priest from St. Louis has been in the buffalo country this season & from the accounts of the Indians, the Lawyer especially, he has already accomplished ten times as much as has been effected from the opposite quarter [i.e., by the Canadian priests], & it gives me reason to expect that the principal point of attack from the Catholics will be from that region & not at Walla Walla . . .[33] A considerable number, the Indians say, a great many children both Flat Head & Nez Perces have been baptized & have been presented with the image of the cross or other emblems of Popery. . .
>
> The Lawyer saw him two days & he says they tried to get the cross on him. He heard considerable from the priest & says the priest inquired of him about the mission and according to him [i.e., the Lawyer's account], he defended the mission very well. . . According to his account, he ridiculed the priests & his doctrines most thoroughly to the interpreter & of course it must have gone to the priest. When they pretended that the cross was God, he said it was only *Kiswi*, like the ring on his finger.
>
> He denied to the interpreter the saving efficacy of baptism & when the priest said it was bad for us to have wives, he in a sarcastic manner asked the interpreter how the priest came into the world, if it was not by means of a father & mother. When the priest pretended that when he got established, he should give the people a plenty of food, he said to the interpreter, "I am very glad, my servant. I will come here & do nothing & load my horses with provisions and go home again." So the Lawyer tells his story. He has no faith in the priest giving so much. But after all, he might fall a prey to Catholicism.

---

[33] Smith assumed that Father Demers was making his headquarters at Fort Walla Walla.

From this report, it is evident that Lawyer understood the basic doctrinal differences between the Protestants and the Catholics. As will be noted, Lawyer tried to prevent the coming of a Catholic priest onto the Nez Perce Reservation in 1865 during the administration of Indian Agent, James O'Neil, a Catholic. Spokane Garry took a similar firm stand against the Catholics at Spokane. It may be that Garry shared his anti-Catholic views with Lawyer when they met at Fort Colville in the spring of 1830.

A CLASH OF CULTURES

The clash of cultures between the Indians and the Whites began when the English Puritans landed at Jamestown in 1607 and the Pilgrims at Cape Cod in 1620. Long before the missionaries arrived in Oregon, the United States Government had adopted the policy of persuading the Indians who lived east of the Rockies to give up their semi-nomadic habits and turn to farming and the raising of livestock.

Since Whitman, Spalding, and the other members of the American Board's Mission spearheaded the arrival of white settlers in the upper Columbia River Valley, they of necessity became the advance agents of American civilization. While crossing the plains in 1836, Spalding noted that the buffalo, an important item in the diet of the Indians, including the Nez Perces, were beginning to be decimated by the unrestrained slaughter by the Whites. Writing to the American Board from the Rendezvous on July 8, 1836, Spalding stated: "What is done for the poor Indians of the western world must be done soon. The only thing that can save them from annihilation is the introduction of civilization."

After Spalding opened his mission station at Lapwai, he discovered that his efforts to educate and evangelize the Nez Perces were severely handicapped by the semi-nomadic habits of the people. They were, as he explained, "always on the wing." During one season of the year, the natives would be at the fisheries along the rivers; again on the high prairies digging camas roots; and yet again, many would be in the buffalo country getting meat and hides. Always the constant search for food.

Both Whitman and Spalding enthusiastically endorsed the policy of trying to induce the natives to settle down on farms and turn to agriculture and the raising of cattle. The transition from their former method of finding food to the white man's ways was for both the

Cayuses and Nez Perces a slow, difficult, and at times a painful experience.

Spalding's spectacular success with his garden and field crops at Lapwai was an impressive object lesson for the natives. In his letter to Secretary Greene dated September 11, 1838, Spalding stated that he had harvested that year 80 bushels of wheat, 100 of corn, 58 of peas, 800 of potatoes, and 50 of garden vegetables. His potatoes went 500 bushels to an acre. Spalding also reported that between seventy and eighty Nez Perce families were farming and that some had raised as much as 100 bushels of potatoes, together with considerable amounts of corn, peas, wheat, and vegetables.[34]

Most if not all of the Indians who had started farming were living in the vicinity of Spalding's station at Lapwai. They did so in order to have access to Spalding's agricultural implements and also for the protection of their unfenced crops which a concentration of their fields provided. But this created problems as the influx of Nez Perces from other valleys into the Lapwai area ran counter to the long established customs of the tribe.

When Spalding settled among the Nez Perces, he found the tribe divided into thirty or forty bands which were living along the Snake and Clearwater Rivers and their tributaries. Each band had its own chief or head man.[35] Each band laid claim to the exclusive use of its particular valley and resented the intrusion of other members of the tribe into their domain. The basic reason for this social structure was the availability of food. Until Spalding induced the Indians to settle down and farm, the individual Nez Perce had no sense of private ownership of land.

The head chief of the Lapwai Valley band was Hin-mah-tute-ke-kaikt, also known as Big Thunder, on whom Spalding bestowed the name of James. When Joseph moved from his Wallowa Valley and began farming at Lapwai; and when Timothy moved from his home on Alpowa Creek, likewise to begin farming at Lapwai; and when other natives did the same, Big Thunder was incensed. All were intruders in his valley. Big Thunder blamed Spalding for this new development. A further complication arose out of the fact that Big Thunder was a tewat and as such he was as much opposed to Spalding's teachings of

---

[34] Drury, *Spalding*, p. 185.

[35] Monteith, Obituary. Other estimates claim that there were about fifty bands.

Christianity as was Looking Glass. In Smith's letter to Walker of October 12, 1840, he stated: "Old James is trying also to drive away Joseph & Timothy & all who do not belong there." [36]

Still another situation arose to plague Spalding. On November 20, 1840, he wrote in his diary: "Craig & Larison, two mountain men, have arrived, probably to spend the winter. I have seen enough of mountain men." Larison did not stay long but William Craig settled on Lapwai Creek about eight miles up from the Spalding Mission. Craig had the distinction of being the first non-missionary white settler in what is now the State of Idaho.

Since Craig's wife was a daughter of James or Big Thunder, it was perhaps natural that he should share his father-in-law's anti-missionary attitude. Craig told Big Thunder that he should demand payment from Spalding for the use of his land, water, and timber. When Spalding refused to pay, Big Thunder induced some of the young men of his band to vandalize mission property. On February 3, 1841, Spalding wrote in his diary: "Today the Indians from Old James are busy demolishing the mill-dam. Oh Lord in great mercy stay thy chastising hand . . . Craig has the honor of countenancing this thing. How is it possible for a man born of Christian parents (his parents are members of the Presbyterian church) to be guilty of such deeds of darkness?"

The acts of vandalism were denounced by Timothy, Joseph, and one whom Spalding called Jason. For a time the vandalism ceased but, as Spalding's diary indicates, the enmity of Big Thunder continued. As will be indicated, both Looking Glass and Big Thunder, two prominent tewats, became critics and at times open opponents of Lawyer.

LOOKING GLASS CAUSES TROUBLE

In the meantime a situation developed at Kamiah which paralleled that which Spalding endured at Lapwai. This was inspired by Looking Glass, who traveled from his home at Asotin to Kamiah for the purpose of making trouble for Smith. There Looking Glass induced some of the Indians to demand payment from Smith for the land he occupied. When Smith refused to pay, he was ordered to leave. Of this Smith wrote in his letter of October 21, 1840 to Secretary Greene: "When I last wrote you, little did I think that such trials were near at hand as have befallen us. . . Suffice it to say that on the 13th inst. we were

---

[36] Drury, S. & S., p. 193.

ordered in the most insolent manner & in the most absolute terms to
leave this place. It has happened that it was an attempt on the part of
the Indians to get property [i.e., payment]." In his diary entry for
October 15, Smith identified the ringleader as Atpash Wyakaikt, or
Looking Glass. Smith was so alarmed by the threats made against him,
that he sent a messenger to Spalding and Whitman begging them to
come to his aid.

Describing the events which followed the threats made on the 13th,
Smith wrote in his diary: "Slept but little during the night & this
morning some of the chiefs came to talk with me." Although Smith does
not here name the friendly chiefs, surely one of them would have been
Lawyer, his teacher, and possibly another would have been Ellis. When
Spokane Garry and Kootenay Pelly returned to the Red River school
in the spring of 1830 with the east-bound H.B.C. express, five more
Indian youths accompanied them. The eldest of this group was a Nez
Perce called Ellice, after a member of the London Committee of the
H.B.C. His name was usually spelled Ellis. He was nineteen or twenty
at the time he left for Red River. He remained in the school for about
four years during which time he learned to speak, read, and write
English. Ellis was a man of considerable ability and, as will be told,
was appointed the first Head Chief of the Nez Perce tribe in 1842. His
home was in Kamiah and he and Lawyer were close friends.

While the friendly chiefs were in the Smith home, the two individuals who had caused trouble the previous day came and demanded
entrance.

The door was locked, [wrote Smith in his diary,] Insinmalakin [37]
ordered me to open the door. I asked him what he had come for.
He made no reply but repeated the order again & again & began
to threaten to break the door down. It was thought best to have
the door opened & he and his brother came in full of rage & began
to talk very insultingly. . . the talk continued for a long time,
very warm & some of the time I felt that I was among a company
of friends.

Describing the incident in a letter to Greene dated October 21, 1840,
Smith added: "I never witnessed such a scene in my life. Much passion
was manifested on both sides & it seemed to me that the house was

[37] Also spelled Ute-sin-male-cum, who will enter our story again.

filled with demons from the bottomless pit rather than human beings.
. . After several hours, the scene broke up & they all went home."
Both Asa and Sarah were so greatly alarmed that they then decided to
leave Kamiah as soon as possible.

Smith's announced determination to leave Kamiah had a sobering
effect on the natives for the two offenders visited Smith on the 16th to
apologize. Smith wrote that day in his diary that they "wished to
obtain my favor." The plain-spoken Smith added: "I talked to them for
some time in the plainest manner possible respecting our object in
coming here, the selfishness of the people, their hypocritical practices
& told them they were fast going to perdition   .   .   .   After this plain
talk they left."

Spalding with some of his friendly Indians including Timothy,
Joseph, and Jason arrived at Lapwai on the 16th. By that time the
excitement had died down. Spalding in his diary wrote on that day:
"The Indians confess their faults & wish Mr. S. to remain but it seems
his mind is made up & he will go." Although Looking Glass did not
actually take part in the disturbance, Smith was convinced that it was
he who had influenced the two brothers to act as they did.

The last entry in Smith's diary is dated December 5, 1840. In it Smith
summarized the many difficulties he had faced, not only with his associates in the Mission but also with the natives at Kamiah. He could
have mentioned, but did not, the frail health of his wife Sarah who
was then an invalid with a spinal affliction. Life had become almost
unbearable. Smith closed his diary with these words of utter despond-
ency: ". . . in view of these things, I must say I feel discouraged
& disheartened & know not what to do."

The troubles that Spalding had experienced at Lapwai and Smith at
Kamiah, both inspired by the tewats, marked the beginning of the
division of the Nez Perce tribe into the Christian and the anti-Christian
parties. The latter was often referred to in the contemporary writings
of the missionaries, and sometimes even in the reports of Government
officials, as the "heathen party." [38]

LATER DEVELOPMENTS

The Smiths left Kamiah for Fort Vancouver on April 10, 1841. Since
Sarah was unable to ride horseback, she was taken down the rivers to

---

[38] The term "heathen" was then used as a synonym for "non-Christian."

Fort Walla Walla in a canoe and from there in a larger boat to Vancouver. The couple sailed for Honolulu on July 18. They remained in the Islands as appointees of the American Board for the next four years and then left for New England on October 15, 1845. They took passage on a ship that sailed around Africa. They arrived back in the United States on May 4, 1846, being the only members of the Oregon Mission to circumnavigate the globe.

Although Smith owed much to Lawyer, it can also be said that Lawyer owed much to Smith. While Smith was mastering the Nez Perce language, Lawyer was learning English. Each was a teacher and each a pupil. Lawyer was the gainer in this exchange of instruction since Smith had no need of the Nez Perce language after leaving Kamiah while Lawyer never ceased benefiting from his knowledge of English. No doubt this acquisition of English was a prime factor in his acceptance as Head Chief of the Nez Perces by Government officials sometime in the spring of 1848.

CHAPTER THREE

The Later Mission Period, 1841-1848

A new chapter in Lawyer's life began when, following the Smiths' departure from Kamiah, he moved to Lapwai to work with Spalding. Even as Lawyer had helped Smith learn the Nez Perce language, now he was to render the same service to Spalding, who was in the process of reducing the language to writing. In turn, Spalding was able to further Lawyer's knowledge of English. On July 21, 1841, Spalding noted in his diary that Lawyer had arrived at Lapwai. Then come the following entries:

22. Spend the day with Lawyer. Get many words.
23. Sabbath. Speak of the Prodigal Son. Lawyer appears solemn. Says he can do nothing, is like a dead carcass without head, legs, or arms.
25. Lawyer leaves & is to be back in some 7 or 8 weeks & be my teacher for 8 or 9 months for a cow.[1]

A glimpse into the continuing conflict with Old James is found in Spalding's diary entries for October 29 and 30, 1841. He wrote:

29. Speak on faith. "Believe in the Lord Jesus Christ." Old James seeing too much light for his sorcery rose in a rage & said he had received the Waiikin [2] when young & could not throw it away & by that he had power over the winds & clouds & that he could cause the winds to blow or the clouds to give rain when he pleased. This stirred up the zeal of Timothy who answered him very closely but the old man stopped him by force & attempting to speak, I told him to sit down. The sorcery & many other things convince me that this

---

[1] Drury, S. & S., p. 317.
[2] *See* text in Chap. I, regarding the Nez Perce belief in Wy-ya-kin.

people are very much under the power of the devil. O may his chains be broken & their souls set at liberty.

30. Old James comes early this morning & he says he shall see me no more for a long time & further that Craig tells them that they should demand pay for their lands & that he told them to tear away the mill-dam last winter. Joseph, Luke & Timothy speak very much to the point.

On February 14, 1842, Eliza Spalding, in a letter to a sister, wrote:

Ellis was here during the meeting and remained several weeks, during which time he attended school and was not only a scholar, but an assistant. He has never, before this, seemed favorably disposed. He now seems interested in what we are doing . . . He, with Lawyer have concluded to settle at Kamiah this spring. We hope that Lawyer will receive a heifer calf for his services here this winter. He will if there is no objection on the part of the other members of the mission.[3]

In this letter, Eliza wrote with pride about the new school building which had been erected at Lapwai. "It is 21 by 17 feet," she wrote. "The frame is of sawed timber, the covering is of boards matched.[4] Three, 12 light [i.e., window panes] windows, a writing desk across one side, a stove in the center, and daily it is filled with interesting learners." The Spaldings were not trying to teach the natives to read and write English but rather to master their own language.

A secret of Spalding's success with the Indians at Lapwai is found in the fact that he and his wife won the cooperation of most of the leading chiefs of the tribe. Eliza's letter continues: "A class of adults have made it their business to attend school through the winter thus far. I will give their names as some of them are familiar to you: Joseph, Timothy, Luke, Lawyer, Stephen, Jason, Five Crows (Joseph's brother) . . ." Actually Five Crows was only the half-brother of Joseph. The two had the same Cayuse father but Five Crows had a Nez Perce mother.

---

[3] Since the small herd of American cattle was so highly prized by the missionaries, unanimous consent was needed before any of the animals could be given to natives.

[4] This frame building is evidence that Spalding by this time had a saw mill in operation. This smaller schoolhouse replaced the larger log building mentioned in the preceding chapter.

A Printing Press at Lapwai

On May 13, 1839, Mr. and Mrs. E. O. Hall, missionaries under the American Board in Honolulu, arrived at Lapwai bringing with them a small Ramage printing press large enough to print a page about eight by eleven inches. This came as a gift from the Hawaiian Mission to the Oregon Mission since the former had received a larger press. This was the first American press to be brought to the Pacific Slope of what is now the United States.[5] Before the end of that year, Spalding had printed a Nez Perce primer of sixteen pages which he used in his school. This was the first of eight items to come from this historic press, seven of which were in Nez Perce and one in the Flathead or Spokane tongue. The last and by far the most important of these eight items was Spalding's translation of the Gospel of Matthew in Nez Perce, an eighty-one page book which appeared in 1845.

During the winter of 1841-42, Spalding was at work with Lawyer's help in translating the Gospel of Matthew into Nez Perce. According to his diary entry for January 26, 1842, Spalding sent the translation of the first nine chapters of Matthew to Whitman for his review and comments. In his entry for April 22, Spalding wrote that Whitman had returned the manuscript without comment. By this time, Spalding, with Lawyer's help, was so far advanced in the knowledge of the Nez Perce language that there was no other person in the Mission who was qualified to make corrections.

Whitman suggested that Spalding consult with Lawyer regarding possible corrections and then report to the Annual Meeting of the Mission scheduled to be held at Waiilatpu on May 16. Spalding, in his diary entry for April 22, stated that time was too short for him to go to Kamiah. Moreover, he wrote, he could not ask Lawyer to come to Lapwai as he was then busy "planting his corn, potatoes, and peas." Spalding also stated that "the language of the translation" was Lawyer's.[6]

During the months that Spalding was working on the translation of the Gospel of Matthew into Nez Perce, Elkanah Walker at Tshimakain was busy reducing the Flathead language to writing and in compiling a Spokane primer. In this he had some help from Spokane Garry. By November 1843, Walker felt that his primer was ready to be printed so

---

[5] This historic press is now in the museum of the Oregon Hist. Soc., Portland.
[6] Drury, S. & S., p. 331.

he took his manuscript to Lapwai, arriving there on November 25. Walker was delighted to find that Lawyer was at Lapwai at that time.

Walker wrote in his diary for Sunday, November 27: "Attended the Indian worship today and [spoke] afterwards to them through the Lawyer. I do not like to talk in this way as I do not know what he may say to them." Evidently Walker was somewhat doubtful of Lawyer's ability to make a correct translation from Flathead or English into the Nez Perce tongue. While at Lapwai, Walker consulted Lawyer on the accuracy of his text for the Spokane primer for he noted in his diary on the 27th: "We had a long conversation last night on the language." [7]

After printing 250 copies of his Spokane Primer, Walker started for his home on Tuesday, December 7. This was the first item ever published in the Flathead tongue. Mary Walker called it "a marvellous little book." [8]

SPALDING, SMITH, AND GRAY DISMISSED

Although Lawyer's name rarely appears in contemporary records covering the years 1842-47, events were transpiring within the Nez Perce tribe which later greatlyaffected his career. It is necessary, therefore, to trace out the background in order to appreciate the significance of later events as they affected Lawyer.

The eleven-year history of the Oregon Mission of the American Board can be divided into two periods, each being approximately of the same length. The first period was characterized by dissensions within the Mission which climaxed in a fateful order from the Board dated February 25, 1842, which called for the dismissal of the Spaldings, the Grays, and the Smiths, for the closing of the work at Waiilatpu and Lapwai, and for the Whitmans to move to Tshimakain. The second period was characterized by growing hostility to the missionaries from some of the natives, especially the Cayuses, which climaxed in the Whitman massacre of November 1847.

The basic reasons for the dissensions within the Mission were rooted in personality clashes and in some honest differences of opinion regarding mission policies. Even high-minded and devoted missionaries could quarrel. Spalding's most bitter critic was Smith who, in his lonely station at Kamiah, had plenty of time to brood over his misfortunes and

---

[7] Drury, *Walker*, p. 216.

[8] Drury, *F.W.W.*, Vol. II, p. 241. Only two complete copies are known to be extant. A facsimile was issued by the Arthur H. Clark Co., Glendale, Ca., 1976.

write long letters. Smith wrote seven letters to Secretary Greene in 1840 in which he related in detail his criticisms of Spalding.[9] Smith was also highly critical of the natives, calling them self-righteous, selfish, and avaricious. In his letter of October 21, 1840, to Greene, he recommended that the Oregon Mission be turned over to the Methodists and that the Spaldings and the Grays be recalled.

Both Gray and Rogers also wrote letters to the Board criticizing Spalding. Whitman, with the exception of one minor criticism, refrained from joining this chorus of censure. Be it noted to Spalding's credit, he never wrote a complaining letter about his colleagues until June 1841 after he had learned of what others had written about him. He then wrote in self-defense.

Secretary Greene was stunned when he received four long letters from Smith on October 5, 1841. When these were added to other letters Smith had written and to the letters sent by Gray and Rogers, Greene felt that some drastic action had to be taken. He had to wait until the Prudential Committee of the Board met on February 15, 1842, before any action could be taken.

When the Prudential Committee of the Board met and were shown the correspondence which Greene had received, they were faced with the necessity of making a most painful decision. For several years the Oregon Mission had received extensive publicity through the *Missionary Herald* as being one of the most promising of all of the Board's missions, and now to confess failure was most humiliating. One of the contributing factors to the distressing situation was the time lag involved in their correspondence. It usually took about two years for a letter to go from Boston to Oregon and for a reply to be received, and likewise from Oregon to Boston. After due deliberations on the problem, the Committee voted to recall the three couples mentioned above, and to close the two southern stations.

Greene's problem then was to find some way to send the decision of the Committee to Oregon. The American Fur Company had closed its Rocky Mountain operations. There were no more caravans going to a rendezvous in the Rockies. To send the message by sea around South America would take too long. Then Greene learned that Dr. Elijah White, a newly appointed Indian Agent for Oregon, was planning to lead a party out to Oregon in the spring of 1842. Arrangements were made for White to carry the Board's order to Whitman.

---

[9] Drury, S. & S., contains copies of these letters.

DR. ELIJAH WHITE, OREGON'S FIRST INDIAN AGENT

The history of the evolution of the office of Head Chief of the Nez Perce nation begins with Dr. Elijah White. Dr. White, a member of the reenforcement of the Methodist Oregon Mission of 1837, served only three years before being dismissed by Jason Lee, the Superintendent of that Mission. On October 25, 1840, Lee wrote to Whitman and Spalding informing them of White's dismissal and that White was returning to the States where, Lee feared, he would do "all he can to injure them." [10]

After his return to the States, White was successful in obtaining an appointment as the first United States Indian Agent for Oregon. This appointment reflects more on White's political pull than on the acumen of the Washington officials who authorized the appointment. As long as the Oregon boundary was undecided (and this was not settled until 1846), Old Oregon was held in joint occupancy by England and the United States. Neither nation had any legal right to extend its jurisdiction over any part of the territory. The appointment of White as Indian Agent for Oregon was, therefore, illegal and was not recognized by the Hudson's Bay Company.[11]

After receiving his appointment, White succeeded in raising a party of 105 emigrants to go with him overland to Oregon. The party left the Missouri frontier on May 16, 1842. This was the first sizeable Oregon emigration. They took with them nineteen wagons, none of which was taken west of Fort Hall. From that point, the men, women, and children completed their journey on horseback.

WHITMAN LEAVES FOR BOSTON

White arrived at Waiilatpu on September 9, at which time he delivered the Board's letter to Whitman. Whitman was astounded at the drastic order of the Board. Conditions had so changed within the Mission that the directive simply did not apply. Both Smith and Rogers had left the Mission in the spring of 1841 and Gray was about to leave when White arrived. To Whitman the abandonment of Lapwai and

---

[10] Drury, S. & S., p. 292.

[11] When the H.B.C. Committee in London learned of Dr. White's arrival in Oregon, it wrote to Dr. McLoughlin on Sept. 27, 1843, saying: ". . . no authority emanating from the Government of the United States is to be recognized west of the Rocky Mountains until the boundary question shall have been settled." Drury, M. & N.W., Vol. I, p. 462.

Waiilatpu was unthinkable. The most successful station within the Mission was that at Lapwai. The strategic location of Waiilatpu, which straddled the Oregon Trail, had taken on new significance with the arrival of the White party and the prospect of an ever increasing number of immigrants in following years. The Tshimakain station did not need any more workers. Moreover, if the Whitmans did move there, they would have had to learn another Indian language.

Whitman called a special meeting of the Mission at Waiilatpu for Monday, September 26. All of the four men were present — Whitman, Spalding, Walker, and Eells. Circumstantial evidence indicates that even before the meeting began, Whitman had decided that it would be necessary for him to go back to Boston and intercede personally with the Board. He wanted the Board to rescind the order dismissing Spalding and calling for the closing of the two southern stations. Spalding was quick to acquiesce to Whitman's proposal for he realized that it would be in his interest if the Board reinstated him in its good favor. Walker and Eells, more deliberate by nature, hesitated but finally consented with the understanding that Whitman should find someone to look after the Waiilatpu station before leaving.

Within twenty-four hours after his three associates had left for their respective stations, Whitman made plans to leave for the East on the following Monday, October 3. Whitman was fortunate in securing the consent of A. L. Lovejoy, one of the members of the White party, to travel with him to the States. Both men felt it imperative to leave as soon as possible so as to cross the Blue Mountains and the Rockies before the winter snows became too deep. As it was, they nearly lost their lives while crossing the Rockies in what is now western Colorado.

Whitman arrived back in Boston on March 29, 1843. He was successful in his mission, for the Board rescinded that part of its drastic order of February 1842 which still applied. On his way back to the Missouri frontier, Whitman called on relatives in his former home in Rushville, New York, where he made arrangements to take his thirteen-year-old nephew, Perrin B. Whitman, with him out to Oregon. Perrin was destined to play a prominent role in Oregon's history following the Whitman massacre of 1847.

Whitman and his nephew joined about 1,000 Oregon-bound emigrants on the Missouri frontier in May 1843. This was the first great Oregon emigration. After the long caravan reached Fort Hall, Whitman became its leader and guide. The success of this large immigration, followed by ever larger parties in following years, precipitated a cultural conflict for the Indians of the upper Columbia River country. Mission activities at Waiilatpu were no longer the same as they had been before Whitman went East. Now more and more of his time and energy had to be devoted to caring for the immigrants. In doing so, he aroused the suspicion and finally the resentment of the Cayuses.

INDIAN UNREST, THREATS, AND INSULTS

Before Whitman left for Boston, he made some hasty arrangements for Gray to find someone to stay with Narcissa and look after the Waiilatpu property in his absence. Gray, however, left Waiilatpu on October 4, the day after Whitman and Lovejoy began their journey, leaving Narcissa alone as the only white person at Waiilatpu. With her was John, a Hawaiian laborer, who was in Whitman's employ, and three half-breed children whom the Whitmans had received into their home.

Late in the night of October 6, an Indian tried to force his way into Narcissa's bedroom. She sprang from her bed and tried to hold the door closed, calling at the same time for John who was sleeping in a nearby room. Frightened by her screams and the coming of the Hawaiian, the Indian fled. The next morning a messenger was sent to Fort Walla Walla to inform Archibald McKinlay, Chief Trader at the fort, of what had happened.

McKinlay sent one of his trusted men, Tom McKay, to go out to Waiilatpu and stay with Narcissa until it could be determined what should be done. After some deliberations, Narcissa consented to leave Waiilatpu and go to stay for a time with the Methodist missionaries at Waskopum, also called The Dalles. She was escorted to Fort Walla Walla on Tuesday, the 11th, and from there she went down the Columbia River with her two half-breed girls to Waskopum where she spent the winter. For the time being Waiilatpu was left unattended except for what care John, the Hawaiian, could give.

After some delays, Gray induced Mr. and Mrs. P. B. Littlejohn, independent missionaries who had arrived in Oregon in the fall of 1840, and William Geiger, Jr., who hailed from Narcissa's home town of Angelica, New York, to go to Waiilatpu. In the meantime, however, before these three were able to arrive at Waiilatpu, the gristmill and about 200 bushels of corn and wheat were burned. McKinlay felt that the fire had been deliberately set by one of the Indians.

In Narcissa's letter to her husband written from Walla Walla on October 22, she reported that the Spaldings had experienced trouble with some dissident Indians at Lapwai. Such information was passed on to Dr. White who, in his report to the Indian Bureau in Washington, wrote that Mrs. Spalding had been "grossly insulted" and that a disgruntled Indian had presented a loaded gun, "cocked at the breast of Mr. Spalding" and had abused and menaced him as far as possible without actually shooting him.[12]

White Moves to Institute Laws

Writing in retrospect to the Commissioner of Indian Affairs, Washington, D.C., on April 1, 1843, White explained why he felt it necessary to take some decisive action to prevent the recurrance of such threats and insults. He wrote:

> My arrival was in good season and probably saved much evil. I had but a short season of real rest after so long and toilsome journey before information reached me of the very improper conduct of the upper country Indians towards missionaries sent by the American Board of Commissioners and accompanied with a passport and a desire for my interposition in their behalf at once.[13]

Before the missionaries left the States in 1836 and 1838, they received passports issued by the War Department which not only granted them permission to reside in the Oregon country but also called upon the officers of the United States Army and "the Indian agents" to render such aid as was needed to facilitate "the accomplishments of their objects, and protection should circumstances require it." [14] Evidently it was Spalding who had appealed to White for protection and no doubt it was he who had sent his passport for White to see.

In his report to Washington, White drew attention to this provision in the passport and said that he felt it was "his imperative duty to protect them in their persons at least from outrage." So with this justification, White felt that it was his duty to visit Waiilatpu and Lapwai in November and December 1842 to see what could be done.

Since the Hudson's Bay Company had refused to recognize the legality of White's appointment as U.S. Indian Agent for Oregon, it refused to provide transportation for him to go up the Columbia to

---

12 *M. & N.W.*, Vol. II, p. 17.   13 White file, O.I.B.

14 Drury, *M. & N.W.*, Vol. I, p. 168 gives the full text of the passport.

Fort Walla Walla. White, therefore, found it necessary to hire six boatmen who, he explained, "were armed in the best manner, a sufficient number to command respect and secure the object of our undertaking." [15] Included in the White party was Cornelius Rogers who was to serve as interpreter.

White left the Willamette Valley on November 15, 1842, but, because of adverse weather, did not reach The Dalles until the 24th. There the Littlejohns and Geiger joined the party. The enlarged White party arrived at Fort Walla Walla on the 30th. There the services of Tom McKay were enlisted as a second interpreter.

In company with Archibald McKinlay, White visited Waiilatpu on November 1. With the exception of the burned gristmill and granary, there seemed to have been no other destruction or looting of the premises. Even so, White wrote that he was "shocked and pained at beholding the sad work of savage destruction." To White's disappointment, only a few Cayuses were in the vicinity when he called and none of the chiefs. It seems evident that Tiloukaikt, chief of the Waiilatpu band, being sensitive over the burning of the mill and granary, had fled. White left word that he would return after visiting Lapwai at which time he wanted to meet with all of the Cayuse chiefs.

THE NEZ PERCES ADOPT A CODE OF LAWS

Dr. White and his party arrived at Lapwai on December 6. Spalding was delighted with the assurance that something would be done to curb the lawlessness which had occurred at both Waiilatpu and Lapwai. He sent word to all the Nez Perce chiefs in the vicinity asking them to come to Lapwai to meet Agent White. Two days passed before all had assembled. They numbered twenty-two and included Ellis, Lawyer, Looking Glass, and possibly Joseph and Timothy.

"The chiefs met us," wrote White, "with civility, gravity, and dignified reserve." White opened the council by presenting the need for the Nez Perces to adopt a code of laws which would cover a number of offenses which had occurred at each of the two stations. He was followed by McKinlay,[16] McKay, Rogers, and Spalding, each of whom

---

[15] A. J. Allen, *Ten Years in Oregon* (Ithaca, N.Y., 1848), contains Dr. White's report. All further quotations from White are from this book, pp. 189 ff.

[16] McKinlay was later reprimanded by Dr. McLoughlin for taking part in the White meeting at Lapwai.

emphasized the same need. Among the chiefs, no one was more in favor of the idea than Ellis who, having spent four years at the Red River school, had become acquainted with the white man's method of governing society and appreciated the importance of having laws.

After several days of discussions, White submitted a code of eleven Articles which he had compiled with Spalding's help. Each of the Articles had grown out of a definite situation which had occurred at either Waiilatpu or Lapwai. The burning of the mill and granary at Waiilatpu was reflected in Article 2: "Whoever burns a dwelling shall be hung," and Article 3: "Whoever burns an out-building shall be imprisoned for six months, receive fifty lashes, and pay all damages." Article 5 clearly reflected the attempted assault on Narcissa Whitman: "If anyone enters a dwelling, without permission of the occupant, the chiefs shall punish him as they think proper." Other Articles forbade theft, the destruction of crops, and threatening the lives of white people. Article 11 gave a semblance of impartiality in claiming that the lews applied to the white men as well as to the Indians.[17]

The imposition of this code of laws on the Nez Perces was doomed to fail from the very beginning. A great gulf separated the white man's concept of a sovereign state and the red man's tribal structure. White's code of laws called for sanctions. Here was a glaring weakness, for there were no courts, no police, and no law enforcement agencies among the Indians. Moreover, as has been indicated, the United States by treaty with Great Britain could not set up such legal procedures as long as the two nations enjoyed joint occupancy over the territory.

Several of the Articles called for the use of the lash on offenders. Whipping was a common form of punishment among white people in that generation and even among the Indians themselves. It was an effective form of punishment where there were no jails. Flogging was an accepted form of punishment in the U.S. Navy until 1850. The Hudson's Bay Company, during the mission period, whipped Indians for certain offenses. Therefore, this form of punishment prescribed in the code was not then unusual. Hanging was abhorrent to the Indians.[18]

---

[17] For a listing of the laws, see Allen, *Ten Years,* pp. 189-90; and Gray, *Oregon,* p. 228; and Drury, *M. & N.W.,* Vol. II, pp. 21-2.

[18] The five Cayuses who were found guilty of taking part in the Whitman massacre by the U.S. District Court of Oregon on May 24, 1850, were hanged. The condemned begged to be shot rather than be hanged.

The code of laws did not specify who was responsible for applying the penalties, but presumably the chiefs were to take charge.

ELLIS, FIRST HEAD CHIEF OF THE NEZ PERCES

More important than the adoption of a code of laws was White's success in inducing the Nez Perces to accept a Head Chief for their nation. Up to this time there had been no Head Chief with authority over the forty or fifty scattered bands. Each band had its own head-man or chief and was a unit unto itself. White pointed out the need, from the white man's position, of a centralized authority with whom the Government could deal. According to White's report of this meeting with the chiefs, there was no objection to his suggestion. Indeed, they even asked White to select one of their number and make him the Head Chief. This White refused to do. He insisted that they make the selection.

After several hours of deliberations and after some consultations with McKay and Rogers, the choice was narrowed to two — Looking Glass and Ellis. Looking Glass, the elder of the two, aspired to the position. He prided himself on his prowess as a warrior and wanted to be known as the Warrior Chief. The fact that Ellis had spent four years, 1830-34, in the Red River school and had learned to speak English was a strong argument in his favor.

According to White, the grandfather of Ellis, a venerable old man of ninety winters who was known as Holhots Ilppilp or Red Grizzly Bear, and who had been one to welcome Lewis and Clark, decided the controversy by saying: "Clark pointed to this day, to you, and this occasion. We have long waited in expectation; sent three of our sons to Red River to prepare for it; two of them sleep with their fathers; [19] the other is here, and [he] can be ears, mouth, and pen for us." White also added that Ellis was ". . . a sensible man of thirty-two, reading, speaking & writing the English language tolerably well, has a plantation a few sheep, some neat [cattle] stock and no less than eleven hundred head of horses." By the standards of that day, Ellis was a rich man.

A new era in the history of the Nez Perce nation began with the appointment of Ellis as the tribe's first Head Chief. Lucullus V.

---

[19] The old chief was referring to the death of Cayuse Halket at the Red River school on Feb. 1, 1837, and to the passing of Cayuse Pitt sometime in 1841 after he had returned from the school. Drury, *M. & N.W.*, Vol. I, p. 36.

McWhorter, in his posthumously published book, *Hear Me, My Chiefs,* wrote: "The Nez Perces were inveigled [in 1842] into adopting a centralized government by Dr. Elijah White, whose outstanding contribution was the adoption [by the Nez Perces] of the principle of the head chief." [20] McWhorter, who was an articulate spokesman for the anti-missionary and anti-treaty party among the Nez Perces, claimed that this appointment of a Head Chief marked "the beginning of the disintegration" of the tribe.

A critical appraisal of McWhorter is found in a thesis written by Robert Lee Whitner, submitted in 1948 for an advanced degree at Washington State University, Pullman. Whitner wrote:

McWhorter had a strong antipathy for both the United States Indian policy and the work of missionaries among the Indians. His dislike for church nominations [of Indian agents and teachers] . . . was even more pronounced, particularly as it concerned the Nez Perces. He did not, however, make any comprehensive study of the subject; his remarks on it were in the nature of opinions rather than statements of fact.

With the coming of the white man, the appointment of a Head Chief of the Nez Perces became inevitable. Instead of this being "the beginning of the disintegration" of the tribe, it was in reality another step in the integration of that nation into the white man's society. There had to be such an office for the Nez Perces in order for the tribe to negotiate treaties with the white men and to protect their economic interests.

Spalding was elated with the adoption of the code of laws by the Nez Perces. He hastily made a translation into the Nez Perce language and printed an eight-page pamphlet on the Lapwai press which bears the imprint date of 1842. Dr. White's name was phonetically spelled as "Take Hwait."

After spending nearly two weeks at Lapwai, the White party started back to Waiilatpu on December 20. To White's disappointment only a few Cayuse chiefs had assembled to meet him, too few for any meaningful negotiations. White explained: "Learning what the Nez Perces had done, gave them great concern and anxiety." Even though one of their number, Five Crows, had been at the Lapwai meeting and had approved the adoption of the laws, the other chiefs were suspicious of the designs of the Whites and objected. When given copies of the

---

[20] McWhorter, *op. cit.,* p. 106.

Spalding pamphlet, they threw them disdainfully on the ground. They claimed that the imposition of the laws was "a deep-laid scheme. . . to destroy them and take possession of their country." [21] Had Dr. Whitman been present, their attitude might have been more cooperative. White promised to return in the spring of 1843 when he hoped that the Cayuses would follow the example of the Nez Perces.

WHITE'S RETURN TO LAPWAI AND WAIILATPU, 1843

During the winter of 1842-43, wild rumors spread through the Cayuse tribe, started by a half-breed, Baptiste Dorion. Narcissa wrote of this in a letter to her husband dated March 29, 1843 — a letter that he never received — which remains in the archives of the American Board at Harvard University. She wrote: "Mr. Geiger writes me that the Indians are constantly talking about going to war with the Americans and will not believe anything else but that you have gone home for men to fight them." [22]

The same disturbing rumors which Narcissa heard also reached the ears of Dr. White. These strengthened his intention to return to the upper Columbia country. He no longer could call on Cornelius Rogers to be his interpreter as Rogers had been drowned in a boating accident at the Willamette Falls on February 1, 1843. White turned to two Methodist missionaries — the Rev. Gustavus Hines and the Rev. H. K. W. Perkins — to accompany him in spite of the fact that they did not know the Nez Perce language. It is possible that White was also depending on Ellis to be an interpreter.

The White party, including a bodyguard of twelve men, left the Willamette Valley on April 29, 1843. They arrived at Waiilatpu on May 9 where they were cordially welcomed by Narcissa Whitman, who had preceded them by a few days, and by William Geiger. The Cayuses were still disturbed about the possibility of the Americans making war upon them. In his report to the Secretary of War, dated November 15, 1843, White wrote:

> The Indians flocked around me, and inquired after my party, and could not be persuaded for some time but that I had a large party concealed somewhere near, and only waited to get them convened to open fire upon them, and cut them off at a blow. On convincing

---

[21] Gustavus Hines, *Wild Life in Oregon* (New York, 1889), pp. 177 ff.
[22] Drury, *M. & N.W.*, Vol. II, p. 28.

them of my defenceless condition and pacific intentions, they were quite astounded. . . I actually found them suffering more from fear of war from the Whites, than the Whites from the Indians.[23]

When White called for a meeting of the Cayuse and Walla Walla chiefs to have them consider adopting the same code of laws which the Nez Perces had accepted, a delay was requested. Those present said that they wanted Ellis and some of the Nez Perces to meet with them. White then decided to go to Lapwai where he and his party arrived on May 13.

Spalding was delighted to welcome White back to Lapwai. It so happened that he had prepared nine natives for church membership and felt that it would be opportune to have these received in the presence of his guests. According to the record book of the Mission Church, eight were baptized and made members on Sunday, May 14, 1843. These included Levi, a brother of Timothy; Tamer, the wife of Timothy; and Asenath, the wife of Joseph. The ninth who was absent on that day, listed by Spalding as "Hezekiah, some 28 years old," was none other than Five Crows, who had spent several months in the Lapwai school. A supplemental note in the record book shows that he was received into the church a few weeks later. Five Crow's baptismal name, Hezekiah, never came into popular usage. He was the only one of the twenty-one natives who became members of the Mission Church who had some Cayuse blood. All of the others were Nez Perces.

Two names are missing in Spalding's list of converts — Ellis and Lawyer. No doubt Spalding did his best to get each to join the church but for some reason both held back during the Mission period. It is possible that Ellis had been baptized while a student at the Red River Mission school, although no record of this has been found. As will be stated in the last chapter of this book, Lawyer in his old age was baptized by Spalding in November 1871 and was elected the first elder in the First Presbyterian Church of Kamiah.

During this second visit of White and his party to Lapwai, the Nez Perces put on a show for the entertainment of their guests in which they acted out with stirring realism the Battle of Pierre's Hole, which had taken place in 1832, and in which Lawyer had been wounded. Possibly Lawyer played his own role in the drama. Gustavus Hines wrote the following description of the mock battle:

---

[23] Hines, *Wild Life in Oregon,* p. 143.

A terrible battle had been recently fought by a party of Nez Perces with a party of Blackfeet in which the former were victorious. The battle was acted to the life with the exception that no blood was shed. The scene closed with a war dance conducted by a chief whom the Whites designate by the name of "Lawyer," and in whom is combined the cunning and shrewdness of the Indian with the ability and penetration of the statesman.[24]

Since it was customary for Indian warriors in their war dances to display their trophies, such as scalps taken in combat, we may assume that Lawyer boastfully displayed his Blackfoot scalp mentioned in Chapter I.

Among those who witnessed this stirring drama was six-year-old Eliza Spalding who, many years later, wrote in her *Memoirs:* "The mental picture of that sham battle has always remained a vivid one with me." [25]

Dr. White and his party returned to Waiilatpu on Friday, May 19. Many of the Nez Perces accompanied him, including Ellis, Lawyer, and from four to five hundred others. The Cayuse Council lasted for five or six days. This time the Cayuses were friendly and receptive. After the laws had been explained and recommended by Ellis and other Nez Perce chiefs, they were accepted. Five Crows was selected by the Cayuses to be their first Head Chief. The adoption of a code of laws and the appointment of Head Chiefs marked the beginning of a new era in the history of these tribes.

---

[24] Hines, *Wild Life in Oreg.*, p. 174.
[25] Eliza Spalding Warren, *Memoirs of the West* (Portland, 1916), p. 20.

CHAPTER FOUR

Lawyer Serves as Head Chief, 1848-1855

Now and then some climactic event takes place which dramatically marks the end of one era and the beginning of another. Such was the Whitman massacre of November-December 1847 which took the lives of fourteen white people including Marcus and Narcissa Whitman. This tragedy marked the end of the mission period, which had begun in 1835, and the beginning of the dominance of the Whites over the Indians.

The causes of the massacre were many — the clash of cultures, the Indians' fear of the incoming Whites, the lies of frustrated half-breeds, and finally the devastating effect of a measles epidemic introduced by the 1847 immigrants. According to reliable estimates, the Cayuse tribe suffered a loss of about one-half of its numbers in the fall of 1847 due to this epidemic.[1] The Cayuses could not understand how white people could have immunity against measles and survive while the Indians, both adults and children, usually died. The Indians concluded that Whitman must have been poisoning them in order to get their lands and their horses. As a white medicine man, or tewat, Whitman deserved to be killed.

The Legislature of the Provisional Government of Oregon happened to be in session when the shocking news of the Whitman massacre reached the Willamette Valley on December 8, 1847. The Legislature reacted immediately. A punitive expeditionary force of 500 volunteers

---

[1] Father J. B. A. Brouillet, who arrived at Waiilatpu two days after the massacre, claimed that 197 members of the Cayuse tribe had died of measles in the fall of 1848. This would have been at least one-half of the tribe. Drury, *M. & N.W.*, Vol. ii, p. 209.

was authorized to be raised and placed under the command of Colonel Cornelius Gilliam. They were to march into the Cayuse country and capture, if possible, the murderers. This act was tantamount to a declaration of war against the Cayuse nation and marked the beginning of a series of Indian wars which were to trouble the upper Columbia River country for the next ten years.

In the meantime, through the efforts of Peter Skene Ogden of the Hudson's Bay Company, the forty-seven men, women, and children held captive by the Cayuses at Waiilatpu were ransomed and released on December 29. The Spaldings with their three children and four others, arrived at Fort Walla Walla on January 1, 1848, being escorted there by a company of some forty friendly Nez Perces. The next day all of the released captives started their voyage down the Columbia River to the Willamette Valley to begin life anew.

A skirmish took place along the Umatilla River on February 26, 1848, between some of the Oregon Volunteers and several hundred Cayuses and their allies. A Cayuse tewat, who boasted that he was immune to American bullets, was killed and Five Crows was seriously wounded. After suffering a few casualties, the Cayuses withdrew.

Following this skirmish, the Volunteers marched to Waiilatpu where they arrived on March 3. They were shocked to see the destruction which had taken place. The mission buildings had been burned. Wolves had dug into the shallow graves where the victims had been buried, devoured some of the bodies, and scattered their bones about the premises.

By salvaging adobe bricks from the walls of the buildings, the Volunteers were able to construct a wall around their camp site which was called Fort Waters, after Lieutenant Colonel James Waters, who had become the commanding officer following the accidental death of Colonel Gilliam on March 28. Waters returned to the Willamette Valley a few weeks later and was succeeded in command by Major H. A. G. Lee.

Several expeditions were sent out from Fort Waters in pursuit of the murderers, but always without success. In June 1848, a company of sixty men under the command of Major Joseph Magone was sent to Tshimakain to escort to safety the marooned Walker and Eells families. This marked the end of the Oregon Mission of the American Board.

LAWYER RECOGNIZED AS HEAD CHIEF

Sometime during 1847, Chief Ellis, who was with a hunting party in the buffalo country of what is now western Montana, died of measles. Lawyer was a member of this party. An incident took place on May 28, 1855, during the proceedings of the Walla Walla Council which indicates that Lawyer was with Ellis when he died. It appears that Ellis, realizing that his end was near, wrote out his advice regarding the policies which he recommended that the Nez Perces should follow in their dealings with the Whites. It may be that Ellis felt that Lawyer should be his successor as Head Chief since he gave the written advice to him.

In the official transcript of Governor Isaac I. Steven's report of the 1855 Council, we may read:

Lawyer opened a [note] book containing in their own language the advice left to them by their Great Chief Ellis, and read as follows:

"Ellis said, Whenever the Great Chief of the Americans shall come into your country to give you the laws, accept them. The Walla Walla's heart is a Walla Walla; a Cayuse heart is a Cayuse; as is a Yakima's heart, a Yakima; a Nez Perce's heart is a Nez Perce; but they will receive the same white law. They are all going straight, yes! While the Nez Perces are going straight, why should they turn aside to follow others who are [not] going straight!" [2] [Then Lawyer, evidently turning from the written statement, said:] Ellis' advice is to accept the white law [i.e., a treaty]. I have read it to you to show you my heart.

"Accept the white law," became Lawyer's dominant political guide. Throughout his approximately twenty-five years service as Head Chief of the Nez Perces, Lawyer consistently followed Ellis' dying advice by remaining friendly with the Whites and by refusing to join neighboring tribes when they resorted to hostilities against U.S. troops.

While the Volunteers were at Fort Waters, Major Lee learned of the death of Ellis which had occurred sometime late in 1847 when he was in the buffalo country. Realizing the need for the selection of a successor, Lee called a council of Nez Perce chiefs to meet with him at Waiilatpu during the first week of May 1848. About 100 chiefs and

---

[2] From the transcript of the Proceedings of the 1855 Walla Walla Council. Original in National Archives, Washington, D.C. Copy in Whitman College.

head-men responded. Lawyer, who was then in the buffalo country, was not present.

Again there was a contest, with Looking Glass as one of the aspirants for the office of Head Chief. Major Lee, however, let it be known that he favored the appointment of Richard. Richard was one of the two Nez Perce boys whom Whitman had taken east with him in 1835 and who had spent a few months in a public school in Ithaca, New York, where he had learned to read, write, and speak some English. No doubt this limited knowledge of English was the determining factor in Major Lee's mind when he recommended that the council appoint Richard as Head Chief. In order to appease the ambitious Looking Glass, Lee appointed him War Chief. According to Frances F. Victor, in her *Early Wars in Oregon,* Richard was chosen because of his "superior attainments and good character." [3]

The appointment of Richard as Head Chief did not meet the approval of Colonel James Waters who, on May 24, less than two weeks after the appointment had been made, wrote: "My confidence in Richard is completely gone." [4]

Another who expressed doubts was Joel Palmer who was one of the three Peace Commissioners who had accompanied the military into the Cayuse country, and who was destined to play an important role in the 1855 Council and in the Indian wars which followed. Writing from Fort Waters on June 9, 1848, to officials in Washington, D.C., Palmer said that although Richard was "a very promising young man," yet he was doubtful of the wisdom of the military pressuring the Nez Perces to agree to this selection.

Palmer explained his views: "I doubt the policy of appointing chiefs for a nation who are as competent as the Nez Perces to select one for themselves. They will only respect a chief of our appointing so far as they expect to profit by it. If he is a bad man, we must bear the responsibility; if he be a good one, his acts are only accounted good by them so far as they are benefited." [5]

Richard's tenure as Head Chief was short and ineffective. His own people did not accept him and there is no evidence that the Army officers ever called upon him to exercise any authority as Head Chief. He is known to have joined the Oregon Volunteers, along with some

---

[3] Victor, *Early Indian Wars,* p. 205.
[4] Cayuse War File, o.i.b., Letter #1089.   [5] *Ibid.,* Letter #1100.

other Nez Perces, and there are conflicting reports as to what then happened to him.[6]

The exigencies of the Cayuse War, in which the Nez Perces were cooperating with the Oregon Volunteers in their efforts to capture the Whitman murderers, called for the selection of a Head Chief who commanded not only the respect of the majority of his fellow chiefs but also of the Army officials. Into this vacuum stepped Lawyer who, by virtue of his knowledge of English and by his evident leadership abilities, assumed the duties of a Head Chief even though the Nez Perces may not have held a council to appoint him to this office.

Supporting this assumption is the fact that Robert Newell, one of Lawyer's friends from their fur trapping days and who was one of the three Peace Commissioners, gave Lawyer a large United States flag in recognition of the services that he and his warriors had rendered in the Cayuse War.[7]

The very fact that the flag was given to Lawyer rather than to Richard or to some other Nez Perce chief indicates that Newell, as a Government official, recognized him as being the Head Chief of the tribe. This was the flag that Lawyer so proudly carried when riding at the head of the Nez Perce delegation of some 2,500 when they arrived at the Walla Walla Council on May 24, 1855. (*See* illustration.)

As will be noted in the following chapter, three of the white men — Governor I. I. Stevens, Lawrence Kip, and the artist Gustavus Sohon, recognized Lawyer as being Head Chief at the time the 1855 Walla Walla Council opened. No documentary evidence has been found which shows that the Nez Perces had a council before 1855 at which time Lawyer was elected Head Chief. Of course, it should be remembered that the Nez Perces were not then keeping records.

The historian, Frances F. Victor, who interviewed Lawyer at Kamiah in 1873, wrote that Lawyer had been Head Chief of the Nez Perces "ever since the deaths of Ellis and Richard." [8] Evidently Victor had secured this information from Lawyer himself. Because of this evidence, I have accepted the view that Lawyer became Head Chief in the spring of 1848 either by Richard's death or default, and that he was so accepted by the American [9] officials and by the majority of the tribe.

---

[6] Gray, *Oregon*, p. 563, claims that Richard was "basely murdered by a Catholic Indian," shortly after his appointment. Victor, *Early Wars of Oregon*, p. 203, states that he was killed in the Cayuse War of 1848.

[7] Carey, *Oregon*, Vol. II, p. 574.   [8] Victor, *Early Indian Wars*, p. 337.

As will be stated, the first positive documentation of the Nez Perces themselves accepting Lawyer as their Head Chief occurred when the chiefs met in council during the meeting of the 1855 Council.

A contrary opinion has been expressed by critics of Lawyer who claim that he did not become Head Chief until he was formally appointed by Governor Isaac I. Stevens at the 1855 Walla Walla Council. Lucullus V. McWhorter, in his *Hear Me, My Chiefs,* claimed that the Whites drove in two "bolts" or wedges which divided the tribe, a division which continues to this day. According to McWhorter, the first wedge was the adoption of "a centralized government" and the acceptance of a Head Chief. McWhorter blamed Dr. White for that. Then McWhorter wrote: ". . . the second and decisive bolt was driven on June 11, 1855, when Stevens steered and secured the appointment or election of the famous orator and Christian, Lawyer, to succeed the spirit-broken and diseased head chief, Ellis of mission fame." [10] As will be stated in the following chapter, Governor Stevens did not appoint Lawyer as Head Chief. Rather, Stevens recognized the fact that Lawyer was already Head Chief by the voluntary choice of his fellow chiefs.

The second critic is Allen P. Slickpoo, Sr., who in his recently published *Noon Nee-Me-poo (We the Nez Perces)* wrote: "Lawyer was appointed by the Government as the Head Chief of the Nez Perces because of his knowledge of the English language." Slickpoo maintains that this was done "over the protests of the other chiefs of the respective groups or bands of the Nez Perces," but gives no documentation for this assertion. Slickpoo also claims that before his appointment as Head Chief, Lawyer was nothing more than the village "crier," whose duty it was to go "around the camp daily, to announce any news or activities to be held about the camp." [11] Again, no documentation is given.

Such assertions as McWhorter and Slickpoo have made imply that, even though the Nez Perces had accepted the idea of having a Head Chief in 1842, and even after Ellis had served as such for five years and Richard temporarily, the tribe was content to get along without a Head Chief during the troubled years of 1848-55. In my opinion, such

---

[9] Strictly speaking the natives were more American than the Whites, yet because the term "Americans" is often used to refer to the white people who migrated to Oregon, the term will be used with this connotation.

[10] McWhorter, *op. cit.,* p. 106.   [11] Slickpoo, *op. cit.,* pp. 136-7.

an assumption is too implausible to accept. Contemporary evidence clearly indicates that during these years Lawyer was accepted by American officials as being the Head Chief of the Nez Perce nation.

LAWYER RECEIVED BY THE WHITES AS A WELCOMED GUEST

Having been schooled in the amenities of the white man's social life through his missionary teachers, A. B. Smith and H. H. Spalding, Lawyer became a welcomed guest in the social circles which included distinguished white residents of the Willamette Valley. Contemporary accounts of these visits show that he was received with all the dignity which would have been accorded his position as Head Chief of his nation.

Dr. John McLoughlin sponsored a Fourth of July ball at the Oregon House in Oregon City in 1848 to which Lawyer was invited. A report of the social events included the following:

> A board of managers, of which the venerable John McLoughlin was chairman, sent out invitations months in advance . . .
> The affair began with a sumptuous dinner at noon in the basement of the old tavern, with Governor Abernethy of the Provisional Government as master of ceremonies. On his right sat John McLoughlin and on his left, the friendly Chief Lawyer of the Nez Perce tribe. In the background were the Indians, and the young people, including pretty half-breed girls all anxious for the dancing to begin.[12]

Another, but undated, incident involving one of Lawyer's visits to the lower Columbia River country is found in Edmund S. Meany's *History of the State of Washington*. Meany relates the story of an experience which Lawyer had when dining with some U.S. Army officers at their barracks at Fort Vancouver. Lawyer noticed a man seated at the table with a bushy head of hair, whose face seemed familiar but who, for the time being, he was unable to identify. The man was Colonel Benjamin L. E. Bonneville who, while on leave from the U.S. Army in 1832, had ventured into the Rocky Mountain fur trade. At this time, Lawyer had been associated with Bonneville. Since Bonneville was baldheaded, he was known by the Indians as the "Baldheaded Chief." According to Meany, whenever anyone at the table spoke to this stranger, Lawyer would glance furtively at him straining to recognize

---

[12] From article by Dan E. Clark, *O.H.Q.*, Vol. 52 (1956), pp. 333 ff.

his voice. Finally, the stranger turned to Lawyer and speaking in Nez Perce asked about a certain chief long since dead.

"That was my father," exclaimed Lawyer.

Without betraying his identity, Bonneville then asked about another chief.

"That was my brother."

Realizing that he was unrecognized, Bonneville pulled off his wig, whereupon Lawyer jumped to his feet and shouted: "Baldheaded Chief." [13]

Lawyer's acceptance as an honored guest by such distinguished men as Dr. McLoughlin, Governor Abernethy, and the officers at the Vancouver barracks, speaks eloquently of the esteem in which he was held by his white contemporaries.

PURSUIT AND CAPTURE OF THE WHITMAN MURDERERS

Ever since the settlement of the Oregon boundary with Great Britain in 1846, Congress had procrastinated in establishing a territorial government for the Old Oregon territory. When the ex-mountain man, Joe Meek, another friend of Lawyer's dating back to the fur trapping days, arrived in Washington, D.C., on May 28, 1848, with the news of the Whitman massacre, a dilatory Congress was stirred to act. The bill making Oregon a territory of the United States was given final approval on August 13 and President Polk signed it the next day.

General Joseph Lane, who distinguished himself in the Mexican War of 1846, was appointed Governor of the new territory and Meek was made United States Marshall. The two arrived in Oregon City on March 2, 1849. The next day Governor Lane proclaimed that "the laws of the United States extended over and were declared to be in force in said territory." This meant that the United States Government was free to establish reservations for the Indians, including the Nez Perces, who dwelt within the Territory.

Shortly after Governor Lane's arrival, Chief Lawyer and a few of his closest friends among the Nez Perce chiefs traveled to Oregon City to call on the Governor and to assure him of their friendship. It was then that Lane asked Lawyer to help him in capturing the Whitman murderers, and in the enforcement of the Government's laws among the natives of the upper Columbia River country. Lawyer promised

---

[13] Meany, *op. cit.* (New York, 1909), Vol. II, p. 35.

his full cooperation. After the Nez Perce party had returned from their meeting with Governor Lane, Lawyer told his people: "The murderers of Dr. Whitman must be delivered up to the Whites, that they may be put to death. This is the law." [14]

The arrival of a regiment of Mounted Riflemen consisting of 600 officers and men together with some 700 horses, 1,200 mules, and 175 wagons at Oregon City in October 1849 made it possible for Governor Lane to issue an ultimatum to the Cayuse chiefs who had not been involved in the Whitman massacre. They were either to deliver up to the American authorities those accused of killing the Whitmans or he would invade their country and make war on the whole tribe. Writing from Oregon City on November 9, 1849, Lane, in a letter addressed to Young Chief, wrote:

> If the murderers are not given up, I will have to make war. We have many soldiers and more are coming . . . I do not want to do this. I want the Cayuse nation to exist. It would make my heart sorry to hurt the innocent, but if we have to go to war, how can I discriminate between the guilty and the innocent? You can save your nation from such a calamity by giving up the guilty, that done and we will be friends and brothers.[15]

It should be noted that Lane did not address his letter to Five Crows, who had been appointed Head Chief of the Cayuses by Elijah White in 1842, but rather to Young Chief. Five Crows, although not directly involved in the massacre, had abducted a young woman, Lorinda Bewley, and had taken her to his lodge on the Umatilla River to be his wife. She was later released. Because of this incident, Five Crows had forfeited all respect from the Whites.

Young Chief consulted with two other Cayuse chiefs, Stickus and Camaspelo. After studying Governor Lane's ultimatum, they realized that for the good of their tribe, they would have to cooperate with the Americans and turn the accused murderers over to the authorities. In this decision they had the cooperation of Lawyer who sent Timothy with twenty Nez Perce warriors to help Young Chief capture Tiloukaikt and the other conspirators.

Because of this turn of events, Tiloukaikt and his diminishing band,

---

[14] Josephy, *Nez Perces*, pp. 283-4, quoting from Proceedings of the Treaty Council at Lapwai (1863), p. 64, National Archives.

[15] Cayuse War Correspondence, O.I.B.

including women and children, fled to the Blue Mountains where they were able to subsist for a few weeks. Tiloukaikt was faced with a hopeless situation. His own tribe, with reenforcements from the Nez Perces, had turned against him. Moreover, there was the threat that if he refused to surrender, the American soldiers would come and make war on the tribe. Having spent about two years wandering in the Blue Mountains and in the Snake River country, having lost at least ten members of his band including two of his sons, having lost most if not all of his cattle and horses, being short of ammunition and facing starvation, and finding the mountains covered with deep snow, Tiloukaikt had no alternative but to surrender. This he did in April 1850.

Young Chief with an escort of his warriors took Tiloukaikt and four other accused Cayuses to The Dalles during the first week of May and turned them over to Governor Lane. The accused men were then taken to Oregon City for trial by the U.S. District Court. Only fifteen days elapsed between May 9, 1850, when the grand jury met, and the 24th, when the death sentence for all five was pronounced. They were hanged on June 3.

The events of the Cayuse War of 1848-50 left a heritage of bitter anti-American feeling among the Cayuse, Walla Walla, and Umatilla Indians, which was felt in the Walla Walla Council of 1855 and in the Indian wars which followed. Since Lawyer was so deeply involved in the 1855 Council, he too was affected by these events.

CHAPTER FIVE

The Walla Walla Council of 1855

Beginning with the establishment of Fort Vancouver in 1825 and continuing through December 1847, when the forty-seven captives held by the Cayuses at Waiilatpu were ransomed and rescued, the main influence exercised by the Whites on the Indians to restrain lawlessness and to punish offenders was the Hudson's Bay Company. The leaverage exercised by the Company was largely economic. The natives had come to depend on the H.B.C. for such trading items as guns, ammunition, and blankets. The threat of withholding such items was always a powerful argument used through the chiefs to maintain good relationships between the Whites and the Indians.

Foreseeing the day when the United States would extend its sovereignty over the Oregon country, the Hudson's Bay Company as early as March 1, 1842, directed McLoughlin to establish a new depot on the present site of Victoria, British Columbia. The arrival of the large 1843 immigration caused the Company to accelerate its plan of transferring its fur trade from Fort Vancouver to Fort Victoria. By 1845, Fort Vancouver had become little more than a mercantile establishment serving the needs of all Oregon settlers and immigrants who might apply.

For several years after the Whitman massacre, the United States Government provided a military escort for Oregon-bound immigrants who were passing through Cayuse territory. An estimated 5,000 immigrants arrived in 1848 with some 1,000 wagons. In that one year, more white people entered Oregon than were in the combined Nez Perce, Cayuse, and Walla Walla tribes. As the number of immigrants increased year by year, the Indians became more and more fearful of being engulfed by this seemingly endless stream of white people. This influx of land-hungry Americans was bound to precipitate a conflict.

A first-hand report of the existence of the anti-American feeling in the Cayuse and Palouse country is found in letters that Elkanah Walker wrote to his wife in June 1851. A new Indian Agent for Oregon, Dr. Anson Dart, had arrived in Oregon City on October 12, 1850. Wishing to assess the extent of the losses suffered by the American Board at Waiilatpu and Lapwai, and also to investigate the advisability of permitting the Board to reopen its former stations, Dr. Dart decided to make an inspection tour of the upper Columbia River country. He secured the services of Elkanah Walker and Perrin Whitman [1] as his interpreters.

The Dart party reached abandoned Waiilatpu on June 13. In a letter to his wife, dated June 21, Walker commented on their visit "to the old station." He wrote: "It was gloomy enough. There is no appearance of any living thing about the place. The [rye] grass stands in its primitive greatness. The trails are untrod and the Indians do not visit the place, believing it haunted." [2]

In this same letter, Walker stated that although the Spokane Indians were eager for their former missionaries to return, the hostility shown by the Cayuse and Palouse Indians was such that it would not be safe for them to travel the trails once so freely used. Dr. Dart found the Cayuses strongly opposed to having any American traders, settlers, or missionaries live in their country.[3]

The Dart party then moved on to Lapwai where they were warmly welcomed by 400 "warriors." Although Walker, in his letter to his wife, did not specifically mention Lawyer as one of those who were present, we may assume that if as many as 400 Nez Perces had gathered for the occasion, Lawyer would have been one of them. According to Walker, the Nez Perces were somewhat apprehensive over the possibility of the Government moving them onto a reservation. They were agreeably surprised and pleased when Dart assured them that any proposed reservation would include the lands on which they were then living. After visiting the Nez Perces, the Dart party returned to Oregon City without visiting the Spokanes.

---

[1] During the four years that Perrin Whitman lived with his uncle at Waiilatpu, 1843-47, he learned the Cayuse (i.e., the Nez Perce) language. Perrin was sent to The Dalles shortly before the Whitman massacre and thus escaped being killed. In the following years, he often served as an interpreter for Government officials.

[2] The original Walker letters written to his wife while on this tour are in the Library of Washington State Univ., Pullman.   [3] Dart file, O.I.B.

The friendly attitude of the Nez Perces toward the Americans contrasted sharply with the hostility shown by the Cayuses. This hostility was but the foreshadowing of their behavior when they met with Governor I. I. Stevens in the Walla Walla Council of 1855. Reporting to the Commissioner of Indian Affairs in Washington, D.C., on September 17, 1851, Dart pointed out that the Cayuse, Walla Walla, and Nez Perce tribes claimed a territory larger than that of the combined states of New Hampshire, Vermont, Rhode Island, and Connecticut, an area totaling more than 25,000 square miles. "I would suggest," wrote Dart, "the propriety of early provisions being made by Congress for purchasing these lands." Nearly four years were to pass before this recommendation was implemented.

GOVERNOR ISAAC INGALLS STEVENS

Isaac I. Stevens was born in 1818. He was graduated from West Point in 1839 when he was twenty-one years old, and served with distinction in the Mexican War of 1846. His career shows that he was a talented, aggressive, and energetic man. Evidently he was ambitious and politically minded, for when Washington Territory was created in 1853, Stevens was appointed Governor even though he was only thirty-five years old. Washington Territory then included all of the present state of Idaho. Stevens later served in the Civil War where he attained the rank of Major General. Hence, some historians often refer to him as General Stevens. He was killed in action on September 1, 1862, in the Battle of Chantilly.

Stevens' relationship to the newly formed Territory was threefold. He was not only Governor, he was also Superintendent of Indian Affairs, and was commissioned to make a survey of a possible railroad route from St. Paul to Puget Sound. Associated with Stevens in the survey was Captain George B. McClellan who became the Commanding General of the Union Army for a time during the Civil War. McClellan was appointed to take a surveying party and work eastward from Puget Sound while Stevens with another party worked westward from St. Paul. Stevens left St. Paul on June 8, 1853, and McClellan left Puget Sound a few weeks later. The two met at Fort Colville on October 18.

Even though Washington Territory was then under United States sovereignty, the Hudson's Bay Company continued to operate Forts Colville and Walla Walla as trading posts for the convenience of the

Indians and the incoming settlers. By 1853 both forts had lost their former importance. The fur trade had almost disappeared. The fields and gardens which once had surrounded Fort Colville were lying fallow when Governor Stevens visited it in the fall of 1853. The former large herds of horses and cattle had been drastically reduced and most of the employees of the Company had been dismissed.[4]

Having lost their jobs at the fort, the former employees, most of whom were French Canadians, had turned to farming in order to make a living for themselves and their families. As Stevens rode through the Colville River Valley en route to and returning from Colville, he noted that there was a line of settlements twenty-eight miles long. Stevens discovered that the settlers were eager to become naturalized United States citizens and to secure legal title to the lands they were occupying. Since these men had Indian or part-Indian wives, their settling on Indian lands did not arouse any local opposition from the natives. Stevens realized that no title to land could be given until all Indian claims were extinguished and the Indians settled on a reservation.

From Colville, the Stevens party traveled to Fort Walla Walla. They arrived on November 4, 1853, at the home of William McBean who had served as Chief Trader at Fort Walla Walla from 1846 to 1851. Stevens found McBean living in retirement a few miles beyond the Hudson's Bay Company's farm on the Walla Walla River. Stevens noted that a Roman Catholic missionary, Father Eugene Chirouse, with two Catholic laymen, was living about thirty miles up the Walla Walla River from its mouth. They had opened a mission among the Cayuse Indians which, Stevens reported, was fairly successful.

On November 5, Stevens visited Waiilatpu where he found two settlers, "Bumford and Brooks," harvesting a fine crop of potatoes. That which Stevens had observed at Fort Colville, where former H.B.C. employees had turned to farming, was repeated at Walla Walla, but with one important exception. There at Walla Walla Americans were coming into the country and settling on Indian lands. This boded ill, for the Cayuses and Walla Wallas were far more sensitive to the settlement of the Whites in their midst than were the placid Spokanes. Here, too, the settlers were eager to get clear title to their farms and this could only be done by placing the Indians on a reservation.

Having completed his inspection tour of the upper Columbia River

---

4 When Walker and Eells first visited Fort Colville in September 1838, they noted that twenty men were then employed at the fort. Drury, *Walker*, p. 75.

country, Stevens hastened to Olympia, the capital of the newly established Territory. In his address before the first meeting of the Legislature, the Governor emphasized "the importance of extinguishing the Indian titles" to vast areas within the Territory which had been vaguely considered as Indian country.[5] This could be done only by meeting with the natives in councils, drawing up treaties, and establishing reservations. This was the only legal way by which the country could be opened to white settlers.

Stevens left for Washington, D.C., in the spring of 1854 to report on the progress of the railroad survey and to discuss with authorities the necessity of establishing reservations for the various Indian tribes in the Territory. Traveling by way of the Isthmus of Panama, Stevens arrived in Washington in May. In the consultations which followed, Stevens was authorized to proceed with his plan to meet with the tribes in councils and draw up the necessary treaties which would establish reservations.

Governor Stevens, his wife, a son, and three daughters sailed from New York on September 20. They made the same journey that the Governor had taken on his way to Washington. Two and one-half months passed before the Stevens family reached their home in Olympia. The eldest of the four children was the twelve-year-old boy, Hazard, who in 1901 published his two-volume life of his father, *The Life of Isaac Ingalls Stevens*. This is a primary source of information bearing on the history of the 1855 Walla Walla Council. Among the many documents which Hazard used in the writing of this biography was his father's diary.

PRELUDE TO THE 1855 WALLA WALLA COUNCIL

Within a few days after his return to Olympia, Stevens took steps to implement his plan to draw up the necessary treaties. Since some of the Indians involved in the upper Columbia River country lived in the Territory of Oregon as well as in the Territory of Washington, Stevens invited General Joel Palmer, Superintendent of Indian Affairs for Oregon, to join him in negotiating a treaty for the four Nez Perce-speaking tribes — the Nez Perces, Cayuses, Walla Wallas, and Umatillas. Stevens and Palmer met at Fort Vancouver on April 4-7, 1855, and agreed that the council should be held at the Indians' ancient council grounds at Walla Walla, beginning May 20, 1855.

---

[5] Stevens, *Stevens*, Vol. I, p. 419.

In his official report to the Commissioner of Indian Affairs, Stevens explained that the site was in the Cayuse country "near the place consecrated by the blood of the missionary, Dr. Whitman and his family who were killed in 1847 by the Indians of the Cayuse tribe." The site, now a part of the campus of Whitman College, lies about seven miles east of the former Whitman Mission at Waiilatpu.

After setting the time and place for the council, messengers were sent to the several tribes concerned inviting them to attend. Stevens sent his secretary, James Doty, to the Nez Perces. Santee, in the account of his interview with Lawyer, wrote: "James Doty . . . arrived at Lapwai in April 1855. Doty invited the Nez Perce chiefs to come together in order that he might address them. The Chief Lawyer among them accepted the invitation. On the morning of April 18, the Indians trimmed the branches from a tall pine and using the tree as a staff, ran up the American flag awarded the Nez Perces for their loyalty during the Cayuse War." [6] Doty then made known to the chiefs the request of Stevens that the Nez Perces be represented at the grand council soon to be held at Walla Walla. The Chiefs agreed to this.

On their way up the Columbia River, en route to Walla Walla, Governer Stevens and General Palmer stopped at The Dalles. Stevens had thirty-five men in his party including interpreters, secretaries, and his son Hazard. Palmer had twelve. While at The Dalles, the two Commissioners heard some disturbing news of Indian unrest and even of hostility to their coming. One report referred to some "turbulent conduct of five young men of the Cayuse tribe," who had been annoying settlers "by entering their houses in a threatening manner, breaking down their enclosures, [i.e., their fences], and indicating a bad spirit." [7]

More disturbing than these acts of vandalism were the threats of "violent opposition" to the Commissioners.[8] Father Pascal Ricard of the Yakima Catholic Mission, who happened to be at The Dalles when the Commissioners arrived, warned them "that the Indians were planning to cut off the white chiefs who might attempt to hold a council." [9] These reports of possible trouble and even of violence were so alarming that the Commissioners requested Major C. J. Raines, then in charge of

---

[6] *Washington Hist. Qtly.*, Vol. 25 (Jan. 1934), p. 50. Undoubtedly the flag was that which Robert Newell had given Lawyer in the spring of 1848.

[7] Stevens to Indian Commissioner, June 12, 1855. o.i.b.

[8] *Magazine of History*, Extra No. 39 (Tarrytown, N.Y., 1915), p. 12.

[9] Stevens, *Stevens*, Vol. ii, pp. 28-9.

the Army garrison at The Dalles, for a military escort. Major Raines complied with the request and detailed Lieutenant Archibald Gracie and a company of forty-six men to accompany the Commissioners. This brought the total in the Stevens-Palmer party to ninety-three.

Present at The Dalles when Stevens and Palmer arrived was nineteen-year-old Lawrence Kip. Kip was visiting his friend Lieutenant Gracie with whom he had served as a cadet in the West Point Military Academy, 1853-54. Kip did not remain to be graduated but, nevertheless, was commissioned a Second Lieutenant in the U.S. Army on June 30, 1857 and, as will be stated, took part in the Indian wars of 1857-58. Kip was invited to accompany the Stevens-Palmer party and attended the Walla Walla Council as a civilian observer. This he did and the fascinating diary he kept during the sessions of the Council remains a prime source of information regarding what took place. His diary published under the title, "The Indian Council in the Valley of the Walla Walla," appeared in at least three historical magazines.[10]

The Stevens-Palmer party arrived at the council grounds on Monday, May 21, 1855. The military escort came two days later. A work party had been sent on ahead which pitched tents on the banks of what is now Mill Creek, a tributary of the Walla Walla River. Hazard Stevens, then thirteen years old, later wrote that he remembered: "A wall tent, with a large arbor of poles and boughs in front, stood on level, open ground a short distance from the creek, and facing the Blue Mountains, all ready for the governor. This was also to serve as the council chamber, and ample space was left for the Indians to assemble and seat themselves in front of the arbor." [11]

A small cabin had also been erected to serve as a storehouse for the presents which were to be given to the Indians and also for provisions. A number of beef cattle and a large quantity of potatoes had been purchased from several nearby settlers, especially from Bumford and Brooks who were farming at Waiilatpu.

THURSDAY, MAY 24, 1855

The first of the tribes to arrive at the council grounds were the Nez

---

[10] *Sources of the History of Oregon*, Vol. I, Part II (Eugene, Ore., 1897); *Washington Historian*, Vol. II, No. 4 (July 1901), and Vol. III, No. 1 (Oct. 1902); and *Magazine of History, see* fn. 8 above. All further quotations from Kip's diary, unless otherwise noted, will be from this item under the dates indicated.

[11] Stevens, *Stevens*, Vol. II, p. 13.

Perces. Lawrence Kip has given us the following description in his diary entry for May 24:

This has been an exceedingly interesting day, as about twenty-five hundred of the Nez Perce tribe have arrived. It was our first specimen of this Prairie chivalry, and it certainly realized all our conceptions of these wild warriors of the plains. Their coming was announced about ten o'clock, and going out on the plain to where a flag staff had been erected, we saw them approaching on horseback in one long line.

They were almost entirely naked, gaudily painted and decorated with their wild trappings. Their plumes fluttered above them, while below, skins and trinkets and all kinds of fantastic embellishments flaunted in the sunshine. Trained from early childhood almost to live upon horseback, they sat upon their fine animals as if they were centaurs. Their horses, too, were arrayed in the most glaring finery. They were painted with such colors as formed the greatest contrast; the white being smeared with crimson in fantastic figures, and the dark colored streaked with white clay. (See illustration)

James Doty, the private secretary of Governor Stevens, who was also an eyewitness of those exciting events, wrote in his Journal:

Toward noon, the Nez Perces came in with considerable ceremony. Their Banner — our national Flag, presented to them by the officers of the Cayuse War, was sent forward and planted in the Valley near the Treaty Ground and around this on foot were assembled the Commissioners, Agents, and other Indian officers and a number of citizens. The Indians were gaily dressed and painted and all mounted on fine horses. They approached in columns, two abreast and when at the distance of ¼ of a mile, halted, when the Lawyer and two other Chiefs advanced and dismounting shook hands with the gentlemen assembled to welcome them.

Then came some twenty-five more of the Chiefs and head men and a general shaking of hands took place. Then the warriors to the number of 600 rode by in column, two abreast and passed through our camp and returned to their banner. Many of the young men then entertained us with dancing for an hour, when they mounted again and filed off to the place assigned them for an encampment, opposite our camp and ½ mile distant.

Doty estimated that the tribe then numbered somewhat "less than 3,800.[12]

The small company of principal chiefs who rode forward to greet the Commissioners and the other white men had with them William Craig who was to serve as their interpreter. Judging by the names of those chiefs who took an active part in the proceedings of the council, this advance party of Nez Perces would have included the following, besides Lawyer — Joseph from the Wallowa Valley, Timothy from Alpowa, Big Thunder from Lapwai, Ute-sin-male-cum from Kamiah, and Eagle-from-the-Light from above Kamiah.

One important chief was missing and that was Looking Glass who, according to Doty, had been in the buffalo country for the preceding three years. As will be noted, Looking Glass hurried to Walla Walla as soon as he had learned what was to happen. He arrived at the council grounds on June 8, too late to take part in drawing up the terms of the treaty, but not too late to challenge the chieftainship of Lawyer.

When Lawyer and his party reached the place where Governor Stevens and General Palmer were awaiting them, they were formally presented by William Craig. Kip then described what happened next:

> Then on came the wild horsemen, in single file, clashing their shields, singing and beating their drums as they marched past us. Then they formed a circle and dashed around us, while our little group stood there, the center of their wild evolutions. . . Then some score or two dismounted and, forming a ring, danced for about twenty minutes, while those surrounding them beat time on their drums.

Following these performances, Lawyer, according to Kip, with "more than twenty of the chiefs went over to the tent of Governor Stevens, where they sat for sometime, smoking the 'pipe of peace' in token of good fellowship and then returned to their camping ground." Hazard Stevens, in his account of the Council, wrote that the Commissioners issued provisions to the Nez Perces "at the rate of one and a half pounds of beef, two pounds of potatoes, and one half a pound of corn to each person."

Kip called on Lawyer in his lodge that afternoon of the 24th and then wrote the following in his diary:

---

12 I am indebted to Father Edward J. Kowrach of Veradale, Washington, for his kindness in giving me pertinent quotations from James Doty's unpublished Journal, and to Glen Adams of Ye Galleon Press, Fairfield, Washington, for permission to quote from this Journal. At the time of this writing Adams was preparing the Journal for publication.

He showed us a wound in his side from which he was yet suffering, although several years had elapsed since it was received. It had been inflicted in a fight with their hereditary enemies, the Blackfeet Indians. These are the most dangerous banditti among all the tribes . . . He [Lawyer] showed us also some locks of their hair which he wore about him, not as love tokens, or presented willingly by the former owners, but rather the reverse, as I presume they are the remains of scalps he had taken.

Hazard remembered that Lawyer's wound had broken out afresh and that "he was unable to walk without pain and difficulty." Lawyer also told the boy that he had had his right arm broken in a fight with a grizzly bear. "Wise, enlightened, and magnanimous," wrote Hazard, "the head chief, yet one of the poorest of his tribe, stood head and shoulders above the other chiefs, whether in intellect, nobility of soul, or influence."

Also present at the 1855 Council was the fifteen-year-old son of Chief Joseph, whose Indian name was Hin-mah-too-yah-lat-kekht which meant "Thunder Traveling to Loftier Mountain Heights." [13] Hazard Stevens, who may have had some fellowship with Joseph's son at the 1855 Council, remembered that the youth was called Three Knives. [14] Following Chief Joseph's death in August 1871, the son succeeded him as chief of the Wallowa band and also took his father's name.

FRIDAY, MAY 25, 1855

Even before the Council opened, Gustavus Sohon, the artist attached to the Stevens party, began drawing sketches of the important chiefs present. By the time the Council closed, Sohon had drawn twelve sketches which are reproduced in this volume. Of this number, eight were Nez Perces, two Cayuses, two Yakimas, and one each from the Spokane and Walla Walla tribes. Sohon also sketched some of the events which occurred during the meetings of the Council, four of which are used as illustrations in this work.

Sohon began his series of sketches of the important chiefs by drawing the likeness of Lawyer. Lawyer's sketch is unique in that Sohon pictured him wearing the white man's high silk hat, such as was worn in that day by Government dignitaries. This was the symbol of his office as Head Chief of the Nez Perces. Lawyer, however, wishing still

---

13 Josephy, *The Nez Perces*, p. 696.

14 Joseph T. Hazard, *Companion of Adventure, a Biography of Isaac I. Stevens*, Binfords and Mort, Portland, Ore., 1952, p. 155.

to keep his identity as an Indian, tied three large feathers around the crown of the hat with three bands of ribbons. It became a hybrid hat — half-White and half-Indian. Several of the sketches made by Sohon show the chiefs wearing flat beaver skin caps, possibly of Hudson's Bay Company's manufacture.

After drawing Lawyer's sketch on May 25, Sohon then drew Spokane Garry's likeness on the 27th and Joseph's on the 29th. The combined evidence from Sohon — the priority of the sketch, the high silk hat, and the notation on the sketch that Lawyer was Head Chief of the Nez Perces — clearly indicates that the artist recognized Lawyer as being the Head Chief of his tribe before the Council opened. This refutes the contention of some modern critics who claim that Lawyer did not become Head Chief until he was so appointed by Governor Stevens at this Council.

Kip wrote in his diary for this May 25:

We woke this morning to hear the rain pattering about us, and to be thankful that we were encamped and not obliged to resume our march. At noon it cleared up, when we procured our horses and rode over to the Indian camp to pay another visit to our friend Lawyer. We found the old chief surrounded by his family and reading a portion of the New Testament, while a German soldier of Governor Stevens' party was engaged taking his portrait in crayon.

Kip called Lawyer "the old chief." If Monteith's statement that Lawyer was eighty years old when he died in 1876 is correct, then Lawyer would have been fifty-nine in 1855. Kip's reference to "a portion of the New Testament" is undoubtedly to Spalding's translation of the Gospel of Matthew in Nez Perce which had been made with Lawyer's help. It was printed on the mission press at Lapwai in 1845. Although Lawyer had not joined the Mission Church, he and many others of the tribe were following Spalding's teachings and were holding daily family devotions in their lodges. They also sang the gospel hymns which Spalding had either translated or composed.

That Friday evening, Lawyer called on Kip. "We feasted him to the best of our ability," wrote Kip in his diary, "not omitting the indispensable pipe, and he seemed exceedingly gratified with his entertainment."

Stevens and Palmer entertained thirty or more of the Nez Perce chiefs and headmen this day with a feast which consisted largely of meat and potatoes. According to the sketch that Sohon drew of the event, a long cloth about a yard wide was spread on the ground beneath an arbor. About fifteen of the guests squatted on either side. At the two ends were the two Commissioners who served the food on tin plates (*see* illustration). Without modern day knives and forks, each of the guests would have had to use his fingers or a hunting knife. "Again and again," wrote Hazard, "were the plates passed up for a fresh supply; the chiefs feasted and gorged [themselves] like famished wolves; and the arms of the hosts became so wearied from carving and dispensing the food that they were glad to resign the posts of honor to a couple of stalwart packers." [15] Hazard noted that such a table was spread each day thereafter throughout the Council for the Nez Perce chiefs but that this was the only time the two Commissioners attended.

SATURDAY, MAY 26, 1855

This was an exciting day as it was marked by the arrival of the other three Nez Perce-speaking tribes — the Cayuses, Walla Wallas, and Umatillas. Hazard Stevens estimated that about 400 of the Cayuses and Walla Wallas arrived "in full gala dress, and uttering their war-whoops like so many demons." [16] Kip added more details in his account of their arrival: "They came in whooping and singing in the Indian fashion, and after riding around the camp of the Nez Perces two or three times, they retired to form their own at some little distance. In a short time some of the principal chiefs paid their respects to Governor Stevens and then came down to look at our camp. It was not, as we had reason to believe afterwards, a friendly visit, but rather a *reconnaissance* to learn our numbers and estimate our powers of resistance."

The majority, if not a complete 100%, of the members of these tribes were opposed to any negotiations with the Government which would force them onto a reservation. The Head Chief of the Walla Wallas, Peu-peu-mox-mox,[17] harbored a deep anti-American attitude which led him to be an active participant in the Indian disturbances which followed the 1855 Council. The events of the Cayuse War of 1848-50, which climaxed in the hanging of five Cayuses who had been convicted by a United States District Court for complicity in the Whitman massacre, had left bitter memories.

---

[15] Stevens, *Stevens,* Vol. II, p. 37.   [16] *Ibid.,* Vol. II, p. 38.

[17] His name has been translated as Yellow Serpent or Yellow Bird. The Mox-mox refers to something to be feared.

Delegations of observers from several of the Flathead-speaking tribes from the upper Columbia River country also arrived at the council grounds on this day. Among these was Kam-i-ah-kan, Head Chief of the Yakimas, and Owhi, his wife's uncle. As will be noted, these two were the main leaders of the rebellious Indians in 1856-58.

Among the Spokane visitors was Spokane Garry whose friendship for the Whites was well known. Evidently the artist, Sohon, recognized his importance for he drew a sketch of Garry which bears the date of May 28.

In order to avoid being in any way indebted to the Commissioners, the Cayuses, Walla Wallas, Umatillas, and some of the visitors as the Yakimas refused to accept the provisions which were offered to them by the Commissioners and which the Nez Perces had so gladly accepted. The chiefs of these three tribes even refused the gift of tobacco which Stevens had sent to them as a token of his friendship with the ominous reply: "You will find out by and by why we won't take provisions." Kam-i-ah-kan also refused the presents offered to him by Stevens by saying that "he had never accepted anything from the Whites, not even to the value of a grain of wheat, without paying for it."

Before retiring for the night, Kip paid Lawyer and the Nez Perces another visit and then noted in his diary: "Some of them we found singing sacred music to prepare for to-morrow, which is Sunday."

Sunday, May 27, 1855

It was raining so heavily when Kip awoke on Sunday morning that he decided to remain in his tent until noon when the sun began to shine again. Kip then described what he observed: "After riding over to Governor Stevens' to lunch, we went to the Nez Perce camp, where we found they were holding service in one of the largest lodges; two of the chiefs were officiating, one of them delivering an address . . . and at the end of each sentence, the other chief would repeat it in a louder tone of voice." Governor Stevens, in his Journal, noted that the preacher was Timothy and that he was speaking on the Ten Commandments. Stevens wrote: "Timothy has a natural and graceful delivery. . . The Nez Perces have evidently profited much from the labor of Mr. Spalding . . . their whole deportment throughout the service was devout." [18]

---

[18] Stevens, *Stevens*, Vol. II, p. 39.

Kip also commented:

> There is an odd mixture of this world and the next in some of the
> Nez Perces, — an equal love of fighting and devotion — the wildest
> Indian traits with a strictness in some religious rites which might
> shame those "who profess and call themselves Christians." They
> have prayers in their lodges every morning and evening — services
> several times on Sunday — and nothing will induce them on that
> day to engage in any trading.

For that reason, there were no treaty negotiations on Sunday at Walla
Walla.

Kip concluded his diary entry for the 27th by writing: "After service
we rode through the Cayuse camp, but saw no evidence of Sunday
there. The young warriors were lounging about their lodges, preparing
their arms or taking care of their horses, to be ready for their evening
races. The Christianity among these Indians, we suspect, is confined to
the Nez Perces."

MONDAY, MAY 28, 1855

On this day, the last of the Indians who were expected to take part
in the council or who would attend as observers arrived. Kip wrote:
"To-day, leading chiefs belonging to some of the most distant tribes,
attended by their followers, have been coming into camp, and most of
those for which the Commissioners have been waiting are now represented. Their encampments and lodges are scattered over the valley for
more than a mile, presenting a wild and fantastic appearance. The
Council will probably open tomorrow." Kip estimated that there were
at least 5,000 Indians present making this the largest Indian Council
ever to be held west of the Rockies.

Stevens in his letter of June 12, 1855, to George W. Manypenny,
Commissioner of Indian Affairs in Washington, D.C., gave the following
statistics as to the number in the four Nez Perce-speaking tribes, most
of whom attended the Walla Walla Council:

	Washington [& Idaho]	Oregon	[Total]
Nez Perces	1,950	550	2,500
Walla Wallas	550	250	800
Cayuses	150	350	500
Umatillas	0	200	200
	2,650	1,350	[4,000]

Stevens noted that 367 Nez Perces were reported then to be in the buffalo country, which figure was not included in the above statistics. Judging by both Kip's and Stevens' reports and other contemporary references, we may safely assume that the Nez Perces then numbered about 3,000, which means that it was the largest and most powerful Indian nation in the upper Columbia River country.

Since the Indians were accustomed to take with them most of their belongings when traveling, including provisions for an encampment of several weeks, and their buffalo skin lodges, there must have been at least three horses for each of the 5,000 (Kip's estimate) natives present at the Council. This meant that the total number of horses present would have been about 15,000. In May, the hills and valleys in the Walla Walla country would have been covered with a lush growth of grass, thus giving the horses plenty of forage. Kip was quite correct in writing that the Indian camps, which spread out for more than a mile, presented "a wild and fantastic appearance."

TUESDAY, MAY 29, 1855

Being assured that all were present who had planned to be, including visitors from four tribes not directly involved at that time in treaty negotiations, the Commissioners opened the Council at one o'clock, Tuesday afternoon, May 29. According to Stevens' report, about fifty settlers from the Walla Walla area were also present. They would have included former employees of Fort Walla Walla who had settled on farms in the vicinity. Little was done at this first meeting except to get organized and to appoint interpreters. William Craig was approved as the interpreter for the Nez Perces. Governor Stevens served as the presiding officer.

Kip in his diary entry for May 30 has given us the following description of the arrangements followed for the participation of all concerned: "Directly in front of Governor Stevens' tent, a small arbor had been erected, in which, at a table, sat several of his party taking notes of every thing said. In front of the arbor on a bench sat Governor Stevens and General Palmer, and before them in the open air, in concentric semicircles, were ranged the Indians, the chiefs in the front ranks, in the order of their dignity, while the far back ground was filled with women and children. The Indians sat on the ground, (in their own words,) 'reposing on the bosom of their Great Mother.' There were probably a thousand present at a time."

Included in the Commissioners' entourage were at least two short-hand stenographers who faithfully recorded all that was said. The Minutes of this Council, now on file in the National Archives, contain about 50,000 words.[19] Their faithfulness in recording all that was said is indicated by an incident which occurred on June 9. Evidently one of the chiefs, named Three Feathers, was seated some distance from a speaker whom he could not hear, so he called out: "We cannot under-stand back here. Why don't he speak louder." The fact that this inci-dental remark was included in the Minutes is evidence that the reporters were faithful in writing down all that was being said.

Not only were the white men making a record of the meetings, the Nez Perces, alone of the eight tribes represented, were doing likewise. On Friday, June 1, Kip wrote in his diary: "We learned that two or three of the half-civilized Nez Perces, who could write, were keeping a minute account of all that transpired at these meetings." Among the Sohon sketches is one which shows six Nez Perces, two with pencils, seated on the ground engaged in writing. Sohon's note which was with this drawing stated that they were "preparing the records of the Walla Walla Council." (See illustration.)

We know that Lawyer was able to read and write his native tongue. He was the only one of the fifty-eight Nez Perces who signed the 1855 Treaty by writing his name. All the others made an "X" mark after their names which had been written in by a secretary. Both Lawyer and another chief, Levi, wrote their names on the 1863 Treaty. How-ever, there is evidence that Timothy also knew how to read and write his language even though he did not write his name on either of the treaties. It is possible that he is one whom Sohon sketched as keeping notes on the proceedings of the 1855 Council.

An item in the official report for May 29 reads: "Timothy, a Nez Perce chief acted as crier for his nation and he will also record in their language the full proceedings each day of the council and this will be preserved among the archives of the nation and handed down to future generations." Unfortunately Timothy's records were not preserved. On February 13, 1975, Jack Williams, then Superintendent of the Nez

---

[19] The original Minutes of the 1855 Walla Walla Council are in the files of o.i.b. All further references to the official proceedings of this Council are to this source. A copy of these Minutes is in Whitman College, Walla Walla. They also appear in Slickpoo and Walker, *Noon Nee-Me-Poo*, but the two versions do not always agree since each has material not found in the other.

Perce Historical Park, wrote to Lawrence L. Dodd, a Whitman College librarian, saying: "When Timothy died and was buried at Alpowa in 1890,[20] the family followed the custom of disposing of the deceased's property by giving away and burning. Unfortunately all of his papers were burned and the documents you seek was among them." [21] What a pity!

WEDNESDAY, MAY 30, 1855

The Council reconvened on the 30th at 1:00 p.m. Kip noted in his diary:

> After smoking for half an hour, (a ceremony which with them precedes all business), the Council was opened by a short address from General Palmer. Governor Stevens then rose and made a long speech, setting forth the object of the Council and what was desired of them. As he finished each sentence, the interpreters repeated it to two of the Indians, who announced it in a loud voice to the rest. . . This process necessarily causes business to move slowly.

According to the contents of Stevens' speech, as found in the Minutes of the Council, the Governor carefully stated the purpose of the gathering. "What shall we do at this Council?" he asked. He then answered his own question: "We want you and ourselves to agree upon tracts of land [i.e., reservations] where you will live; in those tracts of land, we want each man who will work to have his own land, his own horses, his own cattle, and his own home for himself and his children.

> On each tract we want an agent who shall be your brother, and who shall protect you from bad white men. . . On each tract we wish to have one or more schools. We want on each tract, one or more blacksmiths; one or more carpenters; one or more farmers. We want you and your children to learn to make ploughs, to learn

---

[20] Timothy died in Lewiston, Idaho, in November 1891. Spalding noted in the record book of the Mission Church that when Timothy was baptized in Nov. 1839, he was then "some 31 years of age." This indicates that he would have been eighty-three when he died. His remains now lie buried in a public park in Clarkston, Wash., overlooking the Snake River where a monument to Timothy has been erected.

[21] The original Williams letter is attached to the Stevens File, Whitman College. Williams stated that he had gotten his information from Mylie Lawyer of Lapwai, the great-granddaughter of Chief Lawyer.

to make wagons, and every thing in your house. We want your women and your daughters to spin, and to weave, and to make clothes. We want to do this for a certain number of years.

In brief, the primary purpose of the Commissioners was to induce the Indians to settle on reservations and turn to agriculture and animal husbandry as a way of life. The proposals involved a drastic change which the Indians found difficult to comprehend. The establishment of reservations meant that the Indians would surrender vast areas to the white men. "We want you to agree with us to such a state of things," said Stevens, "You are to have your tract with all these things; the rest to be the Great Father's for his white children."

Stevens said that the Government would pay them for all lands not included in the proposed reservations. He outlined the proposal: "Besides all these things, these shops, these mills and these schools, which I have mentioned; we must pay you for the land which you give to the Great Father; these schools and mills and shops are only a part of payment. We want besides to agree with you for a fair sum to be given for your lands, to be paid through a term of years as your schools and your shops." Stevens was here referring to what came to be known as annuities, promised for twenty years. Both he and Palmer elaborated on this subject during the following days.

After the long speech made by Stevens on the 30th, the secretary who kept the minutes for that day wrote: "No reply was made by the Indians and the Council then adjourned at 4½ p.m."

THURSDAY, MAY 31, 1855

Governor Stevens made another long speech on Thursday in which he repeated much that had been said the previous day. He was more specific, however, in explaining what the Government would give. He mentioned the Government's intention to give clothing to all, blankets and shirts for the men; blankets, shawls, and calico for the women.

Besides clothing, [he promised,] we would wish to furnish you with tools and implements for the shops; for the blacksmith; for the wheelwright; for the tin-smith and such other tools you might need. We also want to provide you with tools for your farms, with ploughs and hoes and shovels. . . We want in your houses plates and cups and brass and tin kettles, frying pans to cook your meat and bake ovens to bake your bread, like white people.

General Palmer followed the Governor with another long speech in which he concentrated on telling what the Government had done for Indians living east of the Rockies. Again the Indians listened and said nothing. The Council adjourned at 3:30 p.m. The Indians were so disturbed over the proposal of the Commissioners that they surrender some of their lands and move onto reservations that they asked that no meeting of the Council be held on Friday, June 1. The Indians wanted time to discuss the proposals.

That evening the Commissioners invited four of the principal chiefs to dine with them — Lawyer from the Nez Perces, Peu-peu-mox-mox from the Walla Wallas, Young Chief from the Cayuses, and Kam-i-ah-kan from the Yakimas.

SATURDAY, JUNE 2, 1855

The Council reassembled at 11:30 a.m. General Palmer, in his opening remarks, stressed the inevitability of the ever increasing white population, which would in time engulf the country.

> If there were no other Whites coming into the country, [he said,] we might get along in peace. You may ask, why do they come? Can you stop the waters of the Columbia river from flowing on its course? Can you prevent the wind from blowing? Can you prevent the rain from falling? Can you prevent the Whites from coming? You are answered, No! Like the grasshoppers on the plains; some years there will be more than others. You cannot stop them. We cannot stop them. They say this land was not made for you alone.

Palmer also warned the Indians that the day was rapidly approaching when they would no longer be able to get buffalo hides with which to erect their lodges. They would have to build houses out of lumber. He stressed the necessity of them turning to agriculture in order to survive. "Do you want to have plenty of provisions for your women and children?" he asked. "Do you want plenty of blankets and clothing? The deer skin and elk skin cannot always be had to make your clothing. Do you always want to live at peace with all persons? If you want all these things, we are ready to give them to you. When we know your hearts then we shall know whether you want these things or not."

For the first time since the Council opened the previous Tuesday, the Indians began to talk back. Two Cayuse chiefs spoke — Five Crows and Camespelo. Kip noted in his diary that he arrived at the Council as one of them was speaking. "He did not commit himself," Kip wrote, "as to what they would do, but the whole tenor of his address was unfavorable to the reception of the treaty." Peu-peu-mox-mox spoke at some length. He accused the Commissioners of not speaking plainly. "You have spoken in a round about way," he claimed. "Speak straight."

Suspicious, Fearful, and Rebellious

The failure of the Commissioners to outline clearly the location and boundaries of the proposed reservations was a primary reason why the Indians became suspicious and fearful. It was not until Monday, June 4, that Governor Stevens clearly stated that they had two reservations in mind. "One reservation," he then explained, "is in the Nez Perce country, and one in the Yakima country. The reservation in the Nez Perce country to extend from the Blue Mountains to the spurs of the Bitterroots, and from the Palouse River to part way up the Grande Ronde and Salmon River." The Commissioners proposed to place on this reservation the four Nez Perce-speaking tribes and the Spokanes.

Since the Yakima Reservation was negotiated in a separate Council, its history will not be told here. Suffice it to say that the Yakimas in attendance at the Walla Walla Council, as Kam-i-ah-kan and Owhi, realized that what was happening to the Nez Perces and other tribes would also happen to them, and they became fearful and rebellious.

Even though the Commissioners did not speak publicly about the boundaries of the proposed reservations before Monday, June 4, it seems evident that the proposed boundaries had become known to the Indians by Thursday evening, May 31. The Cayuses, Walla Wallas, and Umatillas were alarmed. If the proposal to establish one large reservation for all of the Nez Perce-speaking tribes was to be finalized, then the tribes living along the Columbia, Walla Walla, and Umatilla Rivers would have to abandon all or part of their homelands and move in with the Nez Perces. Hence the members of these three tribes became fearful and even considered the possibility of forceful resistance to the plan. This may have been the reason why Young Chief requested that no meeting of the Council be held on Friday, June 1, thus giving them time to hold their own council. Also, this may have been the reason why the Commissioners invited the four principal chiefs to dine with them on Thursday evening, May 31.

LAWYER MOVES TO PROTECT STEVENS

Unknown to Kip, an exciting event took place either late Saturday evening, June 2, or early Sunday morning. This can be explained by the fact that he had encamped with the military escort and not with the Commissioners. When Kip called on Governor Stevens on Sunday, he could not have avoided seeing Lawyer's lodge pitched next to the Governor's tent. Lawyer had moved his lodge from the Nez Perce camp during the night but Kip was not told the reason for this move.

After the Council had closed and Kip was on his way back to The Dalles with Lieutenant Gracie, he was told of the exciting events which had taken place. On June 11, Kip wrote in his diary:

> We have now ended our connection with the Council and bid adieu to our Indian friends. It is therefore an appropriate place to say that we subsequently discovered we have been all the while treading on a mine. Some of the friendly Indians afterwards disclosed to the traders, that during the whole meeting of the Council, active negotiations were on foot to cut off the Whites.
>
> The plot originated with the Cayuses, in their indignation at the prospect of being deprived of their lands. Their programme was, first to massacre the escort, which could easily have been done. Fifty soldiers against three thousand Indian warriors, out on the open plain, made rather too great odds. We should have had time . . . to have delivered one fire and then the contest would have been over.[22]
>
> Their next move was to surprise the post at The Dalles, which they could also easily have done, as most of the troops were withdrawn, and the Indians in the neighborhood had recently united with them. This would have been the beginning of their war of extermination upon the settlers. The only thing which prevented the execution of this scheme was the refusal of the Nez Perces to accede to it, and as they were more powerful than the others united, it was impossible to make this outbreak without their concurrence.

Writing many years later, relying on his own memory and his father's notes, Hazard Stevens stated that late on Saturday evening, June 2,

---

[22] The soldiers were still using the old-fashioned muzzle loaders which meant that, after firing their guns, they would have to take time to reload. If the Indians attacked in close quarters, the soldiers would not have had time to reload.

Lawyer "came unattended to see Governor Stevens." Hazard then explained:

> He disclosed a conspiracy on the part of the Cayuses to suddenly rise upon and massacre all the Whites on the council ground, — that this measure, deliberated in nightly conferences for some time, had at length been determined in full council of the tribe of the day before, which the Young Chief had requested for a holiday; they were now only awaiting the assent of the Yakimas and Walla Wallas to strike the blow; and that these latter had actually joined, or were on the point of joining, the Cayuses in a war of extermination against the Whites, for which the massacre of the governor and his party was to be the signal. They had conducted these plottings with the greatest secrecy, not trusting the Nez Perces; and the Lawyer, suspecting that all was not right, had discovered the plot by means of a spy with the greatest difficulty, and only just in time to avert the catastrophe.

Lawyer, alarmed by the news, decided not only to warn the Commissioners but also to take positive action to prevent any attack on them and their party. Lawyer knew that if the conspirators carried out their murderous designs, the consequences would be far more devastating to the Indians than that which followed the Whitman massacre.

According to Hazard Stevens' account, after he had told Stevens of the plot, Lawyer said: "I will come with my family and pitch my lodge in the midst of your camp, that those Cayuses may see that you and your party are under the protection of the head chief of the Nez Perces." Although it was then past midnight, Lawyer was able to make the move before daybreak without awakening the suspicions of any of the conspirators.

Hazard added that his father felt it wise to say nothing about this incident to anyone except to his "Secretary [James] Doty and Packmaster [C. P.] Higgins" for fear that "should the party generally learn of it, a stampede would ensue." For this reason Kip was not informed as to what had happened until he was on his way back to The Dalles.

Lawyer was never more eloquent than on the night of June 2-3, 1855, when he moved his lodge from the Nez Perce encampment and pitched it next to Governor Stevens' tent, for actions speak louder than words. By doing so he was telling the conspirators that they would have to kill him first before they could kill the Commissioners. Lawyer knew that any harm which might come to him would bring immediate retaliation from his followers and there were more Nez Perces at the Council than all of the other tribes combined.

Hazard Stevens, looking back over many years to the Council, summarized the importance of Lawyer's role in the Council by writing:

The turning-point in the council was undoubtedly the discovery of the Cayuse conspiracy by Lawyer, and his act of moving his lodge into Governor Stevens' camp, thereby placing the Whites under the protection of the Nez Perces. This was all that prevented the hostile chiefs and braves from striking the blow. They refrained because they knew that if Lawyer was killed in an attack on the camp, which was to be expected in the melee, the whole Nez Perce nation would avenge the slaughter of their blood.[23]

When the conspirators saw Lawyer's lodge standing next to Stevens' tent on Sunday morning, June 3, they realized that their plot had been discovered and that no attack was then possible. Reluctantly, and no doubt with suppressed anger, the dissidents resumed their negotiations. Finally, treaties were negotiated and reservations were established, all because Lawyer had the courage to defy the conspirators.

COWARD OR HERO?

On June 3, 1930, Whitman College, recognizing the 75th anniversary of the dramatic move made by Lawyer when the great Indian Council of 1855 was meeting on what was to become the College campus, dedicated a monument honoring Chief Lawyer. A huge granite boulder, weighing about 35,000 pounds, had been moved from Elk River in northern Idaho to the campus, on which was fastened a bronze plaque bearing the likeness of Lawyer with the dates — June 3, 1855 and June 3, 1930. Below was the following inscription:[24]

HOL-LOL-SOTE-TOTE

Here were encamped from May 24 to June 12, 1855, two thousand Indians of the Nez Perce tribe, with their famous chief, Hol-lol-sote-tote, Lawyer, attending the great council called by Governor Stevens. Discovering a plot of the other Indian tribes to

---

[23] Stevens, *Stevens*, Vol. II, p. 60.
[24] The proceedings of the dedication of the monument appeared in *Whitman College Qtly.*, Vol. 33, No. 2 (June 1930). Although the inscription states that "two thousand" Nez Perces attended the 1855 Council, contemporary accounts indicate that the number was at least 2,500.

kill the Americans, Chief Lawyer moved his lodge and family before dawn on June 3, to the white men's camp thereby protecting them from the attack.

The class of 1930 presents this tablet in honor of Chief Lawyer, the wise, magnanimous, and brave leader of a noble people.

In the letter of invitation to the dedicatory service, which Dr. Stephen B. L. Penrose, President of Whitman College, sent to the general public, was the statement that Chief Lawyer had "saved the lives of Governor Isaac I. Stevens and his white companions." Such a claim aroused the ire of members of the Cayuse, Walla Walla, and Umatilla tribes then living on the Umatilla Reservation.

Some of these Indians held a meeting on the Reservation on April 24, 1930, at which time a committee of eight was appointed to present the "correct" facts to Nelson W. Durham of Spokane, Washington, who was to give the dedicatory address. In its protest, the committee stated that "Chief Lawyer was not a great chief nor deserving of the honor; that the whites saved Lawyer from the rage of his fellow chiefs." [25] In other words, this committee claimed that the non-Nez Perce Indians at the 1855 Council were so incensed at Lawyer's willingness to accept the proposals of the Commissioners to establish reservations that they were ready to kill him. Therefore, learning of this plot against his life, Lawyer with his family fled in fear to the white man's camp for protection. According to this theory, Lawyer was not a hero but a coward. The protesting Indians suggested that if any Nez Perce chief were to be honored, it should be "Chief Joseph, who was the greatest of the Nez Perce chiefs, or to the elder Joseph, who was the first convert at the Whitman mission." [26]

The Umatilla Reservation Indians were in part echoing the views of Andrew J. Splawn who, in 1917, published his *Kam-Mi-Akin, the Last Hero of the Yakimas.* Referring to Lawyer's moving his lodge to the white man's camp, Splawn wrote:

During my residence of fifty years among the Yakimas, I have talked with many old men who were present at the council, some

---

[25] *O.H.Q.*, Vol. 30 (1930), p. 207, referring to a report of the Indian meeting on the Umatilla Reservation which appeared in the *East Oregonian*, Pendleton, April 27, 1930.

[26] Joseph was one of Spalding's converts and was baptized and received into the Mission Church at Lapwai, not at Waiilatpu.

of them prominent in their tribes. All claim that there was no foundation to Lawyer's story and that the Yakimas and Walla Wallas
heard of it only after Lawyer had moved his lodge to Stevens'
camp. Whereupon Kam-Mi-akin, Peu-peu-mox-mox, and Looking
Glass went to the Nez Perce chief and accused him of having a
forked tongue. Personally, I am convinced that Lawyer was play-
ing the game to procure for his people a larger reservation than
the other chiefs would get and that his Cayuse story was "rot." In
any event he gained the end he sought.[27]

In rebutting such a claim, it should be pointed out that there is
abundant evidence to indicate that the dissident tribes were considering taking violent action against the Commissioners even before the
Council began. Three Roman Catholic missionaries warned Stevens
and Palmer of possible trouble. Father Ricard of the Yakima Mission
met the Commissioners at The Dalles and told them that the Indians
"were plotting to cut off the white chiefs." After arriving at Walla
Walla, the Commissioners were given the same warning by Father
Chirouse of the Walla Walla Mission and Father Charles M. Pandosy
of the Yakima Mission.[28] Moreover, Kip's diary carries many references
to the hostility of such chiefs as Peu-peu-mox-mox and Kam-i-ah-kan.
Such evidence supports the testimonies of both Kip and Stevens that
there was a plot to kill the Commissioners and that Lawyer, by his
courageous act of moving his lodge into the white man's camp, foiled
the conspiracy.

Moreover, we have the family tradition of the descendants of Chief
Lawyer. Among those who took part in the dedication of the Chief
Lawyer monument on the campus of Whitman College on June 3, 1930,
was Corbett Lawyer, the grandson of Chief Lawyer. His participation
in the ceremonies is evidence of his approval of the statement on the
plaque to the effect that "Chief Lawyer moved his lodge . . . to
the white men's camp thereby protecting them from attack."

Perhaps the most convincing evidence that a conspiracy did exist
among the Cayuses, Walla Wallas, and Yakimas while the 1855 Council was in session, is the fact that these tribes joined in open warfare
against the Government during the following year.

---

[27] *Op. cit.*, pp. 28-9. The fact that Looking Glass was not on the Council grounds
at the time indicated, and did not arrive until Friday, June 8, casts doubt on the
accuracy of the reminiscences Splawn claimed to have gotten from "many old men."

[28] Stevens, *Stevens*, Vol. II, p. 37.

THE 1855 TREATY

When the Indians gathered on Monday noon, June 4, before Governer Stevens' tent, they could not avoid seeing Lawyer's lodge standing nearby. There was no need for anyone to tell them what it meant. Governor Stevens made no public reference to what had taken place.

For the first time since the Council began its deliberations on Tuesday, May 29, Stevens called on the Indians to speak. "We want you to open your hearts and speak freely," the Governor said. He then called on Lawyer to respond. Lawyer was hesitant. He found himself in a difficult situation. Standing only a few feet from his relocated lodge, he did not want to say anything which would offend either the Commissioners or the dissident chiefs. Lawyer's speech shows that he was ill at ease. He rambled. He mentioned the poverty of the Indians, the good intentions of Government officials, and the necessity of both the Whites and the Indians to listen to "the laws." Then he sat down.

Peu-peu-mox-mox then brought up the key question — what did the Commissioners propose regarding the number of and location of the reservations? Stevens explained that there would be two reservations, one for the Nez Perce speaking tribes and the other for the northern tribes as the Yakimas. During the next two days, June 5 and 6, the Commissioners patiently explained their proposals in repetitious detail. Large maps had been drawn to show the Indians the boundary lines of the proposed reservations.

The Nez Perce Reservation included a vast area in what is now western Idaho, a small segment of southeastern Washington, and a larger section of northeastern Oregon, including the Wallowa Valley, Joseph's homeland. Excluded were much of the areas then occupied by the Cayuse, Walla Walla, and Umatilla tribes, all of whom would have been obliged to move to the east into the proposed Nez Perce Reservation. The very thought of giving up the Walla Walla and Umatilla valleys for white settlements aroused immediate and deep resentment by the tribes involved.

On June 5, Kip wrote in his diary: "There is evidently a more hostile feeling towards the whites getting up among some of the tribes, of which he had to-night a very unmistakable proof. The Cayuses, we have known, have never been friendly, but hitherto they have disguised their feelings. To-night, as Lieutenant Gracie and I attempted, as usual, to enter their camp, they showed a decided opposition; we were motioned back, and the young warriors threw themselves in our way to obstruct our advance. To yield to this, however, or to show any signs of being intimidated would have been ruinous with the Indians, as we were obliged to carry out our original intentions. We placed our horses abreast, riding round the Indians, where it was possible, and at other times forcing our way through, believing that they would not dare to resort to actual violence. If, however, this hostile feeling at the Council increased, how long will it be before we have an actual outbreak?"

On the 7th, the Commissioners spoke at some length giving details regarding all of the benefits the Government would provide for each tribe — schools, blacksmith shops, saw and flour mills, farming tools, blankets, clothing, and "a good house" would be built for each head chief. Moreover, these individuals, including Lawyer, would receive an annual annuity of $500.00 for twenty years.

The promise of such gifts from the Government did not satisfy the Indians, who were called upon to abandon some of their homelands and move onto a reservation. Chief Stickus, long known for his friendly feelings for the Americans, gave vent to his anxieties by asking: "If your mothers were here in this country who gave you birth, and suckled you, and while you were sucking, some person came and took away your mother, and left you alone and sold your mother, how would you feel then? This is our mother, this country, as if we draw our living from her."

At the June 7 meeting, Lawyer spoke for the second time, giving an hour long speech. By this time Lawyer was advocating the adoption of the proposed treaty. Over and over again, Lawyer emphasized the need to adopt the white man's laws. He could safely endorse the boundaries of the proposed Nez Perce Reservation as it embraced all of their ancestral lands. Chief Joseph and his band in the Wallowa Valley were included in the proposed boundaries.

"From the time of Lewis and Clark," Lawyer claimed, "we have known our [American] friends. We poor people have known you as brothers although we were a poor people, a people knowing nothing when we first saw the white chiefs, Lewis and Clark." Lawyer then made reference to the Indian youths who went to the Red River Mission school and, also a possible reference to the Nez Perce delegation which visited St. Louis in the fall of 1831. "From these poor people," he continued, "there were some of them that started in that direction (east) and of these there is only one now living (Spokane Garry).

They went to be taught; they returned after they could see a little and told us about the Great Spirit. They told us the laws for the poor people. . .

"Ellis, our Chief, spoke straight for the white people. The President has sent you here to us poor people." Then, holding up a note book, Lawyer further said: "I want the President to see what I, a poor man, has said. I have got your talk here (pointing to his note book)[29] and although a poor man, I can look at it from time to time." In his closing remarks, Lawyer begged Stevens "to take care of us well."

Even while Lawyer was speaking, the chiefs of the three tribes, who would have had to abandon their homelands and move onto a reservation, were smouldering with resentment. Young Chief spoke up: "I wonder if this ground has anything to say; I wonder if the ground is listening to what is said. I wonder if the ground would come to life and what is on it; though I hear what this earth says, the earth says, God has placed me here."

Five Crows said: "My heart is just the same as Young Chief."

Peu-peu-mox-mox: "I do not know what is straight. I do not [i.e., understand] the offer you have made to the Indians. . . My heart cried very hard when you first spoke to me, the same as if I was a feather." Referring to Lawyer's remarks, he added: "I think my friend has given [away] his lands, that is what I think from his words." Peu-peu-mox-mox begged for more time to consider the proposals of the Commissioners.

How-list-wam-pun, a Cayuse, said: "The Nez Perces have already given you their land. You want us to go there. What can we think of that? That is the reason I cannot think of leaving this land to go there. Your words since you have been here have been crooked."

Five Crows, speaking for the second time that day, said: "We have been as one people with the Nez Perces heretofore; this day we are divided. We the Cayuses, Walla Wallas, and Kam-i-ah-kan's people and others will think over the matter tonight and give you an answer tomorrow."

Before the Council closed at 6:00 p.m. that Thursday, June 7, Governor Stevens stated that the Commissioners were ready to sign the

---

[29] Brackets indicate author's comments. Comments within parentheses contain observations made by the secretary of the 1855 Council and are in the original manuscript.

CARRYING THE FLAG, LAWYER ARRIVES WITH
THE NEZ PERCES, MAY 24, 1855, AT
THE WALLA WALLA COUNCIL (See text p. 94)
A Gustavus Sohon drawing. Original in the
Smithsonian Institution, Washington, D.C.

CORBETT LAWYER, GRANDSON OF CHIEF LAWYER
Holding his grandfather's flag of thirty-four stars.
Courtesy of Mrs. Gordon Alcorn of Tacoma.

GOVERNOR ISAAC I. STEVENS
At age 37 when he conducted
the 1855 Walla Walla Council.
Courtesy of the Washington State
Historical Society, Tacoma.

CERTIFICATE GIVEN TO LAWYER
BY GOV. STEVENS, JUNE 11, 1855,
recognizing him as HEAD CHIEF
of the Nez Perce. See text p. 131.
From the original at Whitman College.

TO ALL PERSONS WHOM IT MAY CONCERN:

WHEREAS, *Nol-lol-sote-tote* otherwise called *Lawyer* an Indian of the *Nez Perce* Tribe, living in the Territory of WASHINGTON, has been this day recognized as HEAD CHIEF of the same; now, therefore, this paper is given to him that he may be known and treated accordingly.

The said chief is held responsible for the good behavior of his people, and is required to inform the Superintendent of Indian Affairs, or the Agent, of all offences committed by Indians against the citizens of the Territory, and to deliver up on demand, all persons accused thereof. In so doing, he is to be assisted by the Sub Chiefs appointed to counsel with him, and will be supported by the government and the Military.

He is also, on behalf of his people, to make complaint of injuries done by citizens or others against them, and particularly of the sale of liquor to Indians. In this the faith of the Government is pledged to sustain him, and do them justice

Should the said chief fail to perform his duty honestly, the Superintendent will remove him and make another Chief.

In witness whereof, I have hereto set my hand this *Eleventh* day of *June* 1855.

I. I. STEVENS,
Governor, and Superintendent of Indian Affairs.

Issued by

Wm. H. Tappan

Agent.

treaty with the Nez Perces the next day so that the members of this tribe could start on their homeward journey. Since the Commissioners had been at Walla Walla since May 21, more than two weeks, they, too, were eager to leave. The situation was tense since nothing definite had been decided upon for the other three Nez Perce-speaking tribes.

That evening, following his usual custom, Kip rode through the Indian encampments. He found many of the Nez Perces gambling and made the following comment in his diary that evening: "They are most inveterate gamblers, and a warrior will sometimes stake on successive games, his arms, and horses, and even his wives, so that in a single night he is reduced to a state of primitive poverty and obliged to trust to charity to be remounted for the hunt."

After visiting the Nez Perce camp, Kip called on the other tribes where, he found: "Everything seemed to be in violent commotion." The situation was ominous for he wrote: "The Cayuses and other tribes are very much incensed against the Nez Perces for agreeing to the terms of the treaty, but unfortunately for them, and probably for us also, the Nez Perces are as numerous as the others united."

THE UMATILLA RESERVATION AUTHORIZED

Stevens and Palmer, aware of the explosive situation, accepted the necessity of working out a compromise for the three dissenting tribes. After consulting with some of the chiefs, including Lawyer, they decided to establish a third Reservation. This would be located on the Umatilla River and would accommodate the Cayuses, Walla Wallas, and Umatilla tribes. Only a part of the Cayuse tribe and the Walla Wallas would have to move under this arrangement.

When the Council opened its sessions at 3:00 p.m., Friday, June 8, it was apparent that the news of the compromise had been spread abroad and that tensions had eased. Stevens opened the meeting by saying: "My friends, judging from your faces, I think you see your way [to sign]." Not altogether happy over the idea of moving onto a reservation, the three dissenting tribes accepted the compromise as being the lesser of two evils.

Before explaining about the third reservation, Stevens invited any of the chiefs present who wished to speak to do so. Young Chief responded: "The reason why we could not understand you was that you selected this country for us to live in without our having any voice in the matter. . . You embraced all my country; where was I to go?

Was I to be a wanderer life a wolf? Without a home, without a house,
I would be compelled to steal, consequently I would die."

General Palmer then arose and in a long speech, which took over an
hour to deliver, outlined the new proposals. He repeated the promises
that the Commissioners had previously made in regard to schools, mills,
etc., but now he added some new benefits. He promised hospitals and
doctors. All of the material benefits promised the Nez Perces would
likewise be given to the tribes occupying the Umatilla Reservation.
Each Head Chief, for instance, would receive an annual annuity of
$500.00, have a house built for him, and have ten acres plowed and
fenced for his use.

After Palmer had spoken, the meeting was again thrown open for
chiefs to respond if any wished to do so. Old Joseph, for the first time
during the meetings of the Council, spoke briefly. He alone of all who
spoke at the Council referred to coming generations. Perhaps he had
his son, Young Joseph, in mind when he said: "It is not for us, it is for
those of our children who come after us. It is good for the old people
to talk together and straight, on account of our children on both sides
[i.e., both Whites and Indians] to take care of each other."

The records of the Council for Friday, June 8, indicate that the compromise offered by the Commissioners had been accepted and the
chiefs had indicated their readiness to sign the treaties, when suddenly an unexpected incident occurred which threatened to nullify all
that had been accomplished. Kip explained what happened: "It seemed
as if we were getting on charmingly and the end of all difficulties was
at hand, when suddenly a new explosive element dropped down into
this little political caldron."

Just before the Council adjourned, an Indian runner arrived with
the news that Looking Glass, the war-chief of the Nez Perces, was
returning from the buffalo country and was near at hand. The news of
the Council meeting at Walla Walla was late in reaching Looking
Glass. As soon as he learned of it, he with two subchiefs and twenty
warriors, left at once for Walla Walla. Even though Looking Glass was
then seventy years old, he and his men rode 300 miles in seven days
including the rugged journey over the Lolo Trail.

About half an hour after the messenger arrived, Looking Glass and
his party dashed up to the place where the Council was being held.
Stevens and Palmer hastened to meet and welcome the chief. Looking
Glass was angry and also misinformed as to the proposed treaty bound-

aries. "Without dismounting from his horse," wrote Kip, "[he] made a short and very violent speech, which I afterwards learned was, as I suspected, an expression of his indignation at their selling the country."

Hazard Stevens has given us the speech: "My people, what have you done? While I was gone, you have sold my country. I have come home, and there is not left me a place on which to pitch my lodge. Go home to your lodges. I will talk to you." [30] Actually, Looking Glass's home at Asotin was well within the boundaries of the proposed Nez Perce Reservation.

James Doty in the entry in his Journal for that day wrote: "Looking Glass was opposed to the Treaty, chiefly it seemed, because he felt his pride and consequence [role] injured, because his people had concluded a Treaty during his absence. He did not like the Reservation. He did not wish to sign the Treaty now." In other words, Looking Glass was angry because the negotiations for a treaty had been carried on in his absence. The Council was immediately adjourned following the War Chief's arrival.

LOOKING GLASS CHALLENGES LAWYER

Ever since December 1842, when Dr. White met with the Nez Perces at Lapwai and induced them to accept a code of laws and select a Head Chief, Looking Glass had aspired to this position. At that time, Ellis was selected. Again, after Ellis had died, Looking Glass again sought the appointment, but instead Richard was appointed. According to Doty's entry in his Journal for June 8, 1855, "Looking Glass was the principal Chief before he went to the Buffalo hunt three years since." This seems to indicate that the Nez Perces had held a council at which time Looking Glass was made Head Chief. Yet Doty in this same entry noted that at the time he arrived at the Walla Walla Council, he was then "a chief second only to Lawyer." This implies that during the long three-year absence of Looking Glass in the buffalo country, Lawyer had been made Head Chief by the Nez Perces. Certainly, as has been indicated, Lawyer's authority as Head Chief of his nation had been recognized in various ways by American officials in Oregon during the seven years leading up to the 1855 Council.

Some of those who belong to the anti-Lawyer faction among present-day Nez Perces claim that Lawyer was not made Head Chief until he

[30] Stevens, *Stevens*, Vol. II, p. 54.

was so appointed by Governor Stevens at the Walla Walla Council. Slickpoo and Walker, in their *Noon Nee-Me-Poo (We the Nez Perces)*, for instance, claim that Lawyer was designated Head Chief by Stevens over the opposition of "many of the chiefs and members of our tribe." [31] While it is true that there was a small minority of Nez Perces at the Walla Walla Council who were opposed to Lawyer, including Looking Glass, yet it is clear from Doty's Journal in his entry for June 8, 1855, that Lawyer had been "elected Head Chief" during Looking Glass's long absence in the buffalo country.

Again quoting from Doty's Journal for June 8: "Considerable discussion was had during the evening [after Looking Glass's return] as to whether Looking Glass, who was principal chief before he went to the Buffalo hunt three years since, would oppose the Treaty concluded without his presence, [and] whether he would contest the authority of Lawyer elected Head Chief during his absence, and if so what effect it would have upon the Indians." Circumstantial evidence indicates that the Nez Perce chiefs and headmen carried on a heated debate throughout a long evening and that Looking Glass failed in his efforts to supplant Lawyer as Head Chief.

Kip, in his diary entry for Saturday, June 9, wrote: "This morning the old Chief Lawyer came down and took breakfast with us. The Council did not meet till three o'clock and matters seem now to have reached a crisis. The treaty must either be soon accepted or the tribes will separate in hopeless bad feeling."

When the Council opened that Saturday afternoon, Looking Glass was still in an ugly mood. He claimed that he was the Head Chief of all the tribes present. Young Chief of the Cayuses supported the claim. The Cayuses then retracted their previous acceptance of the treaty. Governor Stevens then patiently, and largely for Looking Glass's benefit, repeated the salient provisions of the treaties. He announced a new factor. He stated that the Government would pay $150,000.00 to the three tribes which were to occupy the Umatilla Reservation and $200,000.00 to the Nez Perces. These sums would include the promised annuities and other material benefits. He also explained that the treaties would not take effect until they had been ratified by the United States Senate. This took place on April 29, 1859. The long delay brought further complications of which mention will later be made.

In the acrimonious debate which took place in that afternoon session

---

[31] *Op. cit.,* p. 137.

between the supporters of Looking Glass and the friends of Lawyer, Three Feathers threw his support to Looking Glass and claimed that he was their Head Chief. Whereupon, Billy, another Nez Perce chief, replied "I thought we had appointed Lawyer Head Chief and he was to do our talking." Billy's comment implies that a decision had been made in one of their councils, either before or after Looking Glass's arrival, which by majority vote had accepted Lawyer as their Head Chief.

Because of the heated discussions of the afternoon, the Commissioners realized that the treaties could not be signed that day, as had been their desire. Before the Council adjourned late that afternoon, Stevens announced that the treaties would be ready for signature the coming Monday. He then added: "I trust by that time Looking Glass will have thought the matter over and will be able to agree."

Following the adjournment of the Council, Lawyer asked Stevens why he had not rebuked Looking Glass when he claimed to be Head Chief. "Why did you not reply," asked Lawyer, "The Lawyer and not you is Head Chief? The whole Nez Perce tribe have said in council Lawyer was Head Chief. . . Had this course been taken, the treaty would have been signed."

Stevens answered: "We considered all the talk of Looking Glass as the outpourings of an angry and excited old man, whose heart would become right if left to himself for a time. . . Your authority will be sustained. . . The Looking Glass will not be allowed to speak as head chief. You, and you alone, will be recognized." [32]

Kip wrote in his diary for Sunday, June 10: "We understand there has been a great excitement through the Indian camps to-day. The Nez Perces have been all day holding council among themselves, and it is represented that the proposition has been made to appoint Looking Glass head Chief over Lawyer." The attempt failed. Evidence indicates that Lawyer was again reconfirmed as Head Chief by a large majority. Looking Glass was acknowledged as War Chief, second only to Lawyer. Looking Glass bowed to the will of the majority and indicated his willingness to sign the treaty.

As will be noted, an anti-treaty party arose in the Nez Perce nation following the signing of the Lapwai Treaty of 1863. For the most part, the members of this faction accepted the 1855 Treaty but centered their objections on provisions of the 1863 Treaty.

---

[32] Stevens, *Stevens*, Vol. II, p. 56.

Hazard Stevens, commenting on the events of Sunday, June 10, wrote: "Timothy preached a sermon for the times, and held up to the indigation of the tribe, and the retribution of the Almighty, those who would coalesce with the Cayuses and break the faith of the Nez Perces."

THE TREATY SIGNED, JUNE 11, 1855

The Council opened its last session at 11:00 a.m., on Monday, June 11. According to the Minutes of the meeting, Stevens began by saying:

My children, we have met today for the last time. Every man here present has agreed to a treaty in council. The Nez Perces agreed to a treaty. Not one man spoke against it. All agreed that the head Chief would speak for you. You were all called upon to speak. I called upon Joseph to speak and he spoke: "I have a good heart," says Joseph, "what the Lawyer says, let it be."

Then Stevens called on two Nez Perce chiefs, who later became bitter critics of the 1863 Treaty and consequently critics also of Lawyer, to speak. Eagle-from-the-Light said: "The head chief Lawyer has spoken, so be it." And Red Wolf said: "What the Lawyer has said, be it so." A third chief, who became a strong supporter of Lawyer, Ute-sin-male-cum, who had made trouble for Smith at Kamiah in 1840, also spoke: "My chief has spoken for me."

With due observance of Indian protocol, Governor Stevens called on Lawyer to be the first to sign the treaty document. He wrote "Aleiya," and one of the secretaries wrote beneath that name, "Lawyer, Head Chief of the Nez Perces." All of the other fifty-seven who signed made an "X" mark after their individual names as written by the secretary.

What was the meaning of the name, "Aleiya"? The name is known to have appeared once more in a contemporary document. Possibly this was a phonetic transliteration of the Nez Perce effort to pronounce the English word, "Lawyer." Josephy in his The Nez Perces suggests that the word might be a corruption of the Nez Perces "Alaim," meaning "Big Blade," a term once used to describe important persons.[33]

After Lawyer had signed, Stevens called on Looking Glass, Joseph, James, Red Wolf, Timothy, and Ute-sin-male-cum to sign in that order. Following these seven, the other fifty-one came to the table and made the "X" mark, seemingly with no particular order of importance being

[33] Josephy, op. cit., p. 334, fn. 2.

discernible. The Stevens Treaty of 1855, as it came to be known, had the unanimous approval of all the chiefs of the Nez Perce tribe who had attended the Council. There was no dissenting voice.

After Isaac Stevens and Joel Palmer signed, the following witnesses added their signatures: James Doty and William C. McKay, Secretaries; W. H. Tappan, Indian Sub-Agent for Oregon Territory; William Craig and Andrew D. Pambrun, Interpreters; William McBean and George C. Bumford, local settlers; Fathers Eugene Chirouse and Charles Pandosy, Catholic missionaries of the order of Oblates of Mary Immaculate; and Lawrence Kipp and W. H. Pearson, observers.

Separate treaties were drawn up and signed for the three tribes assigned to the Umatilla Reservation, and later for those tribes assigned to the Yakima Reservation.

> Thus ended, [wrote Governor Stevens in his Journal,] in the most satisfactory manner, this great council, prolonged through so many days — a council which — in the number of Indians assembled, and the different tribes, old difficulties and troubles between them and the whites, a deep-seated dislike to and determination against giving up their lands, and the great importance, nay absolute necessity, of opening this land by treaty to occupation by the whites, that bloodshed and enormous expense of Indian wars might be avoided, and in its general influence and difficulty — has never been equaled by any council with the Indian tribes of the United States.[34]

ON APPRAISAL

The 1855 Walla Walla Council, which Governor Stevens described as having ended "in the most satisfactory manner," would not have been so appraised by the Indian tribes affected, not even by the Nez Perces. For the Indians, this marked the end of an era, centuries old, and the beginning of another when a radical adjustment to the white man's civilization was being forced upon them. General Palmer had told them that they could no more stop the white men from coming than they could stop the Columbia River from flowing. The General declared that the white men in numbers were "like the grasshoppers on the plains." Out of a grim necessity precipitated by the arrival of the Oregon immigrants in overwhelming numbers, and by the heavy pressure laid on them by the two Commissioners, the chiefs of the four Nez Perce-speaking tribes reluctantly signed the treaties which had

[34] Stevens, *Stevens*, Vol. II, pp. 58-9.

been written by the white men and laid before them. They had no alternative.

In a revealing letter which Governor Stevens wrote on June 12, 1855, to the Commissioner of Indian Affairs in Washington, D.C., the Hon. George W. Manypenny, he stated that the four tribes, when accepting their two reservations, had ceded all claims to over 30,000 square miles of territory, located in what is now southeastern Washington and northeastern Oregon.[35] Stevens gave the following statistics to indicate the number of square miles ceded:

	Washington (& Idaho)	Oregon	Total
Nez Perces	12,320	11,818	24,138
Walla Wallas, Cayuses & Umatillas	2,908	3,362	6,270
	15,228	15,180	30,408

The total area ceded was about equal to the combined areas of the following states: Connecticut, Massachusetts, New Hampshire, and Vermont as these states together have 31,108 square miles. According to this 1855 Treaty, this vast area was opened for white settlements.

Most of the Nez Perce Reservation lay in what is now western Idaho, with some areas in southeastern Washington and northeastern Oregon. The total area was about 23,666 square miles,[36] although this is only an estimate as no surveys were then made. If we accept the contemporary estimated population of the Nez Perce nation as being 3,000, then this meant that the Reservation contained about 7.9 square miles

---

[35] The original Stevens letter is with the Proceedings of the 1855 Council, O.I.B.

[36] Stevens in his letter of June 12, 1855, stated that the Nez Perce Reservation contained 5,122 square miles, which is very evidently an error. Josephy, in his *The Nez Perces*, p. 334, evidently relying on the Stevens' figure, also estimated that the Nez Perce Reservation contained "approximately five thousand square miles." Erwin Thompson, in his *Historic Resource Study, Spalding Area*, p. 97, quoted from a report written by Calvin H. Hale, who was one of the Commissioners in charge of the 1863 Lapwai Council, which stated that the 1855 Nez Perce Reservation contained 90,000 square miles! All of Idaho has but 82,808 square miles.

Following a suggestion given by a surveyor, I traced out the boundaries of the 1855 Reservation on a road map, cut it out, and weighed it on a delicate druggist's scale. It weighed .980 milligrams. I then cut out the map of the 1863 Reservation, which area is known to contain 1,187.5 square miles. This weighed .04 milligrams, or about 5% of the larger map. Knowing this, then the 1855 Reservation had about 23,666 square miles.

for every man, woman, and child in the tribe. Much of the area, however, was mountainous and unsuitable for agriculture. The Umatilla Reservation was smaller as it provided about one-half of a square mile for each of the 1,500 members of the three tribes assigned to that place.

In his letter of June 12, 1855, which accompanied his official report of the Walla Walla Council, Stevens wrote: "The Reservations may seem to be large, especially that of the Nez Perce tribe. All these tribes own large bands of horses and cattle and have small farms." Stevens estimated that the Nez Perces had 15,000 horses and cattle, while the other three tribes had some 20,000. Actually, the natives had far more horses than cattle.

In order to hasten the civilizing of the Indians, the Commissioners, through the treaties, laid great emphasis on inducing the Indians to turn to farming. The Government was obligated to build mills, shops, schools, and hospitals. No mention was made of churches. The Government was also obligated to send skilled white laborers and/or craftsmen, as farmers, carpenters, and teachers to live with the natives and help them in this period of transition. In pursuing this program of civilizing the Indians, the Government was following exactly the policies which had first been introduced by Dr. Marcus Whitman among the Cayuses and the Rev. Henry H. Spalding among the Nez Perces beginning in 1836.

In spite of their limited financial resources and the initial reluctance of the Indians to change their manner of life, Whitman and Spalding, during their eleven-year residence at their respective stations, accomplished wonders. Writing in the early months of 1866, Spalding, looking back on his mission experience proudly stated:

When we arrived among the Nez Perces in 1836, as their missionaries, we found the people poor, miserable, and indolent. Not a foot of land cultivated; without the first hoe, plow, or cow; without letters, without law, or a knowledge of Christ, Redemption, or the Sabbath; depending upon camas [an edible root], fish, and roots for a miserable existence. At the end of eleven years, when we were driven away . . . we left the following [at Lapwai], viz., one flour mill, one saw mill, two long ditches used for purpose of irrigation and the mills. . . Some fifteen ditches through the country, used by Indians, large bearing orchard, several throughout the country, fragments of which yet remain; a church 56 x 30 feet; school house; weaving and spinning room; granary; work and blacksmith shops . . . printing office.[37]

Spalding also noted the fact that by the end of 1847 a number of natives in the vicinity of Lapwai were cultivating small farms and that some of them owned a few cattle.

What Spalding had been able to do at Lapwai, Whitman on a smaller scale had effected with the Cayuse tribe at Waiilatpu. Out of their limited financial resources, the two had succeeded in inducing some of the natives to make a significant beginning in farming. Now the Commissioners, with the wealth of the Government behind them, were able to promise material aid to the natives on a magnificent scale never dreamed possible by the missionaries.

Although the missionaries and the Commissioners were agreed on the necessity of civilizing the natives, they differed regarding the basic reason for such a program. The missionaries wanted to settle the Indians on farms as this would make it easier to educate and evangelize them. Years after he left his mission field, Spalding had his photograph taken with a Bible in one hand and a hoe and an ax in the other. This symbolized his philosophy. In a letter to the American Board dated April 21, 1838, Spalding explained this philosophy: "While we point with one hand to the Lamb of God which taketh away the sins of the world, we believe it to be equally our duty to point with the other to the hoe as the means of saving their famishing bodies from an untimely grave & furnishing the means of subsistence to future generations." [38]

The Commissioners were not concerned with any efforts to evangelize the natives. Rather they wanted them to move onto reservations and adopt the white man's ways of cultivating the soil and raising cattle, so that in time they could be self-supporting. Also the Commissioners wanted to avoid clashes between the incoming immigrants and the Indians by throwing open for settlement large areas of land which had been claimed by the Indians as their territory.

Lawyer Officially Recognized as Head Chief

At the time the Lawyer monument was dedicated on the campus of Whitman College, June 3, 1930, the late Corbett Lawyer, son of the

---

[37] From an undated clipping, *Golden Age*, Lewiston, Idaho, quoting from a letter Spalding wrote dated May 12, 1866. O.I.B.

[38] *See* Drury, *M. & N.W.*, Vol. II, p. 216, for a reproduction of this photograph.

Rev. Archie Lawyer and grandson of Chief Lawyer, presented to the College the original document given by Governor Stevens to Lawyer on June 11, 1855, the day the Walla Walla Council closed. The certificate reads as follows, (*see* illustration):

To All Persons Whom It May Concern

Whereas, *Hol-lol-sote-tote*, otherwise called *Lawyer*, an Indian of the *Nez Perce* Tribe, living in the Territory of WASHINGTON, has been this day recognized as HEAD CHIEF of the same; now, therefore, this paper is given to him that he may be known and treated accordingly.

The said chief is held responsible for the good behavior of his people, and is required to inform the Superintendent of Indian Affairs, or the Agent, of all offenses committed by Indians against the citizens of the Territory, and to deliver up on demand all persons accused thereof. In so doing, he is to be assisted by the Sub Chiefs appointed to counsel with him, and will be supported by the Government and the Military.

He is also on behalf of his people to make complaint of injuries done by citizens or others against them, and particularly of the sale of liquor to Indians. In this the faith of the Government is pledged to sustain him, and do them justice.

Should the said chief fail to perform his duty honestly, the Superintendent will remove him and make another Chief. In witness whereof, I have hereto set my hand this *Eleventh* day of *June* 1855.

Issued by *Wm. H. Tappan*   *I. I. Stevens*
Agent.   Governor and Superintendent of Indian Affairs.

The original certificate, which measures 8¼ x 13½ inches, is now in the archives of Whitman College. Since it was printed with some blank spaces, which were filled in by pen (such insertions are italicized in the above copy), it is evident that the certificates were printed in advance for the use by both Governor Stevens and General Palmer. We may assume that each of the Head Chiefs present at the Walla Walla Council received one of these certificates. In all probability, Lawyer's copy is the only one extant.

It should be noted that this certificate did not say that Stevens "appointed" Lawyer to be Head Chief of the Nez Perces, but rather he was "recognized" to be such. The selection had been made by the Nez Perces themselves.

CHAPTER SIX

Three Years of Turmoil, 1855-1858

In his letter of June 12, 1855, to George W. Manypenny, Commissioner of Indian Affairs, Washington, D.C., Governor Stevens, having summarized the results of the Walla Walla Council, wrote: "Thus has ended a most difficult and protracted negotiation. . . Its effect on the peace of the country hardly admits of exaggeration. Had no Treaty been effected, there would probably have been blood shed and open war the present year."

Stevens badly misjudged the situation. Actually the treaties precipitated more than three years of turmoil between Government forces and the rebellious or hostile [1] elements in all of the tribes which attended the Walla Walla Council, including some Nez Perces. Looking back on the 1855 Council, Hazard Stevens claimed that such chiefs as "Young Chief, Five Crows, Peu-peu-mox-mox, Kam-i-ah-kan, and their sub-chiefs — all signed the treaties as a deliberate act of treachery, in order to lull the whites into fancied security. . ." and to give the Indians time "for completing their preparations for a widespread and simultaneous onslaught on all the settlements." [2]

Stevens, reflecting the white man's viewpoint, looked upon the treaty signed at Walla Walla as a solemn, binding agreement which could not be broken except by common consent or by a gross betrayal by one of the contracting parties. Signing a treaty with the white man was a new experience for the Oregon Indians. With the exception of Lawyer and his Nez Perce following, most of the other Indians who were at

---

[1] Contemporary accounts of the Indian wars of these years written by white men consistently refer to the Indians who opposed the Government forces as "hostiles." From the Indians' point of view, the white men were the "hostiles."

[2] Stevens, *Stevens*, Vol. II, p. 61.

Walla Walla did not accept the 1855 treaty as binding. Repeatedly in his recorded remarks, Lawyer referred to the treaty as the "law," which had to be obeyed.

These fundamental differences of opinions regarding the 1855 treaty became evident within a few weeks after the Walla Walla Council closed. The three years of turmoil which followed ended on September 5, 1858, when Colonel George Wright inflicted a crushing defeat on the hostiles in the battle of Spokane Plains. During these three years, most of the Nez Perces, under Lawyer's leadership, not only remained friendly with the Government authorities, but at times actually joined forces with Government troops in military engagements against the hostiles.

HOSTILITIES BEGIN

Governor Stevens, having been instructed to visit the Flatheads and Blackfeet in western Montana and negotiate treaties with those Indians, left Walla Walla for that purpose on June 16, 1855. He took with him a party of twenty-one including his secretary, James Doty, and his young son. After three days of travel, the Stevens party arrived at Alpowa, about twelve miles from present-day Lewiston, Idaho, where Chiefs Timothy and Red Wolf lived. Hazard Stevens remembered that the Indians had thirteen lodges at the place, most of which sheltered several families, and that some thirty acres were fenced and under cultivation.

Commenting on this visit to Alpowa, Hazard wrote:

> By appointment, Lawyer met the Governor here, and with the other two chiefs took supper with him, the three devouring the lion's share of a fine salmon, which Timothy had sold at an exhorbitant price — clearly the Nez Perces were fast learning the ways of civilization — and completed the arrangements for sending their delegation to the Blackfoot council. Lawyer gave much information about his people.[3]

In his letter to Manypenny of June 14, Stevens stated that he had hoped Lawyer could accompany him into the Blackfoot country but that this was impossible because Lawyer's old hip wound had "recently broken out." Looking Glass, ranking second in the Nez Perce hierarchy,

---

[3] *Ibid.*, p. 71.

took Lawyer's place as the head of a fourteen-man Nez Perce delegation to go with the Stevens party.

Stevens visited the Flatheads at Hell Gate Ronde, near present-day Missoula, where an acceptable treaty was negotiated. Stevens and his party then moved on to Fort Benton where another treaty was negotiated with the Blackfeet. Stevens then started on his return journey on October 28. On the following evening, a courier from The Dalles arrived with dispatches bearing the alarming news that the Yakimas, Cayuses, Walla Wallas, Umatillas, and Palouses had gone on the warpath.

It appears that immediately following the Walla Walla Council, Kam-i-ah-kan, Owhi, and the latter's son, Qualchen, decided that they would no longer permit Americans to pass through their country and, if Government troops were sent, the Indians would resist. The timing was unfortunate for the Americans as gold had been discovered in the Colville area and the gold-hungry miners were ignoring Kam-i-ah-kan's warning that all who entered the Indian country would be killed. The first recorded instance of actual hostilities came in September, 1855, when Qualchen with five relatives attacked a party of six white men on the Yakima River and killed them all. Soon afterwards, two more miners were killed.

When Indian Agent Nathan Olney, stationed at The Dalles, heard of these murders, he sent one of his deputies, A. J. Bolon, to investigate. Since Bolon had been on friendly terms with the Yakimas, he sensed no danger, so traveled alone. Three Yakima Indians, one of whom was Qualchen, waylaid the unsuspecting Bolon and killed him on September 23, 1855.[4]

When Bolon failed to return, Olney sent an Indian to investigate. The Indian returned with the news of the murder and also of a boastful claim that Kam-i-ah-kan had made to the effect that he had accumulated enough ammunition to last his warriors for five years. When C. H. Mason, Secretary of Washington Territory and Acting Governor in the absence of Governor Stevens, heard the news, he asked for Federal troops.

Major Gabriel J. Haines, in command of U.S. forces at Fort Vancouver, ordered Major G. O. Haller, then at The Dalles, to move into

[4] *Ibid.*

the Yakima country and, if possible, apprehend the murderers. Haller and a company of about 100 men met a large force of Indians about sixty miles from The Dalles on October 5. As a result of intensive agitation among all of the tribes of the interior by Kam-i-ah-kan, Owhi, and Qualchen, about 1,500 warriors had assembled to do battle against the Whites. Lawrence Kip, in his *Army Life on the Pacific*, stated that "Owhi and his son Qualchen are probably the two worst Indians this side of the Rocky Mountains." [5] Peu-peu-mox-mox with some Walla Wallas is reported to have taken part in the fight against Haller.[6]

After a three-day period of skirmishes, and after having had five of his soldiers killed, seventeen wounded, and after having lost a pack train with supplies, Haller retreated to The Dalles. He called for a reenforcement of 1,000 men. The news of the great victory by the Indians over the Whites spread rapidly throughout the Indian country and brought much jubilation among the natives. Many of the Indians, who had been reluctant to take up arms against the Whites, now began to waver, even including some of the Nez Perces.

STEVENS' LIFE THREATENED

The dispatches which the courier, W. H. Pearson, delivered to Governor Stevens on the evening of October 29, contained the alarming news of the Indian uprising and that Major Haller had been defeated by the Yakimas, and that "the Cayuses, Wallah-Wallahs, and Umatillas were hostile. A general Indian war was apprehended." [7] Stevens also heard from Angus MacDonald, Chief Trader at Fort Colville, that the Indians of that area were in an excitable state.

Also among the dispatches was a letter from Acting Governor of Washington Territory, C. H. Mason, who advised Stevens not to return by the overland route but rather to descend the Missouri and return via the Isthmus of Panama.[8] Mason wrote that in giving such advice he had the concurrence of the ranking military officers of the Territory.

---

[5] Kip, *op. cit.*, p. 101. Having been commissioned a 2nd Lieut. in the U.S. Army in June 1857, Kip served in the campaign against the tribes in the upper Columbia River region in the summer of 1858. An account of his experiences is found in his *Army Life on the Pacific*.

[6] Ruby and Brown, *The Cayuse Indians*, p. 229.

[7] Stevens to Indian Commissioner Manypenny, December 22, 1855, published in *Senate Ex. Doc., No. 46, 34th Congress, 1st Session*, p. 3.

[8] Fuller, *Pacific Northwest*, p. 229.

They were fearful that Stevens might be killed if he traveled through hostile Indian country. Stevens, however, rejected this advice and decided to return the way he had come.

After a hazardous march over the Bitterroot Mountains through deep snow and in very cold weather, the Stevens party arrived at the Catholic Coeur d'Alene Mission on November 24. Stevens then learned that a party of Yakimas had been waiting at the Mission to waylay him, no doubt with the intention of killing him, as he was the highest ranking Government official among the Whites. After waiting for some time and being convinced that no one could cross the Bitterroots at that time of the year when the snow was so deep, the Indians had left just five days before Stevens and his party arrived.

In his letter of December 22, 1855, to Commissioner Manypenny in Washington, D.C., Stevens summarized: "Here I paused two days, the animals absolutely requiring one day's rest; collection information, and soothed the spirits of the Coeur d'Alenes. They talked well, but their statements in regard to the war were somewhat uncertain."

While at Coeur d'Alene, Stevens became acutely aware of the persuasive propaganda against the Whites which was being spread abroad by Kam-i-ah-kan and his followers. All sorts of rumors were rife, including one report that Peu-peu-mox-mox had boasted that he would take Governor Stevens' scalp. Realizing that it was vitally important to keep the allegiance of the Nez Perces, the largest and most influential tribe of the region, Stevens sent William Craig, who had been serving as his interpreter, and three of the Nez Perce chiefs, including one called Captain John who became one of Lawyer's most trusted subchiefs, to Lapwai to confer with Lawyer. Stevens wanted Lawyer to call a council of the Nez Perce chiefs to meet with him when he arrived at Lapwai.

Stevens and his party, including Looking Glass, then moved on to a place in the Spokane country which Stevens described as being sixty miles from the Coeur d'Alene Mission. This would have placed him at Tshimakain, the former mission occupied by Walker and Eells. They arrived there on November 20. Stevens at once summoned the chiefs of the area to a council which he described in his letter to Manypenny as follows:

Every chief of the Coeur d'Alene, Spokanes, and Colvilles came. We were in council parts of three days. They were excited. Their minds were poisoned by all the artful stories and tricks of the hostile tribes. They talked freely. I urged them to talk boldly saying I should talk freely in return. In my address, I refuted the thousand lies which had been spread among them; admonished them wherein their duty lay; avowed my intention to protect the Indians who were friendly. It seemed to change the whole current of their feelings. They were apparently soothed and satisfied, and they pledged themselves to protect all white men in their country, and to take no part in the war.

As will be noted, this promise was not kept when many from these tribes joined the hostiles in their attack on Colonel Wright in the battle of Spokane Plains which took place in September 1858.

While among the Spokanes, Stevens received convincing evidence that Looking Glass had sought the aid of Spokane Garry in a plot to entrap him. Although Garry had reason for complaint against the Whites, he, like Lawyer, remained a friend of the white men. Alarmed by what he had learned, Stevens sent another message to Lawyer asking him "to frustrate the designs of the threacherous chief [i.e., Looking Glass] without his suspecting that they had been discovered." [9]

MAJORITY OF THE NEZ PERCES REMAIN FAITHFUL TO AMERICANS

Stevens, in his letter to Commissioner Manypenny of December 22, 1855, wrote: "On the 8th of December, we were fairly under way for the Nez Perce country, and in four days reached Craig's on the Lapwai [Creek], a distance of one hundred and eight miles, traveling the whole time in storm, snow, and rain; the snow at times eight to twelve inches deep. At Craig's we found the Nez Perces in council awaiting my arrival."

Hazard Stevens has given us the following description of the council:

Although it was now in the midst of winter, and the ground was covered with snow, Lawyer had assembled two hundred and eight lodges, containing over two thousand Indians, and able to muster eight hundred warriors. An animated council was at once held. The council lodge was a hundred feet in length, built of poles, mats, and skins, and in this assembled two hundred chiefs and principal men, Lawyer presiding.[10]

According to Hazard, no mention was made of Looking Glass's plot

---

[9] Stevens, *Stevens*, Vol. II, p. 136.   [10] *Ibid.*, p. 143.

to entrap Stevens, and the unanimous resolve of the council "was not only to maintain their friendship to the whites and stand by the treaty, but also to escort Governor Stevens with two hundred and fifty of their bravest and best-armed warriors" to Walla Walla. This decision was of crucial importance to Governor Stevens for without it, not only was the Government policy of settling the Indians on reservations endangered, but his life also.

When Looking Glass sensed the sentiment of the council, he quickly shifted his position from that of opposing Stevens to that of giving him his most enthusiastic support. Hazard reported the chief as saying: "I told the governor that the Walla Walla country was blocked up by bad Indians, and that I would go ahead and he behind, and that's my heart now." No one was to be more loyal to the Americans than he.

In the meantime, stirring events were transpiring in the Walla Walla Valley. Stevens explained in his December letter to Manypenny: "Whilst we were in council, reports rapidly came in of the four days' battle in the valley between the Oregon volunteers and the Cayuses, Wallah-Wallahs, Umatillas, and the Indians thence to the Dalles, and of the death of Pu-pu-mox-mox."

Here is the background for that report. Fearful for the safety of Governor Stevens and his party, six companies of Oregon Volunteers under Lieutenant Colonel James M. Kelly (or Kelley) were sent to the Umatilla. Indian Agent Nathan Olney preceded the troops and persuaded those in charge of the Hudson's Bay Company's Fort Walla Walla to throw their stock of ammunition into the Columbia River to prevent it from falling into the hands of the hostile Indians. The move was well timed as shortly afterwards Peu-peu-mox-mox, with a large band of his followers, captured and plundered the fort.

On December 2, Kelly left the Umatilla for Fort Walla Walla. Finding the fort abandoned, he moved his troops to the Touchet River where he learned the hostiles were encamped. Finding that he was outnumbered by the Volunteers, Peu-peu-mox-mox visited Kelly's camp under a flag of truce. Kelly kept the chief as hostage and sent word to his followers to surrender their arms and ammunition, but this they refused to do. Governor Stevens later claimed that Peu-peu-mox-mox came into his camp in order to give his followers a chance to escape.

The Indians moved to the mouth of the Touchet, on the Walla Walla River, where they were reinforced by some 100 Palouse warriors. This brought the total strength of the hostiles to about 500. An engagement between the Indians and the Volunteers took place on December 7 in which about fifty Indians were killed, and an unknown number of Volunteers.

During one of the engagements, when the Volunteers with several of their Indian prisoners, including Peu-peu-mox-mox, came within shouting distance of the hostiles, the old chief began shouting orders to his men to cheer them on. Fearing that the prisoners would escape, Kelly ordered that all be tied up. The Indians resisted. One of the prisoners drew a knife that he had hidden in his clothing and stabbed a soldier. Peu-peu-mox-mox tried to grab a gun from a soldier, whereupon he was killed. Some of the soldiers, inflamed with anger against the rebellious chief, disgraced themselves by mutilating his body, by scalping him, cutting off his ears, etc.[11]

On December 10, the Indians, learning of the arrival of two companies of reenforcements for the Volunteers, withdrew across the Snake River into the Palouse country. This was the news that reached Governor Stevens at Lapwai just before the council with the Nez Perces closed.

> These reports were confirmed on the 14th December, [wrote Stevens to Manypenny.] I determined to make no change in the plans which I had made in concert with Lawyer, the head chief of the Nez Perces, which was to take with me a portion of his people, well mounted and well armed, and to leave the larger portion in their own country . . . to drive the hostile Indians out of the Nez Perce country, in case they should invade it from the north side of the Snake.

Thus it came to be that the Nez Perces, as allies of the Whites, were willing to do battle if need be against members of neighboring tribes. This meant that Indians would be fighting Indians.

Stevens, his party, and a large company of Nez Perces started for Walla Walla on what Hazard remembered as being "a clear, bright, frosty December morning," Saturday, December 15. Even though there was the possibility of meeting hostile Indians on the way, the company was in high spirits. Hazard has given us the following account of the mingled cavalcade of Whites and Indians:

Here were the gentlemen of the party, with their black felt hats

---

[11] Fuller, *Pacific Northwest*, pp. 228-9.

and heavy cloth overcoats; rough-clad miners and packers; the mountain men with buckskin shirts and leggings and fur caps; the long-eared pack-mules, with their bulky loads; and the blanketed young braves, with painted visage, and hair adorned with eagle feathers, mounted on sleek and spirited mustangs, and dashing hither and thither in the greatest excitement and glee. Each of the warriors had three fine, spirited horses, which he rode in turn as the fancy moved him.

The cavalcade moved down the north bank of the Clearwater River to its confluence with the Snake. There the men were ferried across the Snake in canoes while their animals were made to swim the stream. The party then proceeded along the south side of the Snake. "The demeanor of the young braves on this march," wrote Hazard, "was in sharp contrast to the traditional gravity and stoicism of their race. They shouted, laughed, told stories, cracked jokes, and gave free vent to their native gayety and high spirits. Craig, who accompanied the party, translated these good things as they occurred, to great amusement of the whites."

While crossing a wide, flat plain covered with tall grass, Craig was reminded of an incident in Lawyer's life which he told.

When yet an obscure young warrier, [related Craig,] Lawyer was traveling over this ground with a party of the tribe, including several of the principal chiefs. It was a cold winter day, and a biting gale swept up the river, penetrating their clothing and chilling them to the bone. The chiefs sat down in the shelter of the tall rye grass, and were indulging in a cosy smoke, when Lawyer fired the prairie far to windward, and in an instant the fiery element, in a long, crackling, blazing line, came sweeping down on the wings of the wind upon the comfort-taking chiefs, and drove them to rush helter-skelter into the river for safety, dropping robes, pipes, and everything that might impede their flights. For this audacious prank, Lawyer barely escaped a public whipping.

Hazard added that the "young braves seemed particularly tickled," on hearing about this escapade of their venerated chief who, evidently, was not travelling with them.

The Stevens party reached Alpowa on Sunday, the 16th. There a Cayuse chief, Ume-how-lish, whom Stevens suspected had taken part in the murder of some settlers, was taken into custody. He protested his innocence and later was released. This chief was none other than "the Umatilla chief Umhawalish" whom Spalding, while on his death bed, baptized at Kamiah on May 11, 1874, and to whom he gave the baptismal name of Marcus Whitman.[12]

While at Walla Walla, Stevens wrote his letter of December 22 to Indian Commissioner Manypenny, from which quotations have already been made. Stevens in this letter drew attention to a sharp difference of opinion which had developed between him and General Ellis Wool, then in command of the U.S. Army's Division of the Pacific with his headquarters at Benicia, California. General Wool was seventy years old in 1855, too old to be conducting an Indian war and too far removed to appreciate the situation in the field of combat. He despised volunteer troops and was loath to authorize supplying them with arms and ammunition. In a letter to Governor Stevens, General Wool took the position that the Indians were not to blame for the outbreak of hostilities and dealt at some length on denouncing the outrages "by whites upon the Indians in southern Oregon." General Wool assumed that what had happened in Oregon was likewise true of Washington. Hazard Stevens wrote: "Instead of making use of, or cooperating with the Oregon Volunteers already in the Walla Walla Valley, he denounced them as making war upon friendly Indians." [13]

Stevens, in his letter of December 22 to Manypenny, stated:

> The war has been most treacherous and bloody in its inception and it must be prosecuted with an iron hand. I state, on my official responsibility, that if strong measures are not urged now, and the enemy be not met and beaten before the spring, that there will be great danger of tribes now peaceable breaking into open war. I will vouch for the Nez Perces. They are staunch and entirely reliable. But all the tribes northward from the Cascades to the Bitterroots are extremely doubtful, and rumors are now reaching me that a portion of the Spokanes have already marched to the aid of Kam-ai-kan.

Stevens' hope to pursue the hostiles, then on the north side of the Snake River, with the Volunteers and the Nez Perces during the winter months became impossible because of the unusually cold weather.[14] The thermometer at Walla Walla sank to an incredible 27° below zero. The land was blanketed with a heavy snowfall. On December 29, Stevens commissioned Craig a Lieutenant Colonel in the Oregon Vol-

---

12 Drury, *M. & N.W.*, Vol. II, p. 359.   13 Stevens, *Stevens*, Vol. II, p. 175.
14 Fuller, *Pacific Northwest*, p. 231.

unteers and then sent the Nez Perces back to their country to be
mustered out by the newly appointed Colonel Craig.

STEVENS ADVOCATES FIRMNESS

The history of the Indian disturbances in the upper Columbia River
country during the years, 1856-1858, is complicated. Our interest in
the hostilities of these years will be limited to those engagements in
which the Nez Perces, with Lawyer's consent, were involved.

Stevens, in the December 1855 letter to Manypenny, summarized his
policies regarding the warring tribes as follows:

> My plan is to make no treaties whatever with the tribes now in
> arms; to do away entirely with the reservations guaranteed to
> them; to make a summary example of all the leading spirits, and to
> place as a conquered people, under the surveillance of troops, the
> remains of these tribes on reservations selected by the President,
> and on such terms as the government in its justice and mercy may
> vouchsafe to them.

In sharp contrast to this policy of firmness outlined by Governor
Stevens was General Wool's leniency. Coming up from California to
Fort Vancouver in December 1855, Wool, because of his superior rank,
mustered out the Washington Volunteers, stationed regular Army
troops at The Dalles under Colonel George Wright, denounced the
activities of the Oregon Volunteers, disbanded the company which had
been raised for Governor Stevens' relief, and forbade white settlers
from entering the territory east of the Cascade Mountains.[15]

Thus, at the beginning of 1856, the hostile Indians controlled all of
the upper Columbia River country except the Walla Walla Valley,
where some Volunteers were still stationed, and the Nez Perce country
where Lawyer was able to exercise a restraining authority.

The day after his return to Olympia, Stevens addressed the Territorial
Legislature. He pointed out the fact that the passage by Congress of
the Donation Act of 1848 held out a standing invitation to American
settlers to settle on any unoccupied land they wanted, surveyed or
unsurveyed, without waiting for the Government to extinguish Indian
titles. The Governor emphasized the necessity of extinguishing the
Indian titles in order to maintain peace with the various tribes and
prevent bloodshed.

---

[15] Stevens, *Stevens*, Vol. II, pp. 160-1.

Regarding the origin of the Indian disturbances of the previous fall in the upper Columbia River country, Stevens wrote: "It originated in the native intelligence of restless Indians who, foreseeing destiny against them — that the white man was coming upon them — determined that it must be met and resisted with arms. We may sympathize with such a manly feeling, but in view of it, we have high duties." [16]

History was repeating itself in the Pacific Northwest. Again and again in human history, peoples, superior in numbers, skills, and material goods, have overrun weaker peoples who happened to be in their way. The Indians of interior Washington were faced with this threat. They had been told at the 1855 Walla Walla Council that the white men were coming, that they were as numerous as the grasshoppers on the prairies, and that they could no more be stopped than one could sweep back the flow of the Columbia. This, said Stevens, was the "destiny" of the Indians and that the white man had the "high duty" to subdue the natives.

Even as the two Government officials, General Wool and Governor Stevens, who had authority over the military, held diametrically opposing views as to how they should deal with the Indians, so likewise the two most influential chiefs of the upper Columbia River country, Kam-i-ah-kan and Lawyer, held contrary views as to how the Indians should deal with the white men.

Kam-i-ah-kan, ignoring the overwhelming advantage held by the Whites because of their superior numbers, their military equipment and technical skills, advocated armed resistance. Out of anger and frustration, he instructed his followers to kill any and all white men who ventured into their territory. He was opposed to reservations and annuities. He even refused to take a blanket from a Government official. No gifts of any kind were to be accepted from the Whites.

Lawyer was more realistic. He knew that the Indians were too few in numbers and too poor in material resources to long resist the white man. He was ready to compromise and accept a reservation with the white man's promises to help civilize and educate his people. The hostilities which occurred during 1856-58 between the American troops and the Indian warriors from several tribes demonstrated the fact that Kam-i-ah-kan was wrong and that Lawyer was right.

---

[16] *Ibid.*, p. 163.

PRELUDE TO THE SECOND WALLA WALLA COUNCIL, SEPTEMBER 1856

Writing to the Indian Commissioner in Washington from Olympia on October 22, 1856, Stevens in a 4,000 word letter described the troubled events of that year. One of the most serious developments he reported was the fact that some of the Nez Perces had become disaffected. Stevens explained: "The Nez Perces, entirely friendly last December-January, first became disaffected in consequence of the War Chief of the Cayuses, Ume-how-lish, and the friendly Cayuses going into the Nez Perce country contrary to my positive orders." The "friendly Cayuses" included Chief Stickus and a band of Cayuses who fled to the Nez Perce country to escape the harassment of the hostiles who tried to get them to join in the anti-White movement. Stevens explained that, before leaving Walla Walla in December 1855, he had "ordered the Nez Perces to keep the hostiles out of their country." If the friendly Cayuses were permitted to go, he warned, then the Nez Perces could not keep out the hostiles which would mean disaffection spreading through that tribe.

Regarding the chief, Stevens wrote: "Ume-how-lish, my prisoner, was sent into the Nez Perce country by Col. Wright, and from the time of his arrival there, all the efforts made by Agent Craig to prevent the spread of disaffection were abortive. What I apprehended and predicted actually came to pass." [17]

During the winter of 1855-56 and in the following months, the anti-American spirit both west and east of the Cascades continued to increase. Stevens blamed the agitation on Kam-i-ah-kan. His son, Hazard, wrote: "In this conspiracy and contest, Kam-i-ah-kan was the moving spirit, the organizer, the instigator, whose crafty wiles never slept, and whose stubborn resolution no disaster could break." [18] Indian tribes, west of the Cascades, especially in the Puget Sound area, joined in the war against the Whites. All of Washington Territory was ablaze.

Faced with this alarming situation, Stevens on January 22, 1856, issued a call for 1,000 Volunteers who would serve for a six-months period for offensive action against the hostiles. Over 1,300 enlisted including 236 Indians of which number 113 were Nez Perces. The Indians furnished their own horses.[19]

---

[17] Stevens to Commissioner of Indian Affairs, Oct. 22, 1856. O.I.B.
[18] Stevens, *Stevens,* Vol. II, p. 61.   [19] *Ibid.,* p. 169.

Realizing the strategic importance of maintaining a garrison in the Walla Walla Valley, Stevens sent Lieutenant Colonel B. F. Shaw with 175 mounted men through the Yakima Country to Walla Walla. They made camp on Mill Creek on July 9, 1856. They were joined by a company of seventy-five Nez Perces under Lieutenant Colonel Craig and Chief Spotted Eagle. The presence of this force at Walla Walla was vitally important in order to supply the friendly Nez Perces with arms and ammunition.

The hostiles succeeded in obtaining arms and ammunition by capturing several supply trains of either the Volunteers or of the Regular Army troops. For instance, in February 1856 they captured sixteen wagonloads of supplies which were en route from the Umatilla River to the Walla Walla Valley. In his letter of October 22, 1856, Stevens reported another loss when on July 29, "one of my pack trains mostly laden with Indian supplies was captured by the Indians, a most unfortunate occurance."

SECOND WALLA WALLA COUNCIL, SEPTEMBER 1856

Believing that it would be helpful if he could meet both the hostile and friendly chiefs in council, Stevens called upon them to meet him at the old council grounds at Walla Walla early in September 1856. Stevens knew that he would have the support of Lawyer and most of the Nez Perces and hoped that somehow he could work out some agreement with Kam-i-ah-kan and the other hostiles which would bring peace.

Stevens and his small party arrived at Shaw's camp on Mill Creek on August 21. According to a previous agreement which Stevens had been able to effect with Colonel Wright at The Dalles, Lieutenant Colonel Edward J. Steptoe with four companies of Regulars were to move to Walla Walla and relieve the Volunteers who were still on duty there. Steptoe and his soldiers arrived at Walla Walla on September 5 and made camp on Mill Creek about five miles below the Governor's camp, evidently at Waiilatpu.

Lawyer and a large number of Nez Perces arrived on September 6 and encamped about four miles from Shaw's camp. On the 8th, the Governor received about 300 of the chiefs and headmen of the tribe and that evening entertained the chiefs for dinner. Stevens was distressed to learn that about one-half of the Nez Perces were "unquestionably hostile." Stevens was also aware that all of the other tribes, with but few individual exceptions, were also hostile.

On the evening of the 9th, Father A. Ravalli of the Coeur d'Alene Mission arrived with the news that Kam-i-ah-kan, Owhi, and Qualchen, the three most influential chiefs of the hostiles, would not attend the council. What Stevens did not know at the time was that these three were plotting to attack the Volunteers and kill Stevens and all in his party. Kam-i-ah-kan had frequently boasted that he would lift the scalp of Governor Stevens, his most hated enemy. Kam-i-ah-kan knew of the lenient policy of General Wool and counted on the Government troops remaining neutral if Stevens and the Volunteers were attacked.

In his letter of October 22 to the Commissioner of Indian Affairs, Governor Stevens stated that he faced 500 hostile warriors at Walla Walla. This number included: ". . . all of the Yakimas and Palouses, 200 warriors; the bulk of the Cayuses and Umatillas, 75 warriors; 100 of the Walla Wallas and Indians from other bands." Those from other bands included 125 Nez Perce warriors who had been influenced by dissident Cayuses to join the hostiles. Stevens had faced a most threatening situation.

Stevens had repeatedly urged Steptoe to camp near him, but this Steptoe refused to do since he was under orders from General Wool to remain absolutely neutral.[20] Stevens wanted Steptoe to be near him in order to demonstrate to the Indians "the strength of our people and the unity of our councils."

Since Steptoe would not move his camp, Stevens then invited him to attend the meetings of the council so that he could hear and see at first-hand the attitudes of the Indians. Steptoe, however, declined even this invitation and in a note to Stevens explained the reason: "Permit me to say that my instructions from General Wool do not authorize me to make any arrangements whatever of the kind you wish." The evident rift between the U.S. Troops and the Volunteers inspired the hostiles to greater boldness.

Since the term of the Volunteers expired on September 6, Stevens was obliged to let them return to their homes. Realizing that the refusal of Steptoe to move his troops close to the council grounds, together with the departure of the Volunteers, would place him in a most pre-

---

[20] *Ibid.*, p. 212.

carious position, Stevens induced Captain Francis M. Goff and his company of sixty-nine men, all Volunteers, to remain as a guard. Stevens had fifty men in his party which included his secretary, servants, teamsters, herders, and a few Indian helpers. He also had the Nez Perce company of about fifty warriors under the command of Spotted Eagle and Craig. He could also depend on the loyalty of Chief Lawyer and his faithful band of Nez Perces, of unknown numbers, but even after counting all of these, Stevens was greatly outnumbered by the combined forces of the hostiles.

Stevens opened the second Walla Walla Council on Tuesday, September 11. Only a few chiefs from the Cayuse and Umatilla tribes attended in addition to Lawyer and his followers. According to Hazard Stevens' account:

> The Governor expressed his sorrow at the state of hostilities; reviewed the course of Kam-i-ah-kan, Pu-pu-mox-mox, and the hostiles in accepting the treaties, professing the utmost satisfaction with them, and then murdering whites traveling through their country, and their agent, Bolon, plundering Fort Walla Walla and burning the houses of settlers, and threatening the lives of himself and party returning from the Blackfoot Council.[21]

Stevens invited the chiefs to speak. Several responded. Their common complaint centered on that provision of the 1855 Treaty which called upon them to surrender so much land. Actually, according to figures given in Stevens' official report to Washington, the area ceded by the Indians, approximately 30,400 square miles, was considerably larger than the combined areas of the Nez Perce and the Umatilla Reservations. As previously stated, the Nez Perce Reservation had about 23,666 square miles and Stevens in his report estimated that the Umatilla Reservation had 800 square miles — making a total of 24,466 square miles. Thus the ceded area contained about 6,000 more square miles than were in the two reservations put together.

One of the Nez Perce chiefs, Speaking Owl, asked Stevens: "Will you give us back our lands? That is what we all want to hear about; that is what troubles us. I ask plainly to have a plain answer." The demand that the ceded lands be returned to the Indians was unrealistic in view of the thousands of white people streaming into the territory.

---

[21] *Ibid.*, p. 213.

Stevens called on Lawyer to reply to the critics of the 1855 Treaty. Of this Hazard Stevens wrote: "He produced his commission [i.e., the certificate which Stevens had given him in June 1855] and a copy of the Nez Perce treaty, remarking that he knew that if he cast away the laws, he should be brought to justice." He pointed out to them the boundaries of the area ceded to the Government and of the reservations established. After referring to other provisions in the treaty, Lawyer concluded his remarks by saying that "fifty-eight of the Nez Perces had signed the treaty made at the council of that year, when all fully understood it, and it was his determination to abide by it, and he trusted his people would do the same." Thus Lawyer openly and unequivocally took his stand in favor of abiding by the provisions of the 1855 Treaty.

Hazard Stevens then added: "Timothy and James expressed a similar determination, but Joseph, Speaking Eagle, Eagle-from-the-Light, and Red Wolf denied that they understood the treaty, or even intended to give their land away, and declared that Lawyer had sold it unfairly." Here is the first evidence that some of the Indians, even those who had signed the 1855 Treaty, were accusing Lawyer of selling their lands unfairly.

On Saturday morning, September 13, Stevens sent an urgent message to Steptoe begging him to send a company of soldiers which, he claimed, was essential for the security of his camp. Responding to this appeal, and risking a reprimand from his superior, General Wool, Steptoe sent a company of cavalry, then called dragoons because they served on foot as well as on horseback, to Stevens' camp. Steptoe also suggested to Stevens that if he had reason to believe that the Indians would attack him, then it would be well for him and his party to move to the vicinity of the Steptoe camp.

In view of the threatening situation, Stevens decided to move. This he did on Sunday, the 14th. As the long caravan, consisting of Captain Goff's company of Volunteers, Steptoe's dragoons, Stevens' party of about fifty men with their freight wagons and pack animals, and finally Craig and his company of fifty Nez Perce warriors moved down the trail, Stevens put all on alert, for he was fearful of an attack.

Stevens' precautions were well taken. En route to Steptoe's camp, they unexpectedly met a party of about 100 hostiles under the leadership of Kam-i-ah-kan, Owhi, and Qualchen coming up the trail. The meeting of the two opposing forces was as unexpected for the Yakima chiefs as it was for Stevens. Hazard Stevens, who was a witness to the encounter, wrote that the Indians "clearly meant mischief; but the coolness with which they were received, and the manifest readiness of the Volunteers and dragoons for battle checked them." [22]

Stevens, commenting on this encounter in his letter of October 22, wrote: "Kam-i-ah-kan had unquestionably an understanding, as subsequent events showed . . . to make an attack that day or evening upon my camp. He found me on the road to his great surprise, and had no time to perfect his arrangements."

According to Hazard Stevens, the friendly Nez Perces who had been encamped with Stevens near the council grounds, were informed on Sunday morning of the move to new council grounds near Steptoe's encampment. Lawyer and his followers made the move for Lawyer was present for the reopening of the council on Tuesday, the 16th.

When the hostiles passed Spotted Eagle and his company of warriors on the trail, Kam-i-ah-kan and his followers attempted to provoke a quarrel with them by reviling them for their willingness to serve the white men. It was possible that Lawyer and his party were traveling at that time with Spotted Eagle and his men when they met Kam-i-ah-kan and the other Yakima chiefs. Thus Lawyer and Kam-i-ah-kan, the two leaders of the two opposing factions, would have passed within a few yards of each other when they met on the trail.

Regarding the continued meeting of the council on the 16th and 17th, Hazard Stevens wrote: "The Lawyer and half the Nez Perces were determined in their adherence to their treaty and ancient friendship to the whites, and approved of all the governor said. The other half of the tribe wished the treaty done away with. The hostiles all said, 'Do away with all treaties, give us back our lands, let no white man come into our country, and there will be peace; if not, then we will fight.' " Hazard Stevens blamed "the intrigues of Kam-i-ah-kan and the Cayuses" for the disaffection which spread through about one-half of the Nez Perces. Indeed the disaffection among these Nez Perces became so threatening that Lawyer and others advised Craig to delay his return to Lapwai as he might, under existing tensions, be killed.

Stevens closed the council on the 17th. Nothing had been gained. Indeed the anti-American feeling had hardened. At the end of the June 1855 Walla Walla Council, Stevens had written that the nego-

---

[22] *Ibid.*, p. 218.

tiations had been closed "in a most satisfactory manner." This time, according to his official report, the September 1856 Council had closed in a most unsatisfactory manner.

On September 18, the day after the council closed, Colonel Steptoe met with some of the chiefs including some of the hostiles, at which time he told them he had not come to fight them but merely to establish a military post at Walla Walla. Such a statement gave the hostiles added reason to believe that the rift between the Government forces under Steptoe and the Territorial troops under Stevens was so deep that they could attack Stevens with impunity, and without fear of any interference from the Government troops.

STEVENS UNDER ATTACK

Governor Stevens with his escort of one company of Volunteers and some fifty friendly Nez Perce warriors started for The Dalles late on Friday morning, September 19. "So satisfied was I," wrote Stevens in his letter of October 22, "that the Indians would carry into effect their avowed determination   .   .   .   to attack me that, on starting, I formed my whole party and march in order of battle." This meant that every armed man carried his weapon ready for instant use; that the whole caravan was stretched out with intervals between units to make an ambush more difficult; and that a small advance party preceded the caravan with scouts along the sides.

About one o'clock that afternoon, when the caravan was only three miles from Steptoe's camp, the hostiles began random shooting at it. Stevens continued his march for another mile until he found what he considered to be a good defensible position. There he formed his wagons into a corral and posted guards on surrounding ridges. The exchange of gunfire continued throughout the afternoon.

Angered by the very thought that some Nez Perces were fighting for Governor Stevens, the hostiles warned these Nez Perces to withdraw from the white man's camp. "We came not to fight Nez Perces," they said. "Go to your camp, or we will wipe it out." The camp with the families of the friendly Nez Perces was about a mile distant. Fearful of the threatened reprisal on the women and children of the friendly Nez Perces, Stevens found it best to dismiss them. It may be assumed that these warriors with their families then returned to Lapwai with Lawyer and his followers.

Late in the evening of September 19, Stevens sent an Indian messenger to Steptoe informing him of the pending attack. He asked for help saying that "a company of his troops would be of service." Steptoe's leniency towards the hostiles was shaken by the fact that they had set fire to the heavy growth of dried grass which surrounded his camp. The grass fire not only threatened his camp, it also robbed his animals of needed forage. Steptoe was therefore in a mood to cooperate. He sent word to Stevens suggesting that he return, that they join forces, and that then together they could move to the Umatilla.

Stevens quickly agreed. Steptoe then sent a detachment of dragoons and artillery to escort the Stevens party to his camp. The Regulars took with them a light mountain howitzer which had been mounted on a two-wheel carriage. The soldiers arrived at the Stevens camp about two o'clock in the morning of the 20th. The hostiles kept up their sporadic firing through the night. The tent occupied by Stevens was pierced by bullets.

By sunrise, when Stevens started his march toward Steptoe's camp, the Indians began firing with greater frequency. The soldiers then fired the howitzer. This had perhaps more psychological than lethal effect, for the Indians scattered and retreated. They could not compete with the white man's artillery. Stevens reported that his casualties consisted of one man mortally wounded, one dangerously so, and two slightly. He estimated that thirteen Indians had been killed or wounded.

Reporting to the Commissioner of Indian Affairs, Stevens wrote: "I report to you officially that when the Indians attacked me, they expected Col. Steptoe would not assist me, and when they awoke from this delusion, Kam-i-ah-kan said, 'I will now let these men know who Kam-i-ah-kan is.' [23] One of the good effects of the fight is that the Indians have learned that we are one people, a fact which had not previously been made apparent to them by the operation of the Regular troops."

Stevens and his party, without any of Steptoe's troops, left for The Dalles on September 23 and arrived there on October 2 without further molestation. From there, Stevens moved on to Olympia. Thereafter the responsibility of enforcing the terms of the 1855 Treaty shifted from Territorial to Governmental authorities. Following the departure of Stevens and his men, Steptoe and his troops remained at Walla Walla.

Perhaps the most important result of these skirmishes with Kam-i-ah-

---

[23] *Ibid.*, p. 223.

kan and his followers was an about face on the part of Steptoe. When an emergency arose and the safety of other white men was endangered, Steptoe defied the strict orders he had received from General Wool and took part in armed resistance. As will be noted, Colonel Wright also experienced a change of views regarding the necessity of using force against the dissidents. Such a change of policy did not escape the notice of Lawyer and the friendly Nez Perces, as well as by the hostiles.

STEVENS ELECTED TO CONGRESS

Little happened during 1857 which affected the Indians of the upper Columbia River country. Since the 1855 Treaty had not as yet been ratified, the Government could take no steps to establish the reservations. Early in the year, General Wool was relieved of his command and was succeeded by General N. S. Clarke who for the rest of this year followed the lenient policies of his predecessor. Clarke was in favor of excluding settlers from entering the interior of Washington Territory. He permitted only the Indian Agents, the Hudson's Bay men, and some Roman Catholic missionaries to remain in that part of the country. The troops stationed at Walla Walla under Lieutenant Colonel Steptoe remained inactive and a quasi-peace extended over the country. But this was only the lull before the storm.

Disturbed over the delay of the U.S. Senate to ratify the 1855 Treaty and also the failure of authorities in Washington to support his policy of dealing firmly with the dissident Indians, Stevens decided to run for the office of Territorial Delegate to Congress. He won the office in an election held on July 13, 1858, whereupon he resigned as Governor. The Stevens family moved to Washington that fall.

STEPTOE'S DEFEAT, MAY 1858

During April 1858, Steptoe began receiving disturbing reports of Indian depredations, especially in the upper Columbia River country. Two white men had been killed by Indians in the Palouse country. Forty settlers in the Colville area, some of whom were former Hudson's Bay employees, petitioned for troops saying that their lives and property were in danger. Some of the hostiles were even so bold as to steal thirteen head of cattle belonging to Steptoe's troops at Walla Walla. These are but samples of many reports of disturbing events which reached Steptoe's ears. As a result, Steptoe decided that it was incumbent upon him to march into the Spokane-Colville country to make a first-hand investigation of conditions and to settle Indian unrest by peaceful means.[24]

Steptoe set out on May 6 with 158 men, including three companies of dragoons, some infantrymen, and two mountain howitzers for the Spokane country. The fact that the troops were poorly armed and had a limited amount of ammunition — only forty rounds per man — is clear evidence that Steptoe had no intention of engaging in hostilities. Two of the dragoon companies carried musketoons, which were short muskets with a limited range of less than fifty yards. Some of the men had the old-fashioned muzzle loading pistols. Steptoe's mission was one of peace, not of war.

Steptoe and his troops arrived at Alpowa where, with the help of members of the villages of Red Wolf and Timothy, they were ferried across to the north bank of the Snake River. According to a statement made by Lawyer at the 1863 Lapwai Council: "Timothy and some of my people accompanied him. The number of Nez Perces who joined forces with Steptoe is not known.[25]

When Steptoe crossed the Palouse River on his way north, he was told that the Spokanes and other tribes would resist his march through their country. Disregarding the warning, Steptoe pressed on, passing the site of present-day Rosalia, Washington, on Sunday, May 16. Then Steptoe found himself facing a large number of hostiles, estimated to number from 600 to 1,200. They came from four tribes — the Palouses, Spokanes, Coeur d'Alenes, and Yakimas. Among the Yakimas was Kam-i-ah-kan, and no doubt Owhi and Qualchen.

The hostiles began a strong attack on Steptoe on Monday, the 17th. Steptoe, realizing the seriousness of his situation, decided to return to Walla Walla. The Indians pressed their attack so intensely that Steptoe was forced to defend himself the best he could on a hill near what is now Rosalia. Here he was surrounded by the hostiles. His situation became desperate by nightfall as his men were without shade or water and their ammunition had been reduced to three rounds per man.

Anticipating his danger, Steptoe had on Sunday dispatched one of the Nez Perces to Lawyer with an appeal for help. In his speech given on May 28, 1863, at the Lapwai Council, Lawyer, referring to the attack on Steptoe, said: "In that battle, two of my warriors, with

---

[24] Fuller, *Pacific Northwest*, pp. 243 ff.
[25] From Proceedings of the Lapwai Council, 1863, o.i.b.

others mingled their blood on the ground; therefore I claim that we are in alliance with the white people." The two Nez Perces were only wounded, not killed.

According to a statement made by one of the white survivors, some fifty years after the battle, Timothy discovered an unguarded trail leading from the embattled area over which he guided the surviving troops to safety.[26] By this time, Stevens had suffered a loss of twenty-five men killed and as many wounded. Eighteen of the wounded were taken out by being tied to horses. The two howitzers were buried before the command left the hill. After leaving the hill as stealthily as possible, the troops with their Nez Perce friends made a dash for the Snake River crossing, some eighty-five miles distant. In the meantime, the hostiles discovered early on Tuesday morning, May 18, that the troops had fled. There followed such a frantic contest for the loot which had been abandoned that the Indians failed to pursue Steptoe until it was too late.

When the Steptoe party was one day's march from Walla Walla, after crossing the Snake River at Alpowa, they became aware of a large body of Indians approaching from their rear. At first they were fearful that these were hostiles but when they drew nearer and saw an American flag flying from an advance party, they knew that they were friendly Nez Perces under Lawyer's leadership. In an amazingly short time after learning of Steptoe's defeat, Lawyer had been able to muster about 200 warriors and had started out to render such assistance as was possible.[27]

Lawyer, stunned by the news of Steptoe's defeat and also of the wounding of two of his warriors, urged Steptoe to turn back and attack the hostiles. He assured Steptoe that he could raise 800 Nez Perces who would accompany the soldiers. This promise indicates that Lawyer had regained his leadership influence within the tribe which had been corroded at the time of the September 1856 Council. Steptoe, however, aware of his loss of equipment, including his two howitzers, and knowing that his troops were in no condition to renew the fight, refused Lawyer's offer. He continued his retreat to Walla Walla.

Steptoe's defeat served as a catalyst to the hardening of attitudes of both the hostiles and the Whites. The victorious Indians were jubilant

---

[26] Fuller, *Pacific Northwest*, p. 248. An obelisk monument, dedicated to Timothy, crowns the hill at Rosalia where this engagement took place.   [27] *Ibid.*, p. 249.

and over-confident. They had beaten the vaunted Regulars of the U.S. Army in battle. Elated by their success, the three Yakima chiefs laid heavy pressure on several bands of Indians who tried to remain neutral. These included Spokane Garry's band at Spokane Falls and the Spokanes under Big Star at Tshimakain, the former mission station of Walker and Eells. Even the Catholic Indians of Coeur d'Alene and Pend d'Oreille were induced to join the hostiles. As a result the hostiles were stronger and more belligerent than ever.

In turn, the ranking military officers of the Government had a change of attitude regarding how to deal with the hostile Indians. They had looked somewhat condescendingly upon Stevens' Volunteers as being ineffective civilian soldiers. But when Steptoe's Regulars met with disaster, General Clarke's and Colonel Wright's attitudes changed. They began to plan for immediate and severe reprisals. General Clarke moved his headquarters from California to Fort Vancouver. Hundreds of troops were transferred to the Northwest. Steps were taken to stop the sale of ammunition to the hostiles by the Hudson's Bay Company at Fort Colville.

On August 6, 1858, General Clarke and Colonel Wright met with a group of twenty-one Nez Perce chiefs, led by Lawyer, at Walla Walla. Included among the Nez Perces were Timothy, Spotted Eagle, and Three Feathers. A compact, sometimes referred to as a treaty, was drawn up and signed by those present in which each party agreed not to bear arms against the other and each agreed to render the other aid in case of war.[28]

Commenting on this meeting at Walla Walla, Lawyer, in his remarks given at the Lapwai Council of 1863, said: "Colonel Wright with his gray hairs met us in Council in Walla Walla. He addressed me as chief, and asked me to furnish warriors. I answered, 'By tomorrow.' Colonel Wright then said, 'This is no boys' play. We enter into this truly and solemnly. We will defend and protect this country . . . The Law by which we are governed is unchangeable.' That is what Colonel Wright said and here it is on this paper, I hold in my hand." The document which Lawyer displayed may have been the treaty which he and thirty other Nez Perce chiefs had signed with General Clarke and Colonel Wright.

A company of thirty Nez Perces was formed under the command of Spotted Eagle and all were sworn in as members of the U.S. Army and

---

[28] Josephy, *Nez Perces*, p. 382.

placed under Lieutenant John Mullan. These were the first Nez Perces to become a formal part of the Army. They were given the regulation blue uniforms of which they were tremendously proud.

COLONEL WRIGHT'S CAMPAIGN, AUGUST-SEPTEMBER 1858

Lawrence Kip, who attended the 1855 Walla Walla Council as a civilian observer, and whose diary covering that event throws much light on its proceedings, was commissioned a Second Lieutenant in the U.S. Army on June 30, 1857. After serving for about a year in California, Kip was transferred to Colonel Wright's command at Walla Walla. Thus it came to be that Kip served in Wright's campaign against the northern Indians in the late summer and early fall of 1858. Following this experience, Kip published in 1859 his small book entitled, *Army Life on the Pacific; A Journal of the Expedition against the Northern Indians*. This illuminating eyewitness account of Colonel Wright's campaign equals in importance the record that Kip published of the 1855 Walla Walla Council. In this book, Kip made several references to the Nez Perce scouts who served with Colonel Wright with Lawyer's approval.

Writing in his diary while at Walla Walla on August 1, 1858, Kip stated:

> A few days ago sixty Nez Perces arrived, under an old chief, named Lawyer, whom I knew at the council in 1855. He has been a great warrior in his day, and is still suffering from a wound in his side which he received many years ago in a fight with their heriditary enemies, the Blackfeet Indians. [Kip then added the comment:] The Nez Perces are blessed with a more tractable disposition than most of their brethren, and we have never seen any Indians who appear so willing to be instructed, not only in the arts of civilization, but also in the precepts of Christianity.[29]

According to Kip, Colonel Wright gathered a force of about 700 men at Walla Walla. After leaving about 100 of this number under the command of Colonel Steptoe to garrison the Walla Walla post, Wright with the other 600 and the Nez Perces left on August 7 for the Spokane country. Wright had under his command six companies of artillery with two twelve-pounder howitzers and two six-pounder guns. In the engagements with the hostiles which followed, these artillery pieces spread havoc among the Indians.

---

[29] Kip, *op. cit.*, p. 33.

Moreover, Wright's men were equipped with a new single-shot rifle which fired bullets called minie balls. The minie ball, named after its inventor, Captain Minie of France, was so constructed that when fired, a metal cap at the base of the bullet expanded to fit tightly against the gun barrel. This gave the bullet the full effect of the explosion and as a result provided a longer range of fire than was ever possible in the old-fashioned muzzle loaders. Thus these rifles were called the long-range rifle.

Another distinct advantage which this weapon provided was that it could be quickly and easily reloaded simply by ejecting the spent bullet and inserting another. Thus even a man on horseback could reload withopt stopping his horse. These long-range rifles gave the soldiers a tremendous advantage over the Indians, who were still using the muzzle loaders and bows and arrows.

Colonel Wright's troops met the combined forces, estimated by Kip to have been at least 500 warriors, of the Spokanes, Coeur d'Alenes, Palouses, and Yakimas in two decisive engagements. The first took place on September 1 at Four Lakes and the second on the 5th at Spokane Plains. The Nez Perces skirmished for Wright in each of these engagements. In the latter battle, Ute-sin-male-cum was cited for bravery.[30]

The hostile Indians in these two battles experienced for the first time the devastating effects of the American long-range rifles. The Indians were accustomed to ride up within firing range of their muzzle loaders, shoot, and then hastily retreat in order to reload. The Indians expected the soldiers to do the same and were amazed when the soldiers began killing them before they could come within firing range. Moreover, the soldiers did not have to stop to reload but kept firing one round after another while advancing.

After the first such encounter, the Indians fled in panic. "In all directions," Kip wrote, "were scattered the arms, muskets, quivers, bows and arrows, blankets, robes, etc., which had been thrown away by our flying enemies." In the first engagement, the Government troops suffered no casualties while the losses among the Indians were very heavy. No count was possible as many of the Indian dead and wounded were carried from the field.

In the second engagement, which took place on September 5, Colonel

---

[30] Josephy, *Nez Perces*, p. 383.

Wright captured a large herd of horses which, according to Kip, numbered 900. At first the Indians did not seem to be concerned as they believed that they could stampede the herd and recover their mounts. Wright, however, never gave them this opportunity for he ordered all but about 100 of the animals to be killed. It took two companies of soldiers two days to complete the grim task. This was a devastating blow to the Indians for, as Kip noted: "Without horses, these Indians were powerless."

The Indians then began to sue for peace. Wright decided that in order to insure peace in the future, he would have to hang all Indians who were guilty of murdering white men, or who had plundered white settlements, or who had acted as ringleaders in the uprising. Kip states that sixteen Indians met this fate. The first hanging took place on September 8 when a Palouse prisoner, who had been "proved without doubt" to be the one who had killed some miners the preceding May, was hung.

On the evening of September 23, Owhi rode into Colonel Wright's camp and surrendered. Of this incident, Kip wrote: "This evening Owhi, the brother-in-law of Kamiaken, came into camp, as he said, to make peace. I first saw him, as I did Kamiaken, three years ago at the Walla Walla council, where he opposed all treaties to cede their country, not only with great zeal but with much ability. His speech of which I took notes at the time particularly impressed me. It was thus:

> We are talking together, and the Great Spirit hears all that we say
>> to-day.
> The Great Spirit gave us the land, and measured the land to us.
> This is the reason that I am afraid to say anything about this land.
> I am afraid of the laws of the Great Spirit.
> This is the reason I cannot give you an answer.
> I am afraid of the Great Spirit.
>> Shall I steal this land and sell it? or, what shall I do?
> This is the reason my heart is sad. . . What shall I do?
> Shall I give the land which is a part of my body and leave myself
>> poor and destitute?
> Shall I say, I will give you my land? I cannot say so.
> I am afraid of the Great Spirit. I love my life.
> The reason why I do not give my land away, I am afraid I shall be
>> sent to hell.[31]

---

[31] Kip, *op. cit.*, pp. 58-9. The arrangement of the sentences in blank verse style is the author's.

Owhi was giving expression to what other Indians had said at the 1855 Council. The earth was their mother. Should one sell his mother? Even though Kip paid tribute to Owhi by recording his eloquent speech, he referred to him shortly after by calling him and his son, Qualchen, "probably the two worst Indians this side of the Rocky Mountains." And Kip added that of the two, Qualchen was "more notorious than the father and therefore Colonel Wright has been particularly anxious to secure him. He has kept the whole country on both sides of the mountains, [i.e., the Cascades], in confusion for years." [32]

Using a Catholic priest as an interpreter, Colonel Wright on that September 23 asked Owhi as to the whereabouts of his son, Qualchen. Owhi said that he was at the mouth of the Spokane River. Turning to the priest, Wright said: "Tell Owhi that I will send a message to Qualchen. Tell him, he too shall send a message, and if Qualchen does not join me before I cross the Snake River, in four days, I will hang Owhi." Upon hearing this, Owhi sank to the ground. Great drops of perspiration, betraying his fear, broke out on his face. Although Owhi had voluntarily entered Wright's camp, he was treated as a prisoner and shackled.

The next day Qualchen rode into camp, armed, and according to Kip, with "a fine pistol, capped and loaded." Colonel Wright immediately placed him under arrest and ordered that he be hanged. Kip reported that it took six men to tie the hands and feet of the struggling Indian, and then he was charged with the murder of nine white men. When Qualchen realized that he was to be hanged, he began cursing Kam-i-ah-kan. Among those who helped hang Qualchen were two miners who had been in a party attacked by the chief some months before.

After the execution of his son, Owhi was told that he would be taken as a prisoner to Walla Walla. About ten days later, Owhi made a sudden dash for freedom. According to the official report, he was shot while trying to escape. Thus ended the lives of two of the most influential leaders of the Indian revolt. Kam-i-ah-kan, hearing of what had happened, and knowing that he would suffer a like fate if captured by Colonel Wright, fled to Canada.

Colonel Wright's ruthless reprisals on a defeated people continued. On September 25, the day after Qualchen had been hung, two Palouse

---

[32] *Ibid.,* p. 101.

Indians rode into Wright's camp. They were promptly arrested, shackled, and put in a guard house. After a short trial, six were convicted of having been "engaged in various atrocities," and hung. One of the six had killed a Sergeant William, who had been wounded in the Steptoe fight and who was making his way back to Walla Walla when the Indian found him.

Before starting back to Walla Walla, Wright negotiated treaties with the Coeur d'Alenes and Spokanes in which the Indians solemnly promised to permit white men to travel through and live in their lands without being molested.

On September 30, Wright held a council with a band of Palouse Indians on the Palouse River. In emphatic words, Colonel Wright told them if he caught one of their number across the Snake River, he would hang the culprit. He warned them not to go into the Coeur d'Alene country, nor the Spokane, nor allow the Walla Walla Indians to enter their country. Nor were they to molest white men passing through their country. "If they do not submit to these terms," said Wright through his interpreter, "I will make war on them; and if I come here again to war, I will hang them all, men, women, and children."

Wright demanded the Palouses to surrender two of their number who had killed some miners, "five moons ago." Only one of the two was present and he was promptly arrested. Wright then demanded the surrender of the Indians who had stolen some of his cattle at Walla Walla. Three came forward and were promptly hanged together with the Indian who had killed the miners.

By October 5, Colonel Wright and his troops, including the company of thirty Nez Perces, were back at Walla Walla. Two days later, the Colonel met in council with the Walla Walla Indians. Kip gives the following account:

> They have been exceedingly troublesome, and it was necessary to teach them a lesson. The colonel told them he knew that some of them had been engaged in the recent fights, and that every one who was in the two battles must stand up. Thirty-five stood up at once. From these the colonel selected four who were known to have been engaged in several murders in the valley. One Indian by the name of Wyecat, was particularly notorious. They were handed over to the guard and hung on the spot.[33]

_____

[33] *Ibid.*, p. 124.

Of the sixteen Indians who were hung, one, Qualchen, was a Yakima; eleven were Palouses; and four were Walla Wallas or Cayuses. One, Owhi, was killed while trying to escape, and Kam-i-ah-kan fled to Canada. We do not know the number of Indians who were killed in the Steptoe and Wright campaigns, but their losses must have been heavy. Colonel Wright, in his two engagements, suffered no soldier killed and only one wounded.

Although Kip implies that Wyecat (Waie-cat), who was one of the four who were hung on October 7, was a Walla Walla Indian, the probability is that he was a Cayuse. Wyecat was one of the active participants in the Whitman massacre and the only one of the fourteen conspirators who escaped being apprehended, killed, or executed in the Cayuse War.[34] Undoubtedly Wright was unaware of Wyecat's involvement in the Whitman massacre. According to Kip, Wyecat was simply a "particularly notorious" individual. With his hanging, the account of what happened to the conspirators in the Whitman massacre is completed.

LAWYER APPROVES

News of Steptoe's defeat and Wright's victories was sent to Isaac I. Stevens in Washington. Writing to J. W. Denver, Commissioner of Indian Affairs, on November 20, 1858, Stevens told of receiving a letter from Lawyer who evidently approved of the stern measures taken by Colonel Wright. Stevens wrote:

> I have just received a letter from my old friend, "Lawyer," head chief of the Nez Perces from which I make the following extract: "At this place three years since we had our talk [referring to the meeting with Stevens in the early fall of 1855 following Stevens' return from Montana] and since that time, we have been waiting to hear from our Big Father. We are very poor. It is other people's badness. It is not our fault, and I would like to hear what he has to say. If he thinks our agreement good, our hearts are thankful.
> "Colonel Wright has been after the bad people, and has killed some of the bad people, and hung sixteen, and I am in hopes we will have peace."

---

[34] See Drury, M. & N.W., Vol. II, pp. 302 ff., for an account of the discovery of the portrait of Wyecat by John Mix Stanley which was painted in the fall of 1847 shortly before the Whitman massacre. The painting is reproduced in this work, Vol. II, p. 261.

Stevens then added: "The Lawyer's opinions are entitled to more weight than those of any other Indian in the Territory. His people want the treaty [of 1855] confirmed, and are rejoiced that the Indian murderers have been brought to justice." [35]

1855 TREATY RATIFIED

Ever since Stevens arrived in Washington, D.C., in the fall of 1858, he had pressed for the ratification of the 1855 Walla Walla Treaty by the U.S. Senate. Ratification had been delayed by General Wool's prejudices against the treaty. Word of Steptoe's defeat and then of Wright's victories, changed the attitudes of the members of the Senate's Indian Committee, thus making it possible for the Senate to ratify the treaty on April 25, 1859. President James Buchanan signed the document on April 29. Thus the Cayuse-Walla Walla-Umatilla and the Nez Perce Reservations finally became legal realities.

---

[35] *Annual Report of the Commissioner of Indian Affairs,* 1858, p. 191.

CHAPTER SEVEN

The Lapwai Council of 1863

A new era in the history of the Nez Perces began with the ratification of the 1855 Treaty by the U.S. Senate in March 1858. The long
delay of nearly four years between the signing and the ratification was
then characteristic of the dilatory actions of the Government in fulfilling its treaty provisions. As far as the Nez Perces were concerned,
months and even years passed before any annuities were paid, schools
built, teachers provided, or lands plowed for the chiefs. According to a
report from the Commissioner of Indian affairs, no annuity funds were
paid from 1859 through 1861. A payment of $6,396 was made in No-
vember 1862 which was diverted into white men's pockets.[1]

Lawyer became aware of the fact that the Indians were being
cheated of that which had been solemnly promised and he made fre-
quent protests, as this chapter will detail. Following ratification, the
Government made no immediate move to force the Indians who lived
outside of the boundaries of the two reservations to move within their
limits. Several years passed before such action was taken.

An event of major importance in the history of the Nez Perce nation
occurred in 1860 when Elias D. Pierce discovered gold on Orofino
Creek within the Nez Perce Reservation. The news of this discovery
sparked a gold rush which lured thousands of white men onto the
reservation, all of which was in violation of the 1855 Treaty. Additional
gold discoveries were made on the South Fork of the Clearwater River
and on the eastern and southern sides of the reservation. This sudden
and overwhelming influx of white men proved to be a disaster for the
Nez Perces, but they were unable to prevent it.

Following the ratification of the 1855 Treaty, the Government ap-

---

[1] *Report of Commissioner Indian Affairs*, 1865, p. 236.

pointed A. John Cain Indian Agent for the Nez Perces. Cain succeeded William Craig, who had been serving as such in an unofficial capacity. Since Cain had his headquarters in Walla Walla, he appointed Charles H. Frush as his subagent for the Nez Perces. Frush established his office at the old Spalding mission site at Lapwai. This marked the beginning of the Lapwai Indian Agency.

Cain visited a large number of Nez Perces in July 1859, when they had gathered on their camas root grounds on Weippe Prairie near Kamiah. According to information which he then received, Cain estimated the tribe to number 3,700, including 800 men, 1,200 women, and 1,700 children.[2] This estimate is larger than other contemporary accounts.

NEWSPAPER ACCOUNTS DESCRIBE LAWYER

An item in the *Weekly Times* of Portland, Oregon, for November 24, 1860, tells of difficulties that Lawyer was experiencing with the "war party" within the tribe. This would have included Looking Glass and Big Thunder. The item, referring to the Nez Perces, follows:

> These Indians are among the most wealthy and powerful on the Pacific Slope. . . Lawyer is their chief and is an intelligent and educated Indian. He is friendly to the Whites and will do all in his power to maintain friendly relations. But his influence and power is resisted by a strong party of the tribe, who seek every pretext to find fault with the conduct of the government in the manner of fulfilling their treaty stipulations, and with white citizens who go upon their lands. The war chiefs are constantly seeking to undermine the influence and power of Lawyer . . . and convert the great majority of the tribe to a state of inveterate hostility to Americans.

The exciting news of the discovery of gold on the Nez Perce Reservation prompted a number of newspaper reporters to visit the area and describe what they saw. One of these, C. L. Goodrich, visited Lawyer at Lapwai, March 24-April 1, 1861, and then wrote the following:

> At the Agency, the head chief, "Sawyer" [Lawyer] has his lodge. I had a long talk with him; it appears to me that he is not entirely

---

[2] *Ibid.*, pp. 214 ff. Stevens, in his report of the Walla Walla Council, estimated the Nez Perces to number only 2,500. *See ante,* Chap. IV, under heading, "Monday, May 28, 1855." I have arbitrarily used a medium figure of 3,000.

satisfied that the Whites should come into his country. After asking him three separate times, he refused to answer. The conversation was through the interpreter. "Sawyer" says that he tells his people that they are rich now, but if they should go to war with the Whites, they will lose all their horses and cattle as the Cayuses have, and become reduced to poverty; that the Whites are too strong for them, but yet most of the sub-chiefs are complaining to him, while many of the people are understood to be satisfied that the miners come in.

The rub appears to be in the fact that the portion of the reserve, where the mines are, is entirely useless to the Nez Perces and they want to sell it to our Government. From all I could learn in my conversation with "Sawyer" and others of the tribe, they want to sell out that portion of their domain for a "big price." [3]

Goodrich learned that some of the Nez Perces were profiting from the sale of garden produce and beef cattle to the miners, and, therefore, were quite content to let the Whites move onto the Reservation.

Goodrich's reference to Lawyer's "lodge" at Lapwai is evidence that at the time of his visit, the Government had not yet erected a house of the Head Chief at the Agency which had been promised in the 1855 Treaty. A frame dwelling was erected for Lawyer a year or so later after the Government built a saw mill at Lapwai. An early map of the Agency area shows Lawyer's house standing on the west side of Lapwai Creek near the Clearwater River. The map also shows an area of about ten acres near the house marked "Lawyer's Field." [4] Just exactly when this house was erected is not known, probably in 1862.

A second newspaper man who visited Lawyer at Lapwai was Henry Miller. When he arrived in June 1861, he noted that "five or six log buildings" had but shortly before been erected. Since there was no saw mill then in operation, there were no frame structures. Regarding Lawyer, Miller wrote:

This interesting Indian gentleman is apparently fifty years of age. He is about five feet, eight inches in height, and awkwardly framed. His features are rather more oval than common among Indians, with a nose straight but not high. Eyes small and expressive and a smile always about the corner of his mouth, completed

[3] *Idaho Yesterdays*, Vol. III, No. 4 (Winter Issue, 1959-60), p. 26.

[4] Erwin N. Thompson, *Historic Resource Study, Spalding Area*, G.P.O., 1972, Appendix map #3.

the picture. His whole bearing is extremely amiable. He wore elegantly beaded mocassins, blue cloth pants, calico shirt, alpaca sack [i.e., a thin loose-fitting coat], and a preposterous white plug-hat; closely resembling in shape the one recently worn by Gov. [I. I.] Stevens. He carried a plain hickory cane, the usual three-tailed pouch, and an Indian pipe. I must say that his character for justice and intelligence is far above that of his white brethren of the [law] profession. I had a *wa-wa* with him of considerable duration but further than vouching for his dignity, amicability and intelligence, I cannot speak.[5]

This is the best description of how Lawyer looked and dressed that has been found. Miller was mistaken about Lawyer's age. If 1796 is the correct year of his birth,[6] then Lawyer would have been sixty-five in 1861. The fact that Miller thought he was about fifty years old, shows that Lawyer was carrying his years very well. Miller's reference to a "white plug-hat" refers to a term used in that generation for the high-crown "stovepipe" hat, such as he wore at the Walla Walla Council in 1855 when the artist Sohon drew his sketch.

Lawyer looked upon the high-crown hat, such as was worn by Government officials of his day, as a symbol of his office. In addition to the Sohon sketch, we have a photograph of Lawyer wearing such a hat.[7] The three-tailed tobacco pouch mentioned by Miller refers to a deer-skin bag which had been decorated with three squirrel tails.

When Edward R. Geary,[8] then serving as Superintendent of Indian Affairs for the State of Oregon and for Washington Territory, learned of the discovery of gold on the Nez Perce Reservation, he knew that a gold rush was inevitable. This would raise serious problems, for the second article in the Walla Walla Treaty specifically stated that the Nez Perce Reservation was for "the exclusive use and benefit" of the

---

[5] *Idaho Yesterdays*, Vol. iv, No. 4 (Winter Issue, 1960-61), p. 20.

[6] For comments regarding the year of Lawyer's birth, *see* Chap. i.

[7] Through the kindness of Douglas Riley, Historian, Nez Perce Nat. Hist. Park, Spalding, Id., I received a copy of a photograph of Lawyer wearing a "stovepipe" hat and holding a cane in his right hand while standing before his house at Lapwai. In the background are the bluffs on the north side of the Clearwater River. The picture is too indistinct to be reproduced. Probable date, 1870.

[8] Geary was a pioneer Presbyterian minister who arrived in the Willamette Valley in April 1851. He became one of the founders of Albany College, the fore-runner of present-day Lewis and Clark College, Portland. In order to supplement his meager salary as a home missionary, he served as Indian Agent for several years.

Nez Perces. White men were forbidden to live on the Reservation except those in the employment of the Indian Department or those who had the "permission of the tribe and the superintendent and agent."

Geary realized that some adjustment would have to be made to legalize the presence of the miners. Therefore, Geary called upon Lawyer and his subchiefs to meet with him and Agent Cain at Lapwai early in April 1861. Since the gold rush had taken place in the country occupied by the northern Nez Perces, no move was made to include Chief Joseph and others from the southern Nez Perces.

The Lapwai meeting was held and four articles were adopted which can be summarized as follows: The first article defined the areas of the reservation which would be opened to the Whites. These included the mining areas on the northern and eastern side of the Reservation. Article II forbade Whites living elsewhere on the reservation unless permission had been granted by the proper parties. Right of way to the mining districts through the reservation was granted. Article III forbade white men from engaging in trade without first securing a license to do so.

Perhaps the most important provision of this supplemental treaty was Article IV which called for the establishment on the reservation of a military post of sufficient strength "to preserve the quiet of the country and to protect the Nez Perces in the rights secured to them by treaty." Thus, by a strange turn of events, troops, which once were sent into the Indian country to protect the Whites from the Indians, were now to be used to protect the Indians from the lawless Whites.

In his official report, Geary stated that Lawyer, "Head Chief of the Nez Perce nation and forty-seven others" signed the supplemental agreement to the 1855 Treaty.[9] Lawyer was the only one whom Geary mentioned by name.

With the rapid increase of miners flocking onto the Reservation and with the introduction of river steamers on the Columbia and Snake Rivers, the establishment of a shipping and supply center became a necessity. The logical site was at the confluence of the Clearwater and Snake Rivers where the present-day city of Lewiston, Idaho, is located. Even though the Whites had settled there late in 1860, the site was not under consideration when Geary and Cain met with Lawyer and

[9] *Report of Commissioner of Indian Affairs*, 1862, p. 13.

his subchiefs the following April. The failure to consider this brought some problems in later months.

According to one authority, the town site of Lewiston was laid out "with the consent of Lawyer and his headmen, who received some compensation for their reasonable attitude." [10] McWhorter, in his *Hear Me, my Chiefs,* relates the following strange story regarding the acquisition of the Lewiston site by the Whites:

> The legend says that Paukalah [a Nez Perce], returning from Alpowa late at night and reaching the mouth of Lapwai Creek, caught a glint of light at the window of the Indian Agency office and dismounted to see what it meant. The door was not locked, and entering, he saw that the windows were covered with blankets, and at a table, on which was a pile of gold coins, sat the agent and interpreter with Chief Lawyer and a few other headmen. Lawyer immediately handed him a twenty-dollar gold piece with the admonition, "Take this one piece and go about your business. Speak no word of what you see here." Paukalah, deeming it safer to do as told, hurried away, and aside from confiding in his wife how he came by the money, kept silent.[11]

By his own statement, McWhorter called this story, "a legend." The sad truth is that a legend often repeated becomes to many an historical fact and, in this instance, a blot on Lawyer's reputation.

By October 1861, Lewiston is reported to have had a population of 1,200. When Idaho Territory was erected in March 1863, Lewiston became its capital and continued as such until December 1864 when the Territorial offices were moved to Boise.

Pursuant to the fourth article of the amended 1855 Treaty, the Government established a military post in the Lapwai Valley about four miles up the creek from the old Spalding mission site, then occupied by the Agency. There the valley widened out to give plenty of room for the military establishment. In time, the community which grew up around the military post took the name of Lapwai while the original site became known as Spalding.

THE TWO-YEAR INTERVAL, APRIL 1861-JUNE 1863

During the two-year interval between the signing of the amend-

---

[10] H. H. Bancroft, *History of Washington, Idaho, and Montana, 1845-1889* (San Francisco, Calif., 1890), p. 238.   [11] *Op. cit.*, p. 154.

ments to the 1855 Treaty and the opening of the Lapwai Council in May 1863, a number of national events took place which affected the Nez Perces. Abraham Lincoln was inaugurated President in March 1861, and the Civil War began the next month. The financial demands of the War is one reason why the U.S. Government was unable to meet all of the promises made in the 1855 Treaty. Congress was loath to appropriate funds for some far-away and little known tribe of Indians as the Nez Perces.

Following Lincoln's inauguration, a number of changes were made in the Department of Indian Affairs which affected the Pacific Northwest. A. J. Cain was replaced as Indian Agent for the Nez Perces by Charles Hutchins on June 13 of that year. Hutchins was the first of the Agents to take up residence at Lapwai. E. R. Geary was relieved of his duties as Superintendent of Indian Affairs for Oregon and Washington and was succeeded on Septembe 19, 1861, by B. F. Kendall.

Shortly after his appointment, Kendall visited Lapwai. In a report to the Commissioner of Indian Affairs in Washington, D.C., dated January 21, 1862, Kendall made a scathing criticism of Cain's administration. Although Cain had had ten white employees on his payroll and had spent some $60,000.00 for administrative purposes in one year, "the visible results of the liberal expenditures," wrote Kendall, "are meagre indeed." Kendall also wrote: "I sought in vain to find me one foot of land fenced or broken by him or his employees; and the only product of the agriculture department that I could discover consisted of three tons of oats in the straw." [12] Although the 1855 Treaty had promised the Nez Perces schools and teachers, by 1862 not one schoolhouse had been erected or one teacher hired.

John B. Monteith, who was the Indian Agent at Lapwai during the Chief Joseph uprising of 1877 commented in his report to the Commissioner of Indian Affairs for 1877 on some of the causes which led to the uprising. He mentioned especially the failure of the Government to fulfill its promises made in the 1855 Treaty. He noted the following:

In 1862 only 247 blankets were furnished the tribe or one blanket to six Indians and 4,393 yards of calico, which was less than two yards to each Indian. Giving one blanket to one Indian works no satisfaction to the other five who receive none, and two yards of calico to each Indian affords but little help and advance-

12 Thompson, *Historic Resource Study,* p. 90.

ment; yet this was all that could be distributed owing to the meagre appropriations allowed.[13]

Calvin H. Hale succeeded Kendall as Superintendent of Indian Affairs for Oregon and Washington in the summer of 1862. He transferred Hutchins to the Flathead Agency and appointed J. W. Anderson to the Nez Perce post. Anderson, who began his duties at Lapwai on August 25, wrote his first report on the following day. Although he had not then met Lawyer, he stated that the Head Chief was "often actually in want of the necessities of life." Anderson also wrote: "No part of the treaty stipulations with respect to him has been carried out by the government in good faith." [14]

Superintendent Hale, speaking before the Lapwai Council on May 27, 1863, reported that on his first inspection trip to Lapwai he was surprised "to see so little improvements made, in view of the large appropriations, which I knew have been made." [15] Hale had the following to say about the failure of the Government to fulfill its promises to Lawyer: "Your head chief had no house built, and no farm fenced or ploughed. The money for this has been appropriated, but did not come into my hands." Beginning with the ratification of the 1855 Treaty in 1858, Lawyer was supposed to receive an annual salary of $500.00 but, according to Hale, was given only a small unspecified amount which Agent Hutchins had received.

A further financial difficulty experienced by the Agents at Lapwai was the fact that the Government was making payments with vouchers instead of gold coin and that these vouchers were being discounted 50% by merchants and others. Hale, in his remarks at the Lapwai Council, mentioned the fact that a Steamboat Company refused to carry machinery for the saw and grist mills that were to be erected at Lapwai until they were paid the delivery costs. The Government had made no appropriation for such an expense and, as a result, the erection of these mills was delayed.

In his report to the Indian Commission in Washington dated Sep-

[13] *Report of Commissioner of Indian Affairs*, 1877, p. 9.

[14] Thompson, *Historic Resource Study*, p. 92.

[15] The Proceedings of the Lapwai Council, May 13-June 8, 1863, are now on file in the National Archives, Washington, D.C., Record Group 75, Treaty File. All subsequent references to remarks by the Commissioners or by Indians at this Council are from this source. The copy used by the author has been deposited in the Idaho State Hist. Soc., Boise.

tember 30, 1862, Hale stated that while Lawyer was still friendly, Big Thunder (Old James) was "quite upset by the Government's failure to live up to the terms of the 1855 Treaty." Hale warned the Commissioner: "These Indians are neither fools nor children — they know what they have received, and to what they are justly entitled."

Hale further stated:

> They have not received their Annuities at the time, and in the manner specified. The goods furnished were bought at exhorbitant prices, the invoices fell short even then, and . . . the goods did not always come up to the quantity charged, whilst many of them were absolutely useless. The first payment of $60,000 for . . . fencing ground, building houses, etc. . . . has been more or less diverted from its proper objects.[16]

These repeated failures of the Government to fulfill its treaty obligations fueled discontent among the Indians, brought difficulties to Lawyer as Head Chief who wanted to believe in the integrity of the Government, and, as will be noted, made it very difficult for Superintendent Hale and other Government officials to induce the Nez Perces to agree to a new treaty which was designed to reduce drastically the size of their 1855 Reservation.

DEATH OF ELDER LOOKING GLASS

On January 6, 1863, Looking Glass died in Lawyer's lodge at Lapwai. He was a medicine man or *te-wat*, and as such was anti-missionary and anti-Christian. At times he was anti-American. He aspired to be Head Chief but had to be content with a secondary role, that of being War Chief.

An undated newspaper clipping in the library of the Oregon Historical Society, Portland, contains the following story:

DEATH OF AN INDIAN CHIEF

The annexed obituary I clip from the Oregonian. The defunct, chief, of old Looking-Glass, was a mighty man of war in his day. Death found him dethroned and in obscurity, and it must have been a relief to have been called away to the spirit hunting ground, as the cloud without the silver lining is extending its dark shadow over his doomed race.

Looking-glass, once a war-chief of the Nez Perces, is dead. He

---

[16] Thompson, *Historic Resource Study*, p. 92.

belonged to that element of his tribe which is called the "buffalo Indian," or was one that made a practice of going over into the Crow country to hunt the bison. . . During Col. Wright's Spokane campaign, Looking-glass was suspected of being a friend to Kamiakin, and when a great council of the Nez Perces was held at the close of the war, he did not appear at the first meeting of it. For this contemptuous conduct towards the whites, his name was stricken from the roll of Nez Perce chiefs. . . This broke his heart. The old man begged to be reinstated, but it was never done.

The Lawyer is an unmitigated old humbug, whose only redeeming quality is his amiability. He and Looking-glass were reconciled a short time since, and the humbled war-chief died in the house of the cunning aboriginal politican, fitly named Lawyer. His death took place on the 6th of January.[17]

Looking Glass's son succeeded him in the chieftainship of his band. The son hung his father's small trade mirror around his neck, and also took his father's name. The son did not take part in the 1863 Lapwai Council, but he did become one of the most important of Young Joseph's warriors in the uprising of 1877.

The reference to Looking Glass dying in the "house" of Lawyer indicates that a house had finally been erected for the Head Chief at Lapwai. Even though Lawyer hailed from Kamiah, he felt it advisable to live at Lapwai in order to be as near as possible to the resident Indian Agent.

Pressure Grows for Treaty Revision

When Looking Glass unexpectedly arrived at the Walla Walla Council on Friday afternoon, June 8, 1855, just after Commissioners Stevens and Palmer had succeeded in winning the consent of the four Nez Perce-speaking tribes to sign the proposed treaty, they were obliged to postpone the signing ceremony until the following Monday. During the special meeting of the Council held on Saturday, the 9th, the Commissioners patiently explained for Looking Glass's benefit the provisions of the treaty. The minutes of that meeting show that the old chief asked some penetrating questions. Here are some extracts from the records of that day:

---

[17] Judge Matthew Deady Scrapbook, O.H.S., #112, p. 29. My attention was drawn to this item by the Rev. Paul Hovey, Portland, Ore.

Looking Glass: "I want to know if an Agent will stay in my country?"

Gov. Stevens: "As long as there are people."

Looking Glass: "Will you say . . . the Agent will keep the whites out?"

Gen. Palmer: "None will be permitted to go there but the agent and the persons employed, without your consent."

When the Commissioners agreed to that provision in the 1855 Treaty which gave the Nez Perces exclusive use of a reservation containing over 23,600 square miles, they could not foresee that within five years the discovery of gold within the reservation would radically change the situation. When the Whites began surging onto the reservation in 1860 and following years in overwhelming numbers, the Government authorities were powerless to keep them out. All the assurances given to Looking Glass became idle words.

A Government official, who visited Lapwai and other points on the reservation in May and June 1862, reported that approximately 18,000 Whites were then living on Nez Perce land. He stated that Lewiston then had a population of 2,000 and the two principal mining centers, Pierce City and Florence, had 3,514 and 9,200 respectively.[18] Although these two cities had been excluded from the boundaries of the reservation by the amendments to the 1855 Treaty, still there were over 5,000 Whites illegally living within the reservation including the residents of Lewiston. The continuous disregard of the treaty provisions by the Whites necessitated, from their viewpoint, a drastic reduction in the size of the reservation.

The high financial returns from the mines inevitably stimulated the influx of Whites onto the Reservation. The Portland *Oregonian* of January 1, 1862, reported that $3,000,000.00 worth of gold had been brought to Portland from the Idaho mines up to that date. Gold was then selling for $16.00 an ounce. Now (February 1978) it sells for more than ten times as much or $180.00 an ounce. Thus a reported return of $3,000,000.00 in 1860 and 1861 would now be ten times as much. This was a fabulous sum considering the relatively few who were actually mining the precious metal. And the rich harvest continued for a few more years.

---

[18] Josephy, *Nez Perces*, p. 412, quoting from Giddings Report, Aug. 28, 1862, *House Executive Document, No. 1, 37th Congress, 3rd Session.* Giddings was Chief Clerk of the Surveyor's General's Office in Washington Terr.

By the spring of 1862, the sentiment in favor of a greatly reduced Reservation was becoming more and more insistent on the part of the Whites, including the military at Fort Vancouver and the Indian Agents and Commissioners. The tremendous size of the 1855 reservation, which contained over 23,600 square miles for a tribe numbering about 3,000, had to be drastically reduced.

Spearheading the drive in Congress for the calling of another council of the Nez Perces for the purpose of negotiating a new treaty was Senator J. W. Nesmith of Oregon who made the astonishing claim: "The Indians are anxious to dispose of the reservation and remove to some point where they will not be intruded upon . . . They can be taken to some valley which will be more removed than the present position which they occupy, [away] from the line of travel across the continent." [19] On May 14, 1862, the U.S. Senate approved an appropriation of $50,000.00 to cover the cost of a council to be held with the Nez Perces for the purpose of negotiating a new treaty in which the Indians would relinquish "a portion of their present reservation, or its exchange for other lands."

Calvin H. Hale, Superintendent of Indian Affairs for Washington Territory, which then included what is now northern Idaho, was authorzed to call a council of Nez Perces and to negotiate a new treaty. Hale selected two Indian Agents to serve with him as Commissioners. One was Charles Hutchins, who had served as Agent at Lapwai for about a year, 1861-62, and the other was S. D. Howe, Indian Agent for Washington Territory. After consultation with Lawyer, Hale called for a council of Nez Perces to meet at Lapwai beginning May 10, 1863. Hale then made arrangements with the military at Fort Lapwai to establish a huge tent city along Lapwai Creek between the Agency and the fort large enough to shelter some 3,000 Nez Perces whom Hale optimistically estimated would attend. This number would have included women and children.

Dr. George Whitworth,[20] a pioneer Presbyterian minister in Washington Territory, was asked to serve as secretary and H. C. Hale, possibly a brother of Calvin Hale, as clerk. Since Henry H. Spalding had taken a claim near present-day Prescott, Washington, in 1859, near

---

[19] *Ibid.*, p. 410.

[20] Whitworth migrated to Washington Territory in 1853. He was the first Presbyterian minister to work with white people north of the Columbia River. Whitworth College, Spokane, has been named for him.

one taken by his daughter Eliza and her husband, A. J. Warren, Hale asked him to attend the council as interpreter. Also asked to serve as interpreter was the former mountain man, Robert Newell, a friend of Spalding and also of Lawyer. Judging by the extensive notes made of the speeches given at the 1863 Council, at least one member of Hale's staff was able to record the proceedings in shorthand.

PREPARATIONS FOR THE LAPWAI COUNCIL, 1863

Hale and Howe arrived at Lapwai on May 10, 1863, and Hutchins came on the 20th. In a personal report to the Commissioner of Indian Affairs, Washington, D.C., dated June 30, 1863, Hale stated that when he arrived at Lapwai only a few of the Indians had arrived. Lawyer was present as his house had been erected near the Agency by the Government.

Hale also stated in his letter of June 30: "We also ascertained that evil disposed persons had been busy in the circulation of false reports among the Indians, for the purpose of delaying or preventing their coming in; such as these, that the Commissioners would not come and that the soldiers, then stationed at Fort Lapwai, were there for the purpose of driving them from their lands by force. These with other reports of a similar nature operated upon their minds very unfavorably, so that they knew not whom to believe, or what to do. Many of them had heavy hearts in looking forward to the Council, knowing that its object was to induce them to consent in relinquishing a part of their lands to which the great body of the tribe were manifestly very averse."

On Wednesday morning, May 13, the Commissioners met with Lawyer and three of his closest associates — Ute-sin-male-cum, Spotted Eagle,[21] and Captain John — at the Lapwai Agency. Hale was eager to dispel any erroneous impressions which had been spread abroad in order to secure the confidence of the Indians and "induce them to listen to the propositions we had to make."

Since one of the rumors claimed that the Commissioners did not have governmental authority, Hale stressed the fact that President Lincoln had indeed authorized the negotiations for a new treaty. He insisted that the Commissioners had not come to drive them from the Reserva-

---

[21] Spotted Eagle came from Kamiah and was one of the fifty-eight chiefs who signed the 1855 Treaty. He was in command of the company of Nez Perces who assisted both Colonel Steptoe and Colonel Wright.

tion, "but to consult with them as to what was best to be done under the circumstances and to devise such means as would be best adapted to secure to them more full and ample protection for the future." From such comments, it is evident that the Nez Perces were aware that the Government was determined to reduce the size of thier reservation, and were afraid.

According to the official report of the Council, another object of the meeting was to consider the request of the Indians to have Perrin Whitman,[22] the nephew of Dr. Marcus Whitman, serve as the chief interpreter rather than Spalding, Craig, or Newell. "They expressed full confidence in all the Interpreters mentioned," noted the secretary in his official report of the Council, "with this exception, that they might very naturally be led to soften some of the harsh expressions which might be used . . . in order to avoid disagreement or difficulty. Especially they desired that the labor should not devolve upon Mr. Spaulding, as he was their Teacher, and they did not wish to put harsh words into his lips."

Lawyer and his subchiefs had good reason for asking for a change of interpreters, for they remembered that some of the troubles which followed the 1855 Walla Walla Council occurred because some Indians felt that the interpreters in that Council had not accurately translated what had been said. Lawyer knew that Spalding and Newell were friendly with the treaty Indians and that, consequently, the non-treaty Indians would suspect their interpretations. Spalding was known to be hostile to the non-treaty party.

The Commissioners, accepting the reasonableness of Lawyer's request, dispatched the local Agent, J. W. Anderson, to get Whitman, who was then living at Salem in the Willamette Valley. In a personal letter to Whitman, Hale explained why he was needed and assured him that the Government would give "ample remuneration" for his services. The invitation led to Whitman's steady employment as an interpreter at the Lapwai Agency.

In his remarks before the Lapwai Council on Tuesday, May 26, Hale stated: "We are here by the authority and under the instruction of our Government." Hale did not specify what those instructions were but, judging by subsequent events, we must assume that the Commissioners had been instructed to reduce drastically the size of the 1855 Reserva-

---

[22] See Chap. v, fn. 1.

tion. It is inconceivable that the Commissioners would have made the drastic reductions in the size of the Reservation on their own initiative and without knowing precisely what Washington had mandated.

As has been stated, the 1855 Reservation provided about 7.9 square miles for each man, woman, and child in the Nez Perce nation, whereas the Umatilla Reservation allotted only about one-half of a square mile for each person in the three tribes sent there. As will be noted, the boundaries of the 1863 Nez Perce Reservation, as fixed by the Commissioners, allotted only .4 of a square mile to each member of that tribe, thus bringing it more in line with what was provided on the Umatilla Reservation.

The responsibility of delineating the precise boundary lines of the Reservation was distinctly that of the Commissioners, based on their interpretation of instructions from Washington, D.C. Perhaps no better qualified men could have been selected to negotiate the new treaty than the three appointed — Hale, Hutchins, and Howe. Each had spent several years in the Indian service of the Government in the Pacific Northwest and each was familiar with the geographical areas involved.

Realizing that they would have some extra time on their hands while waiting for Perrin Whitman and Charles Hutchins to arrive, Hale and Howe decided to make an inspection tour of the Kamiah country to take note of possible boundary lines. They left Lapwai on May 14. In his report to Washington dated June 10, 1863, Hale wrote:

We passed over much beautiful fertile country. The spots of land suited for agricultural purposes, though numerous, were not very extensive. At all such points, we found Indian villages or camps with their patches of wheat, corn, peas, and potatoes. The largest of their villages is called Kamiah, situated on the south bank of the Clearwater, extending along the stream for a distance of about ten miles, and varying from half a mile to two and a half miles in width.

It is nearly evenly divided by a beautiful stream, about half the size of the Lapwai, coming in from the South West through what is known as Lawyer's Canyon.[23] With this stream, they are able to

[23] Today a highway from Lapwai to Kamiah passes through Craigmont and then follows Lawyer's Creek through Lawyer's Canyon to Kamiah. About midway between Craigmont and Ferdinand on U.S. Highway 95 is a roadside park called Lawyer's Canyon Park. This occupies a narrow strip of land paralleling the highway and creek for approximately one mile.

irrigate the entire plain, which is dotted with numerous Indian farms, exhibiting encouraging signs of thrift. Their wheat, corn, peas, and potatoes were growing luxuriantly, especially the two former, and gave promise of excellent crops.

Hale summarized his observations: "Well pleased with the information thus obtained by direct observation, we were well satisfied that the valleys of the Clearwater and the Lapwai contained within a reasonable compass sufficient amount of agricultural lands for the whole tribe and that the intervening and adjacent hills and table lands would furnish sufficient grazing for their horses and cattle." Years later it was discovered that these "adjacent hills and table lands" could produce, by dry farming methods, excellent crops of wheat.

Since Spalding was the first to introduce the white man's methods of agriculture among the Nez Perces, and since it was he who helped them get their first cattle, the small farms and herds of cattle which Hale and Howe saw were far more the direct result of Spalding's teachings and example than from any promised benefits embodied in the 1855 Treaty.

While on this exploratory trip, the two Commissioners studied the location of the possible boundaries of their new proposed reservation. "In determining these limits," Hale wrote, "we had to be governed not only by consideration of capacity, but so frame it that it should include within it, the greater part of their villages, and especially, as many as possible of that portion of the tribe who are considered disloyal or disaffected — known as Big Thunder's party." Writing after the 1863 Treaty had been signed, Hale added: "The boundaries of the new Reservation, as fixed in the Treaty, embraces within them about three-fourths of the whole tribe and at least two-thirds of the disaffected bands."

When the Commissioners returned to Lapwai on or before May 19, they found about 1,000 of the Nez Perces encamped in the valley. The weather turned rainy and cold. Hale wrote: "Many of the Indians were taken violently sick with influenza, of which 3 or 4 suddenly died." Since no doctor was available at the Agency, Hale was obliged to call upon a physician from Lewiston to come. He was paid $15.00 a day for his services and he succeeded in stemming the epidemic.

Agent Charles Hutchins, one of the Commissioners appointed to negotiate the new treaty with the Nez Perces, arrived at Lapwai on May 20. The three Commissioners then met in conference and evidently agreed on the location of the boundaries for the new reservation in accordance with instructions received from Washington. According to a subsequent survey of the 1863 Reservation, it contained 760,000 acres or 1,187.5 square miles.[24] This meant that the 1855 Reservation had been reduced by about 95%. Eliminated were the Wallowa, Inmada, and Grande Ronde Valleys of northeastern Oregon, the valleys along the Snake and Salmon Rivers, such places as Asotin, Alpowa, Lewiston, the upper waters of the Clearwater and its tributaries, and the trails that led over the Bitterroot Mountains. The decision, evidently made in Washington, to make this drastic reduction in the size of the 1855 Reservation made the eliminations of these areas mandatory. All that the Commissioners could do was to fix the boundaries for the new reservation.

As later events proved, the elimination of the Wallowa Valley, the ancestral home of Chief Joseph and his band of about 400, became the primary cause for the Young Joseph uprising of 1877. The March, 1977, issue of the *National Geographic*, (p. 415), states that: "What was once Joseph's domain is now Wallowa County, Oregon — 3,178 square miles of mountains, rugged canyons, and some of the finest natural grazing country in the United States." This statement is somewhat misleading as Wallowa Valley itself is only a part of the larger Wallowa County. Although no statistics are available to show approximately the area claimed by Joseph as his homeland, it may safely be assumed that the number of square miles involved was more than that allotted by the Government to the 1863 Reservation.

The Commissioners had a difficult decision to make. Not only was the Wallowa Valley too large compared to the Lapwai Reservation, for the number of Indians living there, it was also too far away to be administered by the Indian Agent located at Lapwai. Moreover, the size of Joseph's band was too small to justify the establishment of that area as a separate reservation with a resident Indian Agent. It is possible that the Commissioners did not appreciate the deep antipathies which existed in that day between the Lower Nez Perces, which included Joseph's band, and the Upper Nez Perces, which embraced

---

[24] See Chap. v, fn. 36, for reference to the 1855 Reservation containing 23,666 square miles. The acreage of the present Nez Perce Reservation was given to me by Douglas J. Riley, Historian of the Nez Perce National Historical Park, in a letter dated May 21, 1977. He also stated that of the 760,000 acres, only approximately 87,000 are actually owned by the Nez Perces.

those members of the tribe who lived along the Clearwater River and its tributaries. But even so, if the Commissioners were given instructions to significantly reduce the 1855 Reservation by up to 95%, then there was no alternative but to make these drastic eliminations. Wallowa Valley had to be thrown upen for white settlers.

Hale, in his official report, noted that some of the disaffected chiefs were reluctant to attend the Lapwai Council. He wrote: "On the 23rd of May, being informed that some of the remote and disaffected Indians, especially White Bird's band, either had not been notified or did not deign to respect a summons which seemed to come only from that portion of the tribe [i.e., Lawyer's] on whom they looked with disdain, we deemed it advisable to send a special messenger to notify and invite them in." A white man who knew the Nez Perce language was sent and he was able to persuade White Bird, who lived along the Salmon River in an area which was to be eliminated, to attend.

Although Agent Anderson and Perrin Whitman had not arrived at Lapwai by May 25, the Commissioners felt the necessity of opening the council without them. For the time being, the Commissioners and the Indians present, agreed that Spalding and Newell could serve as interpreters. Since Whitman did not arrive until June 4, and the council closed on the 9th, Spalding and Newell served longer as interpreters than did Whitman.

Big Thunder, who claimed the Lapwai Valley as the home of his band, was very sick when the Lapwai Council convened. Following the death of Looking Glass, the previous January 6, Big Thunder became Lawyer's main opponent among the Upper Nez Perces. Although he was himself a tewat, or medicine man, Big Thunder was persuaded by Hale to accept the services of the Lewiston doctor who had been employed by the Commissioners. Perhaps because of his illness Big Thunder played only a minor role in the events of the council.

An Eyewitness Account of the Lapwai Council

In the early fall of 1934, shortly after I began my search for source materials bearing on the life of Henry H. Spalding, I called on the two elderly daughters of Perrin Whitman who were then living in Lewiston, Idaho. They were Mrs. Charles (Frances) Monteith and Mrs. Sophia Mallory. Charles Monteith was the brother of John B. Monteith, a bachelor, who was appointed Indian Agent at Lapwai in February, 1871. Charles served for a time with his brother at the Agency. I remember that when I called on these two ladies, it was a chilly autumn evening and that they had a fire burning in their fireplace. After explaining my intention to write Spalding's biography, I asked if they had any of their father's papers.

"Oh, why did you not come a few weeks ago," one exclaimed. "We sat here one evening before this fireplace and burned the papers from two of our father's small trunks."

My heart sank within me as I asked: "Did you not save anything?"

"Yes," she answered. "We did save one bundle of papers just before it was burned." She then went into an adjoining room and brought back a packet of folded documents about four inches thick which had been charred by the fire around the edges. The first document that I examined was a letter from General W. T. Sherman, then in San Francisco, to John B. Monteith giving directions regarding the Chief Joseph uprising. Other documents related to contemporary events then taking place in the Nez Perce tribe. I was able to secure possession of the papers which I turned over to the Spokane Public Library.[25]

I had the rare privilege of visiting the old Spalding mission site with Mrs. Monteith in January 1935. She told me that when her father, Perrin Whitman, arrived at Lapwai on June 4, 1863, he had with him his family. Thus as a little girl, ten or twelve years old, Frances Whitman witnessed the exciting events which marked the closing days of the council. As we walked over the field, just west of the site where the Spalding cabin had once stood, she said that it was there where the Commissioners met with the Indians. And also that it was there where Spalding used to hold his religious services when the congregations became too large for the log church.

Blessed with a clear memory, Mrs. Monteith recalled many incidents which had occurred there nearly seventy-two years before. She pointed out the site of Lawyer's house at the mouth of the creek. She remembered seeing the long line of tepees and tents which stretched out along Lapwai Creek from the old mission site almost to Fort Lapwai. She recalled especially how sullen and even angry were the anti-treaty chiefs because they had learned that their homelands were to be excluded from the boundaries of the new reservation. Since the Whitman family arrived at Lapwai at least a day before Old Joseph left in anger, she had an opportunity to see the chief. She remembered that

<hr>

[25] See Drury, Tepee, p. 197 for further details about this incident.

he attended a meeting of the council while carrying his gun under his blanket.

Looking back on that rare experience, which took place nearly forty-three years ago at the time of this writing, I realize with regret that my knowledge of the importance of the 1863 Council was then too meager for me to ask intelligent questions.

Proceedings of the Lapwai Council, 1863

Writing to Washington on June 10, 1863, Hale explained that he and the other two Commissioners had decided to open the council on May 25 even if Perrin Whitman had not then arrived or if some known anti-treaty chiefs as Red Owl, White Bird, Eagle-of-the-Light, and Joseph also had not come. Hale mentioned in this letter the presence of a band of about fifty Palouse Indians who were encamped a few miles from the Agency on the banks of the Clearwater. "As they were found visiting Big Thunder," wrote Hale, "we had reason to believe their presence boded no good. Their demeanor became so insulting that Hale found it necessary to instruct the military to order them to leave.

The drama of the 1863 Lapwai Council began at 11:00 a.m., Monday, May 25. "At which time," wrote Hale, "all the friendly Indians of Lawyer's party were present. There were also present some from Big Thunder's camp." Big Thunder was more anti-Lawyer than he was anti-treaty. Hale, summing up the purpose of the Council in his opening remarks, with Spalding serving as interpreter, said:

> My friends — You see us here as your friends, sent by the President of the United States to talk with you. We have thought it best to speak to you now, rather than to wait until Mr. Whitman arrives, and to tell you what we have to propose, that you may have time to think about it and consider it well. You may use your own pleasure in regard to answering or talking to us, until Mr. Whitman arrives. . . As your friends, we propose to you to relinquish to the United States a part of your present Reservation, and to take a new Reservation, smaller than the one you now hold.

Hale then explained the necessity of stationing troops at Fort Lapwai.

> The Government of the United States desires to act justly towards you against the injustices of men who would wrong you and do you harm. It is for this that your Great Father, the President of the United States, has placed troops here. They are to protect you, to

see that justice is done to you, and not to drive you away from your homes, as some bad men have told you. The soldiers are here to prevent bad men from driving you away.

We do not propose that you should leave your own country. We do not wish it. We only desire that you would relinquish such portions of your Reservation as you do not really need, and instead of being scattered in small bands over a large extent of country, we wish to bring you nearer together, so that your rights, your lives, and your property can be better protected, than it is possible to do whilst you continue as you are.

Hale then outlined in detail the boundaries of the proposed new Reservation. He assured the Indians that the boundary lines would be surveyed and marked so that both the Whites and the Indians would know. He also promised that the valley lands would be surveyed into lots or farms "so that each of you can have a farm in his own right and have it secured to him by a paper [i.e., a title deed], just as the Whites do, then nobody can disturb you." Hale explained that the owners would have the right at their deaths to bequeath their property to their heirs.

The Commissioners repeatedly assured the Nez Perces that the provisions of the 1855 Treaty were not to be abrogated, except for the changing of the boundary lines. All of the other rights and benefits were to be honored. Hale also stated on this day, May 25, that the Government was prepared to buy that part of the former reservation which was to be given up and that: "Those of you who live on that portion of it, which is to be relinquished, will be paid for the improvements you have made, such as your fields that are enclosed and cultivated." He added: "Think about what has been said, and see if it is not best for you to settle down as we propose, and become a farming people."

TUESDAY, MAY 26

The Council reconvened at 10:00 a.m. with Spalding serving as interpreter. Agent Hutchins was the first to speak. He amplified what Hale had said on the previous day and assured the Indians that the Government would carry out all of the provisions of the 1855 Treaty such as the payment of annuities, the building of mills, and the providing of teachers to show them how to farm. He assured them that each family would be given a twenty-acre farm which would be plowed and fenced by the Government. Since the horses and cattle owned by the Indians were to graze on the uplands, a twenty-acre farm was all that one man could cultivate using the methods then common.

Hutchins also stated that the Government would pay the first year after the Treaty was ratified $81,200.00 for the erection of a mill at Kamiah (one had already been erected at Lapwai); two schools and boarding houses; a blacksmith shop at Kamiah; a hospital at Lapwai; and other improvements. Indian children were to be given clothing, board and room while attending the schools. All claims for services rendered by the Nez Perce warriors to the Government in the Indian wars of 1855-58 were to be paid.

Indians living outside of the boundaries of the new reduced Reservation were to be given one year to move onto the Reservation. Hutchins also explained:

> No white man is to be permitted to come and live on your new reservation, except those who are connected with or under the control of the Indian Department for the purpose of carrying out the provisions of the Treaty. No white man will be permitted to own any land within it. The land is to be yours, and every thing that grows upon it, the grass and the trees are to be yours.

After Hutchins had spoken, Hale asked if there were any questions. Ute-sin-male-cum, the old chief from Kamiah, then asked: "When did the order for this proposition you have made come from your Government? I feel responsible to the Government, and wish to know if this came from it." Here is a suggestion that perhaps the Indians thought that the idea of a reduced reservation came from Senator Nesmith of Oregon and not from the Government in Washington. The Indians were assured that the order had originated in Washington. Ute-sin-male-cum then wanted to know when the order arrived — "in the fall, in the winter, or this spring. State it distinctly for we wish to know." Hale patiently explained:

> About a year ago the Government was informed of the discovery of numerous gold mines in and around your Reservation. Knowing that white men would rush in to work the mines before it would be possible to send a force of soldiers sufficiently strong to prevent them, and that there would be men who would violate the laws framed for your protection by introducing whiskey for sale, and thereby produce difficulties, the Government at once began to

inquire as to the best way to preserve peace, and protect you fr[
suffering wrong.

Hale's letter of June 30 to the Commissioner of Indian Affairs in Washington threw further light on the problems the Indians were facing.

The great reduction in the size of their reservation, [he wrote,] was, at first, very unsatisfactory, their ideas being so different to ours as to the amount of land sufficient to answer every needed purpose. It was manifest that, at the most, they had only thought of relinquishing a small spot of ground around Lewiston, and at a few points in the mountains around the mining towns and camps, while the great body of the Reserve would still be theirs.

The drastically reduced size of their reservation was the main issue which troubled the Indians at this May 26 meeting. In his endeavor to explain to the Nez Perces why the Government had decided to reduce the size of the 1855 Reservation, Hale said,

Knowing that you were friendly to the Government and perceiving by the maps that the Nez Perces had a much larger reservation than they could use, so large, too, that it would be impossible for the United States to protect you with an army of soldiers, a larger number than could be spared [i.e., during the Civil War], the President thought you would be willing to make your reservation smaller, and by being paid for it, relinquish such portions as contained the gold mines.

Hale also explained that he and the other Commissioners had been appointed in the fall of 1862 to study the problem and to meet with the Nez Perces in council to draw up a new treaty. "We are here," he declared, "by the authority and under the instruction of our Government."

Lawyer then arose and spoke as a lawyer. Here he was at his best. He was in a court of law. The Government, because of its many broken promises made in the 1855 Treaty was the defendant; the Nez Perces were the plaintiffs; and the three Commissioners were both jury and judges. Forceably and sometimes sadly, in a transcribed speech of about 700 words, Lawyer reviewed instances of repeated Government failures to fulfill its solemn obligations. Lawyer was a deeply religious man. His inherent sense of justice had been nurtured and intensified by his understanding of Christianity taught him by the missionaries. To him, all men, both Whites and Indians, had a solemn obligation to obey both the laws of man and the law of God.

After addressing each of the Commissioners and after reminding them that he clearly understood all that they had proposed, Lawyer continued:

As for me and my Chiefs, we are governed by law. We are here today to adhere to the treaty that has been made and which we, on our side, have kept. Not one of us is grasping at shadows or the simple sayings of an outsider. We once had a principal Chief [Ellis] and we remained under his influence as regards his law. The Great Creator of the universe, that governs all things, lives under the decrees of his laws. We are under the same sacred influence.

The head of your Government has now spoken to us through you. . . In the same manner that my people receive the law of God as binding, so do we acknowledge and consider the law of your Government as binding on us and on you, for the law is sacred.

As for me and my people and these Chiefs, they have all understood what you have said; we understand that these propositions you have made come from the Government, through you, and that they are the last. We are not going to shrink, we will squarely face the whole thing, and when we come to an agreement, we intend to be bound by it. . . Here are my Chiefs and they like me are under the sacred influence of the law from above. Those who will cast off all law, if any do, I will not acknowledge as belonging to me. They would be considered by me as outlaws.

Your propositions are now before us. Your Government previously (alluding to the Stevens-Palmer treaty) marked out our boundaries. That was your proposition. We still adhere to that law, and to the law of righteousness. You have broken the treaty, not we. When you broke through the treaty, it did not make my heart sad and sore. I only wondered why you did it.

Now I am called upon to look on this proposition of yours, after the Americans have broken their treaty so often. That engagement was made with us for 20 years by your Government.[26] We understand very well what 20 years mean. We were given to understand at the time we made the treaty that we should have the guar-

---

[26] Lawyer was referring to a statement in Article v of the 1855 Treaty which stated that the Government was to pay certain annuities to the Nez Perces for 20 years.

antees secured to us for 20 years, and that the treaty would be observed. By adhering to that treaty, we were told that we should become as white men. We have been looking on; we have been waiting. Many articles in that treaty have not been fulfilled by the Government. This winter we were told that Col. Nesmith was in Congress at Washington. We learned what he said there. I understand that there was a division of opinion on Col. Nesmith's proposition. . . Here we are listening to what you say again, before this 20 years are ended. Now we are anxious to know what you have to give us; when you have done this, we will then show our hearts.

Perhaps by contemplation, you will find something that is wrong in your propositions; we will examine into what we shall propose, and if there is anything wrong, we will correct it so that the law, and the treaty, and the engagement to be entered into shall be just and straight and upright.

We are but Indians, miserable, and ignorant, and need a law that is just and right. I have shown you my heart thus far.

Hale's reply suggests that he was somewhat embarrassed by Lawyer's remarks. He made no attempt to justify the Government's failures. He did propose going over the 1855 Treaty with them the next day. "Perhaps," he said, "we do not understand it right; Perhaps you do not understand it." Hale reassured the Indians that: "We are instructed not to do anything which will injure the Nez Perces. We are to seek their good in the treaty we propose. We are expected to fix upon such boundaries as can be understood and protected, and to make such a Treaty as can be carried out." Here was the strongest argument that the Commissioners could make for a smaller reservation. In view of the overwhelming numbers of Whites surging into the country and onto the Nez Perce Reservation, it was impossible for the Government to protect the Indians by excluding the Whites, as long as the boundary lines enclosed so vast an area.

WEDNESDAY, MAY 27

The Council reconvened at 10:00 a.m. on Wednesday with Spalding still serving as interpreter. The discussions of this day centered around the 1855 Treaty. In his opening remarks, Hale frankly admitted: "We do not claim that in all respects the Treaty has been carried out." He insisted, however, that much had been done. He mentioned the fact that Congress had appropriated $91,250.00 for Nez Perce projects in

1861, but was unable to explain how this money was spent. He did not explain why there was a two-year delay following the ratification of the Treaty in 1859 and the first appropriation in 1861.

During 1862, the Government appropriated $26,000.00 and the same amount for 1863. Such sums were spent on annuities, wages and salaries of employees, and for some material improvements. Hale stated when he became Superintendent of Indian Affairs for Washington Territory in the summer of 1862, he tried to find out what had been done with the moneys previously appropriated but without much success. He frankly told the Indians that: "I found there was not as much done as you had the right to expect, nor as much as the United States Government supposed."

Hale referred to his first inspection trip to Lapwai made in the summer of 1862 and confessed:

> I was surprised to see so little improvements made, in view of the large appropriations which I know have been made. Your Head Chief Lawyer had no house built, and no farm fenced or ploughed. The money for this had been appropriated but did not come into my hands. Your Head Chief Lawyer was entitled to receive pay. The money had been appropriated but I found none had been paid to him, except what Mr. Hutchins paid.

Hale did not specify how much this was.

Hale continued with his list of Government failures: "I found that you had no school house, altho a teacher had been sent; that you had no hospital; and your mills were not finished. This was not the fault of Mr. Hutchins. He had done what he could to complete the mills, although he had received no money either for mills, hospital, or school."

Hale then summarized what had been accomplished.

> I made arrangements to have the machinery and the mill stones forwarded at once. By this means, your mills were finished and are now sawing lumber and grinding your grain. These are not permanent for that purpose. Your Chief's house has been built. He is living in it. His salary has been paid. A portion of his land has been ploughed and fenced, and arrangements are made for ploughing and fencing the rest. The school house is built and nearly completed, and we are carrying out the provisions of the Treaty as rapidly as possible.

Hale admitted that there were "deficiences in the expenditures of the first years' appropriations, but he was unable to determine how much.

He assured his hearers that the Government would continue to appropriate $26,600 annually throughout the following seventeen years, thus fulfilling the provisions of the 1855 Treaty to make such payments over twenty years.

Hale made only an indirect reference to the new boundaries which were to be drawn by saying that the Government would pay for all land relinquished. The Nez Perces had nothing to say about the drastic reduction of their 1855 Reservation by about 95%. The decree for such a reduction had come from Washington, and was simply for the Commissioners to implement. With this exception, Hale maintained that the 1855 Treaty "was binding and that our Government is endeavoring to fulfill it." After Secretary Whitworth had read the text of the 1855 Treaty, Lawyer again addressed the Council.

Lawyer's remarks carried a double meaning and perhaps he so intended. With his strong emphasis on law, he might have been rebuking the Government for unilaterally abrogating the 1855 Treaty which, for him, was a sacred law. Or Lawyer, recognizing the impossibility of the Nez Perces to overrule what had been decided in Washington, was making an appeal to his people to accept the inevitable and obey the new law which was being imposed upon them.

According to the minutes of the meeting, Lawyer said: "It seems that what you say comes from the Government. I have ever looked upon treaties as laws that are made for the control of evil, as well amongst the Whites as Indians. Our Chief Ellis, while he lived directed us to live according to the laws." Lawyer then referred to an incident which occurred in the 1855 Council when Governor Stevens addressed the Nez Perces as "his children." Lawyer, taking a notebook from his pocket, said: "I have it here as I took it down at the time." Then Lawyer read from the notation he had made quoting Stevens: "My children, we have assembled today. The Creater is looking down upon us, and I expect to say the truth." Lawyer then seemed to contrast what Stevens had so solemnly declared with that which Hale was saying: "I have heard what you have said, and we show you our hearts. This is what I have to say on this occasion."

Upon this note, the Council closed for the day.

THURSDAY, MAY 28

This was a day of excitement, of harsh words, and bitter feelings. Although it had been agreed that no meeting was to be held this day, the chiefs sent an urgent appeal to Hale early in the morning requesting that a meeting be called at once. Some white squatters had gone beyond the city limits of Lewiston, had staked out claims, and had begun to build fences and houses. The Indians were alarmed. "The Indians were much excited by the news which was brought into the camp last night," wrote the secretary in his official report, "of white persons having gone onto some of their lands and taken possession." The Indians asked: "If this could happen at Lewiston, might it not also happen elsewhere on their Reservation?"

The Commissioners acted promptly by asking Colonel Justus Stein- berger at Fort Lapwai to send troops to eject the squatters, to pull up the surveyor's stakes, and to tear down any improvements that had been made. This the soldiers did, throwing the lumber and logs into the river.

> If there had been any failure in this respect, [wrote Hale to the Commissioner in Washington,] the Council would have speedily broken up, and the Indians have returned in haste to their respec- tive homes, fearing that during their absence, white men were settling upon their lands and taking possession of their fields. The promptness with which the Col. acted to use the necessary force to execute the request, . . . gave satisfaction to the Indians, quieted their fears, and soon restored their confidence.

The Council reconvened at 10:00 a.m. with Spalding still serving as interpreter, since Perrin Whitman had not yet arrived. Of all the days when Whitman should have been present, this was the one, for never before had the Indians spoken with such frankness.

The chief event of the morning was a long and eloquent speech by Lawyer which contained about 2,500 words. Considering the time it would have taken Spalding to do the interpreting, the speech could well have consumed two hours. In his remarks, Lawyer gave an excel- lent summary of Nez Perce contacts with the Whites beginning with the arrival of Lewis and Clark, whom he evidently remembered. Law- yer gave a chronological catalog of the many times the Nez Perces, acting under his direction, had assisted the white men. Then with evident sadness, he mentioned a few of the failures of the Government in its dealings with the Nez Perces. He closed with the blunt statement that he could not give up "the country you ask for." This speech is so important that it is here given almost in its entirety.

Clark and Lewis were the first white men who came among us,

and our people immediately understood that white men were good
men. Your fathers and ours, from that moment were in friendship
and have been ever since. . . We become still more acquainted
with the Whites, and with their usages, by sending from different
parts of our country, some of our children to the Red River school.
Through these [including Ellis], when they returned, we became
better instructed in the usages of the Whites. . . We learned
that the Whites were the work of God, that by him they were
planted on the earth, that he gave to them the different metals for
use, that he gave them science and knowledge. . .

It seems that the red man is from the same source, and that he
has been placed on the earth where there is gold. The Creater has,
in this respect, placed the White and the Red man on equal
grounds. This we learned in part from those who attended that
school, and the rest from other sources. We have also learned that
these discoveries of gold in the country of both White and Red
now require legislation.

[After referring to the return of Spokane Garry and Kootenai
Pelly from the Red River school in 1829, Lawyer continued:]
Subsequently four of their number, including two chiefs went East
[i.e., to St. Louis] as a delegation to the States.[27] The result of
their visit was that Dr. Whitman came to the mountains,[28] and the
next year the missionaries came. From that time we became instructed that God was our Creator.

Dr. Whitman established himself in the valley of the Walla
Walla and Mr. Spalding came here.[29] I and my chiefs were much
rejoiced that we should now be able to become better acquainted
with the laws and usages of the Whites. We learned a correct
knowledge of law from Mr. Spalding and Dr. Whitman, as we
believe, but when Dr. White arrived, he said, "I came to make
known to you the laws."

At that time Ellis was our chief. He was well instructed and
understood other languages than our own. In his understanding
and knowledge of the usages of the Whites, we had great confidence. He went into the buffalo country and there died. Then we

---

[27] Lawyer modestly refrained from saying that he was the connecting link between Spokane Garry and the Nez Perce delegation which went to St. Louis in
1831.

[28] A reference to the exploring tour of Dr. Whitman and Rev. Samuel Parker in
1835. See subhead in Chap. II: "The Exploring Tour of Whitman and Parker."

[29] It is interesting to note that Spalding was serving as interpreter for Lawyer at
this time.

were without one to lead or direct. We had lost our chief. We had other chiefs but there was none that had the knowledge and understanding of Ellis.

Upon the heels of the death of our chief, the word came, and we heard it, that Dr. Whitman and his wife were killed. We were perfectly bewildered, and knew not which way to turn. Our best friend was killed. I was confident that there would be fighting amongst the Indians of this country. I sent word to my people here to have nothing to do with the war that would arise from this murder.

My friends, do not let your heart jump. I deem to speak to you the truth, be not offended. I went to Oregon immediately after I returned from the buffalo country and saw Governor Lane. He said to me: ,'My friends, you must now put the law in force." I addressed my people, and Timothy and his people, and my brother,[30] now dead, and his people. I said to them: "There is a great work for us to do. The murderers of Dr. Whitman must be delivered up to the Whites that they may be put to death. This is the law." They were taken and delivered up.

At a later date, when the Snake Indians were murdering the emigrants who were passing through their country, Major Haller was sent to take and punish the murderers.[31] Immediately, on my advice, Captain John and Jason, with some of their people, went into the Snake country to assist Major Haller. They killed some of the Snakes and delivered others up at The Dalles. Here now, are two of our acts showing our friendship to the Whites, and our respect for law.

It was in accordance with these principles and with the knowledge of these facts, that Governor Stevens and General Palmer met with us in Council, [1855]. At the beginning, they said: "We came by the authority of our Government and present you a law and this law is to be permanent for the Whites and Red men." At that time, I knew that gold had been discovered in California and that roads had been forced to it.

Governor Stevens said to me: "How much country do you need for yourselves, for you and your children?" I replied frankly and decidedly, and bounded the reservation as is in the Treaty. That boundary I named for myself and my people and that according

---

[30] See Chap. IV, "Lawyer Received by the Whites as a Welcomed Guest," for another reference to this brother.

[31] A reference to a punitive expedition led by Major G. O. Haller against the Shoshone Indians in 1854.

to law.[32] It was defined, written down, and prescribed as the Reservation of the Nez Perce people, agreed to, finished and sealed.

The Governor then said, "I have done this work, and now I wish to go to the Flathead country." I said, here are my chiefs who are acquainted with the country and who will accompany you, — Captain John and Looking Glass. . .

I then heard of Mr. Bolon being killed. An express to give notice to Governor Stevens came to my camp in the night. . . I told the messenger, take my horses, follow after Governor Stevens. The prospect was fair for war. All the tribes were in commotion. A council was immediately called and the question was what shall we do? The neighboring tribes are in commotion and [some of] our people are with Governor Stevens. We called upon Craig for his advice, and he took the lead in directing us. About that time, Governor Stevens was returning with our brethren, and was near at hand. I then gave another horse to send word to Governor Stevens, to inform him of his danger, and direct him to leave his intended route, and return by the way of our country.

He was found surrounded by about twenty Spokanes, who with my people brought him in safety to us. Governor Stevens then said to me: "My friend, Lawyer, what shall I do?" I replied, Governor Stevens, we will take you in our arms as a child, and as a child, deliver you safely to your own people, and I only ask of you in return for our care of you, that you will deal as kindly and tenderly with me and my people, as I now deal with you, and as I conduct you through this danger to safety, so do you conduct me and my people when we need your aid.

Eighty of my warriors were supplied with arms by Governor Stevens. We carried him safely to Walla Walla. When he arrived there, he was met by [U.S.] forces, and the Governor said to them: "My white friends, I introduce you to our true friends, who have brought and delivered us here in safety. These who are with me are here as representatives [of the Nez Perce tribe.]"

After this Colonel Cornelius [Gilliam] had his horses taken from him, and he made request to us to furnish him with other horses to replace them.[33] Over forty horses were furnished, and he was

---

[32] Lawyer here made claim that he was primarily responsible for drawing the boundary lines for the 1855 Reservation.

[33] Lawyer was here referring to an incident which took place in the Cayuse War of 1848 when the Nez Perces replaced forty horses which had been stolen from Colonel Gilliam's command by the Cayuses. The Nez Perces had not been paid for these horses up to the time of the 1863 Council.

enabled to proceed and fight the Indians who were hostile, and many were killed both of men and horses. This is our third act in defense of law.

Colonel Steptoe came into my country. Timothy and some of my people accompanied him. The whole people of the North met him in battle array. In that battle, two of my warriors, with others mingled their blood on the ground; therefore, I claim that we are in alliance with the white people.

Afterwards, Colonel Wright with his gray hairs, met us in Council at Walla Walla. He addressed me as a chief and asked me to furnish warriors. I answered: "By tommorow." Colonel Wright said: "This is no boy's play. We enter into this truly and solemnly. We will together defend and protect this country that is not yet in a state of war. The law by which we are governed is unchangeable." This is what Colonel Wright said. Here it is on the paper I hold in my hand, [referring to a paper which he held.]

Ute-si-mal-a-kin, Spotted Eagle, and many others accompanied Colonel Wright. They accomplished their object and returned in safety. I rejoiced at it, because it was in defense of law. This is another instance. . .

[Lawyer then turned to some of the violations of the 1855 Treaty.] I now turn to the other side. There is a ferry kept by white men near the Alpowa. I am about to ask, what shall I receive for the privilege? There is another at the mouth of the Clearwater; another across the Snake River. What are we to receive for the town of Lewiston? What for the ferry at the North Fork of Clearwater? There is a mining town at Oro Fino, what are we to receive for it? What for Elk City? [Lawyer listed three other ferries operating on rivers within the Reservation without receiving Nez Perce permission or paying any compensation.]

I have named these grievances, these violations of the Treaty, of the law, by the side of our services to the Whites. I want now to know what we shall receive for all these? We wish not to be offended and we want you to keep nothing back. Let us know. I intend you shall know my heart. I think you do know it.

In the old treaty, there are many things promised. I see only the flour and saw mill and you see what is yet unfulfilled. With my own eyes, I have seen lumber go from the mill [at Lapwai] to Lewiston, and by reason of these grievances from day to day, I am caused to shed tears. I am anxious to get at that point, where I know I am safe and straight, and can feel assured that I and my people shall rest securely.

I hear you say that the land is to be divided up, so much for one, and so much for another. I fear there would not be enough, then there will be crowding. I present this for your consideration.

I have friends in Lewiston, but I have said nothing to them about this. I have not prevented miners and others from going through my country. We have all been willing for this, and we said, My friends, dig the gold. The time is coming, I am convinced, when the law will regulate these matters. I am willing for any to look back on my doing and see if there is any fault with my past conduct.

Lawyer was not afraid of letting future generations judge his conduct. He closed his long speech with these memorable words:

This is my heart, and I show it to you. My friends, we are to be governed by law in these things. I want you to understand that I have all along been governed by law. I want the President and all white men to understand.

I will now give you the great answer. Dig the gold and look at the country, but we cannot give you the country you ask for.

Ute-sin-male-cum then spoke up: "I have heard you, Mr. Hale. You have heard what Lawyer has said. . . You have heard what we have done for the Whites and in support of laws. That boundary then made, we consider permanent, sacred, and according to law. . . We thought it was to remain forever. . . You trifle with us. . . We understand that the whole of our reservation was for us, to cultivate, and to occupy as we pleased." We can easily imagine Ute-sin-male-cum shouting out his closing words in anger: "We cannot give up our country. You trifle with us. We cannot give you the country. We cannot sell it to you."

Then Hai-haich-tuesta, also known as Billy,[34] spoke. He, too, stressed the feeling that the 1855 Treaty was "sacred." He doubted if the proposals brought by Hale actually came from the Government. "It cannot

[34] Billy, a faithful follower of Lawyer, was also mentioned in the Proceedings of the 1855 Council, but his Indian name was not given. Billy was the second after Lawyer to sign the 1863 Treaty. Among those whom Spalding baptized on November 12, 1871, were Lawyer and "William," the latter of whom might have been Billy. Kate McBeth, in her *The Nez Perces Since Lewis and Clark,* p. 234, mentions "Jonathan Williams," better known as Billy Williams, an elder in the Kamiah church. According to McBeth his Indian name was Ku-ku-loo-ya, whereas his name on the 1863 Treaty is given as Ha-haich-tnesta. The Nez Perce names are often confusing as the same person could have different names. On the other hand, there may be in this case two different persons known as William or Billy.

be," he said, "it is so different from what Governor Stevens said to us as to our boundary. . . You say our country is a large one, and that you will give us a smaller country. . . Yet you profess to speak according to law. It does not look good. It looks crooked."

The strong stand taken by the friendly chiefs threw Hale and the other Commissioners on the defensive. They had not been the ones who decided that the size of the reservation had to be reduced so drastically. That decision had been made in Washington. All that they could do was make some minor adjustments in the boundaries. Hale and his two associates were left to defend to the best of their ability what had proved to be a most unpopular treaty.

In his rebuttal, Hale confessed: "What you say about Governor Stevens is true. When he entered into this treaty with you, it was not expected that the boundaries then made would need to be changed." Hale then drew attention to a provision in Article vi of the 1855 Treaty which provided that "the President may assign lots of permanent homes to such individuals or families, as should be willing to avail themselves of this privilege." On this somewhat slender legal basis, the Government was now assigning lots, or farms, to members of the tribe within the boundaries of the reduced reservation. Hale stressed the fact that since they had agreed to the 1855 Treaty, the Nez Perces were bound by this Article, although no one then dreamed that it would be applied in this manner.

Hale dealt with the matter of authority by saying:

> If I understand you aright, you deny our authority; you do not recognize us as being sent, and empowered to enter into any arrangement with you. If so, we are only talking in vain, when we talk. It is not for the benefit of the Government so much as it is for yours, that we have proposed to make your reservation smaller. How can the Government protect you from the lawless and bad, scattered as you are over so large a reservation? To protect your borders would require an army of 20,000 men [this during the Civil War], and then it would be impossible to prevent some trespassing upon your lands and injuring you. . . By making the Reserve smaller, it is believed that you can be the better protected.

Hale again assured the Indians that: "If your improvements are within the boundaries we have mentioned, you lose nothing; if they are outside, you are to be paid for them." Regarding the ferries mentioned by

Lawyer, Hale said that this was a matter which could be adjusted.

Regarding the illegal actions of some squatters who staked out lots and started building on Indian land near Lewiston, Hale reported that soldiers had been sent to evict them. He added: "We have also had men arrested who are charged with selling whiskey and have had them placed in confinement." Article ix of the 1855 Treaty provided that "any Indian belonging to said tribe who is guilty of bringing liquor into said reservation, or who drinks liquor, may have his or her proportion of the annuities withheld from him or her for such time as the President may determine." Strangely, the Treaty made no mention of white men bringing in liquor. Hale admitted that this provision of the Treaty was practically impossible to enforce.

The proceedings of the day closed with a short speech by Timothy who said: "While we were assembled here yesterday, we heard that lands were staked off and white men were taking our homes. We tell you that this must stop. The country is still ours and our children's. What Lawyer has said is the heart of all the people."

Looking back on those days Hale, in his letter to Washington, wrote:

After several days had been spent in Council, without arriving to any conclusions, or seeming to make any progress toward the negotiation, I became satisfied that the Chiefs were, to some extent at least, copying after the style of a certain class of politicians; they were making speeches in the Council for buncombe, out of which nothing would be likely to result. Instead of declaring their own views and opinions as to what would conduce most to the interests and welfare of the tribe, they were doing little more than re-echoing the opinions of the great part of their people, who did not consider their future, or that of their children and who, Indian like, were averse to any change that looked to the circumscribing of their boundaries.

Realizing that he was not winning the support of the Nez Perces in open council meetings, Hale shifted to a different strategy. "I therefore concluded," Hale wrote to his superiors in Washington, "to try private conferences with the Chiefs, whereby by direct questions and answers, there would be better opportunity of ascertaining their true feelings, meeting their objections, removing their doubts, and explaining to them such matters as they were liable to understand."

Hale, through these private conferences, became increasingly aware of the many personal animosities which divided the tribe. A few, including Big Thunder, were so anti-Lawyer that they became anti-treaty. "It is truly to be regretted," wrote Hale, "that this people should be so divided." Unfortunately, some of those divisions which existed back in 1863 have continued to the present day.

FIVE DAY RECESS, FRIDAY, MAY 29-TUESDAY, JUNE 2

In order to provide time for his private conferences with individual chiefs, and also to give further time for Perrin Whitman to come, Hale arranged for a recess to extend from Friday, May 29, through Tuesday, June 2. During these days, several of the disaffected chiefs with their followers arrived including Eagle-from-the-Light, Old Joseph, and White Bird. The first of these lived on the South Fork of the Clearwater River. His home, therefore, was within the boundaries of the proposed new reservation. The homelands of Joseph and White Bird lay outside of the new reservation. With the arrival of these bands, the total number of Nez Perces assembled at Lapwai must have been close to 2,000.[35] This number would have included women and children. Hale reported that some Indians from each of the adjoining tribes were also present.

Spalding was delighted when Hale invited him to serve as an interpreter at the Lapwai Council. Since Hale had asked the Nez Perces to assemble at Lapwai on or before Sunday, May 10, this would have given Spalding four Sundays in May and the first Sunday in June in which he could hold religious services for these Indians. Agent Anderson, who was present at Lapwai when Spalding returned, has given us the following description of the enthusiastic welcome the veteran missionary was given by the Nez Perces:

> At the time of his arrival a great part of the tribe was collected at the Agency and I must say they seemed highly delighted at seeing Mr. Spalding again. This was more particularly the case with many of the old Indians who had known Mr. S. when he came amongst them as a missionary many years before. . . Every Sabbath the Indians in great numbers attended Mr. S's preaching & I was greatly astonished at the orderly & dignified deportment of the congregation.[36]

---

[35] The records of the 1863 Council give no figures as to the number of Nez Perces in attendance with the exception of Hale's reference to 1,000 being present when the Commissioners returned to Lapwai on May 19 from their trip to Kamiah. After that date other bands, including the non-treaty Indians, arrived.

[36] Drury, *Spalding*, p. 376.

Spalding's great appeal to the Nez Perces assembled there at Lapwai lay in the fact that he had been their missionary for over eleven years. He could speak their language and needed no interpreter. His audiences met in the open air. It was there in December 1838 and January 1839 that he had conducted a series of revival meetings which resulted in the conversion of Joseph and Timothy who were baptized and received into the Mission Church on November 17, 1839.

Perhaps still standing at Lapwai in 1863 was a small log building which once had housed the printing press which the American Board missionaries in Hawaii had sent in 1839 to their co-workers in Oregon. It was on that press that Spalding had in 1845 printed the translation he had made, with Lawyer's help, of the Gospel of Matthew into Nez Perce. Among those to whom Spalding gave copies were Joseph and Timothy.

As has been stated, the Provisional Government of Oregon took action following the Whitman massacre to apprehend the murderers. Accompanying the Volunteers sent to Waiilatpu were three Commissioners who called for a meeting of some chiefs who had not taken part in the massacre. Among those summoned was Joseph. Apprehensive as to what might happen to him, Joseph took with him his copy of the Nez Perce Gospel of Matthew.

On March 6, 1848, while meeting with the Commissioners, Joseph is reported to have said:

> When I left home, I took the book in my hand and brought it with me. It is my light. I heard the Americans were coming to kill me. Still I held my book before me, and came on. I have heard the words of your chief. I speak for all the Cayuses present, and all my people. I do not want my children engaged in this war, although my brother [Five Crows, a half-brother] is wounded. You speak of the murderers. I shall not meddle with them. I bow my head. This much I speak.[37]

When Old Joseph traveled to Lapwai to meet Hale and the other Commissioners, he carried his Nez Perce Matthew with him. To him it was a symbol of his trust in the white man's religion and in the white man's justice.

Hale made good use of the recess by meeting with the chiefs individually. Of this he wrote in his letter to Washington: "Private conversations thus held separately with the chiefs of each faction, resulted

---

[37] Gray, *Oregon*, p. 526.

satisfactorily. On the part of the friendly ones, an agreement to accept the terms proposed by the Commissioners, with some slight alterations as to boundary . . . was at length had."

"On the part of the disaffected bands," wrote Hale, "their chiefs gave an unequivocal assent to the main features of the Treaty as far as they were concerned, only that their pride would not permit them to come out with the Lawyer party and sign the Treaty." Hale then mentioned Eagle-from-the-Light and Big Thunder, whose lands lay within the proposed new borders. Hale wrote:

> Each came of his own accord, in private conference, and asked that it might be reported to their Great Father at Washington, that they did not refuse to sign the Treaty out of disrespect or want of friendly feelings towards him, to the Commissoners, or to the people of the United States, but that their refusal was solely on account of difficulties among themselves. Besides, they alleged, that it was not necessary for them to sign it, as they were not called upon by the conditions of the Treaty to surrender anything to the Government, as their lands were almost entirely included in the proposed new Reservation.

Hale made no mention in this letter of having had any interviews with Joseph or White Bird.

WEDNESDAY, JUNE 3-FRIDAY, JUNE 4

Perrin B. Whitman having arrived, the Council was reconvened on June 3 with him serving as interpreter. Since the assembly had been swollen with the arrival of the disaffected bands, the Commissioners found it necessary to repeat much that had been said during the previous days.

Hale addressed the Council on the 3rd. He stressed the fact that many of the difficulties which the Indians had experienced in their contacts with the Whites arose out of the tremendous size of the old Reservation.

> Whilst you continue in this way," [he said,] it is impossible to protect you as we wish, and it is important for you that it should be [protected]. If it were not for the discoveries of gold in the mountains, there would be no necessity of making it any smaller at the present time. Now it is necessary for your own good and for your own protection and especially for the preservation of your children.

Howe repeated what had previously been said: "We ask you to relinquish a part, for which the Government will pay you. We are satisfied that it is impossible to protect you properly in any other way than by reducing the size of your reservation, and each one taking his own farm and receiving a paper [i.e., title deed] for it." Howe then bluntly stated: "If you refuse to accept it, we shall be compelled to close the Council and return home."

The chiefs asked to be allowed to retire in order to deliberate among themselves regarding what should be done. The request was granted. After an unspecified length of time, the chiefs returned and stated: "They could not relinquish their country or consent to reduce their Reservation to the size proposed by the Commissioners, but they would be willing to relinquish those portions where gold had been discovered and the place where Lewiston was situated."

Upon hearing this, the Commissioners "at once informed them that they could not entertain such a proposition." They were adamant. The Government was insisting that the reservation be reduced in size. The chiefs had no choice but to accept the terms dictated by Washington.

The Council reconvened Thursday morning, June 4, with Hutchins as the first speaker. He addressed his remarks especially to the anti-treaty chiefs. He pointed out the fact that "no power could prevent men from digging gold wherever they could find it." Then, speaking for the Government, Hutchins confessed that it was powerless to prevent the white men from overrunning the 1855 Reservation. He argued that the proposed smaller reservation "was well adapted to their wants, retaining for them one of the finest and richest bodies of land within their whole country." He insisted that, although the new reservation would seem small in comparison with the old, still it was "amply sufficient for all their wants."

Hutchins assured his hearers that they would be free to hunt, to fish, and to gather roots and berries where they pleased, even outside of the new reservation. They were to be as free as the Whites to travel through the country. "In concluding his remarks," wrote Secretary Whitworth, "he urged them to accept the propositions made, for the sake of their children, who were to be the most benefited, and assured them that if they did not, they were in danger of being utterly ruined and destroyed as a people, for the Whites will come in as thick as grasshoppers and crickets." He emphasized the desire of the Government to protect and preserve them as a tribe and urged them to accept the propositions made.

Whitworth then added in the minutes: "Two or three of the disaffected chiefs said a few words, but in such a haughty and inconclusive manner as to be unable to understand half of what was said." Eagle-from-the-Light complained: "You have talked without me." Hale responded by saying that he and the other chiefs had been invited to be on the grounds by May 10 and that the Council had not opened until the 25th, two weeks later than had been planned, and still they were late. The chief's complaint was, therefore, without merit.

Big Thunder, a tewat, brought up the religious issue. He opposed Lawyer because he was a Christian, although not at that time a member of the Mission Church. Hale answered by saying: "We have asked Lawyer and his party to go and settle the differences with you. Are you willing to try and settle it? There should be no difficulties between you as to your religion. No man should be required by others to give up his views on that manner. That is between him and his God."

However, the religious issue remained. The anti-Christian, the anti-treaty, and the anti-Lawyer parties were all factions of the same opposition party, and, judging by those who signed the 1863 Treaty, they were only a small minority.

The minutes of the meetings held on June 3 and 4 do not indicate that either Joseph or White Bird spoke. Evidently they sat in sullen silence. Sometime during these days, possibly on the 4th, when Joseph realized that there was no hope of having his Wallowa Valley included within the boundaries of the new reservation, he took the printed copy of the 1855 Treaty which he had and tore it into pieces and threw them at the feet of the Commissioners. This was his dramatic way of saying that he had completely lost faith in the integrity of the Government.

The tearing up of his copy of the 1855 Treaty was followed by an even more dramatic gesture when Joseph tore his copy of the Nez Perce Gospel of Matthew into pieces.[38] This symbolized his repudiation of the white man's religion which he had accepted on that very spot more than twenty-four years earlier and where he had been baptized and received as one of Spalding's first converts into the Mission Church. The Nez Perce Gospel which he tore up had also been printed on that

---

[38] John B. Monteith to Indian Commissioner, F. A. Walker, Aug. 27, 1872. Reference furnished by Dr. Merle Wells, Idaho Hist. Soc., Boise.

same site. Here was the beginning and the end of Joseph's acceptance of Christianity.

LAST DAY OF THE COUNCIL — FRIDAY, JUNE 5

Having been in session for almost two weeks, the Lapwai Council closed its deliberations on Friday, June 5. Joseph and White Bird had departed after being present for only a few days. Only three of the anti-treaty chiefs were present at this Friday meeting including Big Thunder, Red Owl, and Eagle-from-the-Light. The day was spent in open discussion with the Commissioners answering the complaints of the anti-treaty party.

Commissioner Hale opened the meeting this day by commenting on some of the incidental aspects of the Treaty which was about ready to be signed. Hutchins then spoke, addressing his remarks especially to the three anti-treaty chiefs. Hutchins bluntly accused Big Thunder of being a trouble maker.

> We know, [said Hutchins,] that you are striving to make your young men break the law. While your Head Chief, Lawyer, is a good man and has the respect of the Great Father, and has been doing all that he could to benefit his people, you have defied him, and tried to undo the good he has done. But you shall not poison the hearts of the other Nez Perces. The Government will protect them from your bad designs. . . You spoke a little yesterday, but you did not say much when you spoke. . . You spoke your tongue but kept your real words in your belly. . . We know that you understand us. . . but you answer us with crooked words.

Hutchins reminded Big Thunder that he had signed the 1855 Treaty and that immediately "you went home determined to break the law." Big Thunder was one who had refused to accept free beef and flour from the white men and then had spoken "contemptuously of the good Nez Perces who did accept them." Hutchins warned Big Thunder that the white men were "more numerous than grass on the hills," and then asked: "Do you think that your power is greater than the white man's? . . . Do you think that because you have refused the annuities, the beef and flour, that the Treaty is less binding on you? We tell you that this treaty is binding on you, whether you accept these things or not. Your refusal makes no difference."

Hutchins continued:

You have told the Nez Perces that when they take the blankets and clothing given them by the President, that they are putting their lands on their backs and when they eat the beef and the flour, that they are eating up their country. When you say that you lie. . . You have been trying to persuade the Nez Perces not to accept [the Treaty]. You have been giving them bad advice. Take our word for it, and time will prove it, Lawyer and his chiefs who wish the welfare of their people begin to see that it will be wise and good to accept our propositions.

Hutchins then laid down the ultimatum:

And if you do not choose to make the arrangements with them, we will make it without you. You will not be compelled to receive the benefits against your will. When the new arrangement is made, the good Nez Perces will be wise and rich and happy, you will be poor and miserable, and you will make your children poor and miserable. They will see that you have caused it, and when you are dead, they will curse you, because you did not secure these things to make them happy, as the wise chiefs did for their children.

Big Thunder did not have much to say in reply. Again, he questioned the authority of the Commissioners to negotiate a new treaty. He objected to the proposal that each adult Nez Perce man receive only twenty acres to farm.

I have never thought of living on so small a piece of land as that you have marked out for me," he said. "I can hardly get about on it. . . Let us have time to think about it. Mind! I don't say No! to your propositions; I want to think of it slowly. I do not take your goods or your provisions. I want to wait. Don't be in such a hurry. It is not for me to go in and join the other Indians, [i.e., Lawyer's followers].

Robert Newell, who served as a Commissioner at the conference held with the Nez Perces at Waiilatpu in March 1848 and who was in attendance at the Lapwai Council, then spoke emphasizing the fact that the Commissioners had come to Lapwai with Presidential authority. Then Big Thunder said: "I am very sick, and spitting blood, excuse me." Secretary Whitworth noted that Big Thunder then left the Council. He was followed by Red Owl.

Lawyer then spoke again:

No one doubts your power, [he told the Commissioners.] From

the time the law was passed, it was well known everywhere that you were the people to settle this matter up. Our Father in Heaven caused it for fear that we Indians would be blinded to our own interests. [Lawyer then quoted Governor Stevens who, stressing the inevitableness of the white man coming in overwhelming numbers, said: "Here is a law for you to keep; hold to it and observe it. It is to keep the Whites out of your country. . . My children hold to this law. We can assure you it is for your good. Now the wind blows, no one can prevent it; the crickets move along the grass, no one can impede their progress. The Government is desirous for you to hold on to the treaty and abide by it as the Americans will come here as thick as grasshoppers and crickets, and no one can stop them."

Lawyer, then turning to the Commissioners, said:

You will, I think, soon be going home. The Government will know how long we have been here. The records of this treaty will go back, and it will be well kept. My friends! I am poor, the Lawyer [39] is poor. . . You see the Whites all around me, and those at Lewiston, too. You see the many travellers that are going to the mines, and those that are there already. . . You speak of causing my people and children to settle down permanently. You know the size of the proposed reservation. Please add a little more to it, and make it a little larger. . . As long as the mountains exist, so long you must have pity on my children, till the end of the earth. Year after year, when I am dead and gone, you will remember what I have said.

Lawyer was bowing to the inevitable. He was a man of peace. He realized that it would be folly for the Nez Perces to resist the incoming white men by force. His moving plea for a larger reservation went unheeded. After Lawyer had concluded speaking, seven of his most loyal followers spoke. All endorsed what their Head Chief had said. In accepting the new treaty, each promised to adhere to its provisions.

Ute-sin-male-cum said: "I understand that the President and the Congress and all are working for our good. . . I am poor, weak, and feeble, both in body and soul. I throw myself on the protection of the law and the Government. . . What the Lawyer has said, that I accede to as much as though I had said it myself."

Spotted Eagle said: "I grabbed the law Governor Stevens gave us

---

[39] *See* Chap. i, fn. 13.

with both my hands, and held on to it fast. . .   The Whites are our friends as if from the same family and, therefore, let us not do anything that would harm each other. . .   I will not deviate from what Lawyer has said."

Billy: "It is not for us to turn from what you have told us, but for us to follow your advice and counsel. We want to settle down permanently. You talk with justice to us. I don't except to anything you have said."

Jason: "Governor Stevens . . .   brought us a law and told us to follow it. The things that were promised in the treaty, we have never seen. . .   I hope you will make the boundaries of the reservation a little larger."

Although Timothy and his band, who lived at Alpowa, were on land not included within the boundaries of the new reservation, special permission had been granted to them to remain where they were. Using expressions which reflected his knowledge of the Bible, he said:

> As the Lawyer says, be merciful to our children and see that they are attended to as long as the mountains stand. It is well for us to receive goods from year to year. We hunger and thirst after the right way to do good. Attend to us rightly; do justice to us, and it will be like meat and drink to our children. The preacher says, we must be bound in affection to each other. I have not long to live for the good of my children. . .[40] All the Whites know I have tried to do right and to obey the law. These are my feelings.

Captain John: "I will tell you my heart. My elders, my chiefs have talked; they are older than I and I cannot depart from what they have said. That is all."

Levi, a brother of Timothy:

> You make me frightened at so small a piece of land as you propose. . .   The country is very large with its mountains, rocks, and snows; there is no chance for farming on them and that's the way you frighten me. Lawyer says, make the boundaries a little larger and add a little more to it, that's what I say too. . .
> Governor Stevens promised to build us a church to worship in, also school houses for our children . . .   and we should have farms. None of these things are here. When I see the churches,

---

[40] Timothy lived for another twenty-eight years after the Lapwai Council. *See* Chap. v, fn. 20.

I shall know it is there; when I see the school house, I shall know it; when I see the proposed farm, my friend, I shall know it.

Answering the criticisms of some of the chiefs regarding the small side of the new reservation, which averaged 256 acres for each man, woman, and child in the tribe, Hale said: "You speak of it being small. We know it is large. If it is rightly managed, it will sustain twenty times the number of present Nez Perces. If we thought it too small for you, we would make it larger." Hale then drew attention to the fact that the Government intended to assign twenty acres of farm land to each adult male, and added: "Twenty acres is a large piece of land which we assign each of you to have." It should be remembered that in that generation, when a farmer used a walking plow and separated the wheat from the straw by a flail, twenty acres was about all that one man could handle. The treaty provided grazing and forest lands in addition to the farms.

Commissioner Hale closed the Council on this day by saying: "I understand you accept our propositions. I am satisfied you will never regret it. We have now to draw up the papers and make the final agreement." Hale then requested twelve of the leading chiefs to meet with him to clarify some minor points in the treaty. The Council then adjourned to meet Tuesday morning, June 9, 1863, for the signing.

The 1863 Lapwai Treaty — An Evaluation

The 1863 Treaty was signed on the appointed day. Following the signatures of the three Commissioners, Lawyer wrote his name, under which one of the secretaries noted: "Head Chief of the Nez Perce Nation." Then came the names of Ute-sin-male-cum, Ha-haich-tuesta (Billy), and forty-nine others, making a total of fifty-two. In addition to Lawyer, Levi also printed his name. All of the others made an "X" mark beside the names which had been phonetically spelled and inscribed by a secretary.

Not one of the five anti-treaty or anti-Lawyer chiefs signed. As has been noted, Joseph and White Bird had left several days earlier. The other three dissident chiefs — Big Thunder, Red Owl, and Eagle-from-the-Light — after telling Hale that they favored the treaty, since their lands fell within the boundaries of the new reservation, refused to sign simply because they were anti-Lawyer. No information is available to indicate how many subchiefs belonging to these dissident bands also refused to sign. Agent John B. Monteith, writing in 1878, stated that only twenty of those who signed the 1855 Treaty also signed in 1863.[41]

What happened to the thirty-eight who signed in 1855 but not in 1863? Among these were the five dissident chiefs who attended the latter Council but who either left before the signing took place or who remained and refused to sign. With these five might have been some subchiefs who had signed in 1855. During the eight-year interval between the two councils, a few, such as Looking Glass, had died. Perhaps another possible explanation to account for the difference is the fact that the Indians often had more than one name. The secretaries for the respective councils could well have differed in the way these names were spelled. Hence it is possible that Monteith's statement that only twenty who signed in 1855 did so in 1863 is well below the actual number.

As has been stated, Lawyer was given an American flag in the spring of 1848 in recognition of the services he rendered the Oregon Volunteers in their efforts to apprehend those guilty of the Whitman massacre. Lawyer was inordinately proud of that flag. He carried it at the head of the long procession of his followers as they approached the council grounds at Walla Walla in May 1855. Again, he carried the flag where he and his warriors rode to the relief of Colonel Steptoe when the latter was retreating from his defeat by the northern Indians in May 1858. We have references in contemporary writings to him flying his flag from a pole in front of his home in Kamiah in his old age. Displaying the flag in processions or before his home was to Lawyer a visible symbol of his position as Head Chief.

Without a doubt, the flag was flying from a pole in front of Lawyer's house at Lapwai when the 1863 Council met. Possibly it was Newell who noticed that the flag, which he had given to Lawyer at Walla Walla in March, 1848, was out-of-date. Four more states had been added to the Union during the intervening years. And perhaps it was Newell who suggested to the Commissioners that a new flag with thirty-four stars be given to Lawyer. Extant is a picture of Lawyer's grandson, Corbett Lawyer, holding a flag with thirty-four stars.[42] The flag is still treasured by one of Lawyer's descendants.

[41] *Report of Commissioner of Indian Affairs,* 1877, p. 214.

[42] Corbett Lawyer, as an employee of the Indian Bureau, had his office in Moscow, Idaho, during the 1930s when I was serving as pastor of the First Presbyterian Church of that city.

Following the closing of the Lapwai Council, Lawyer and one of his chiefs known as Captain John visited Portland, perhaps making the trip down the Columbia River with Commissioner Hale and his party. Writing on June 15, 1863, Judge M. P. Deady passed on the following news to Senator J. W. Nesmith:

A treaty was concluded with the Nez Perces on the 9th, except Big Thunder. . . Lawyer and one of his staff, Capt. John, came down. They were at church today. Came home with us and paid us a visit of state L[awyer] said Big T[hunder] did not amount to much. He only had three chiefs, while he L. had 46. L. speaks pretty good English, walks with a cane . . . and I think prides himself more upon diplomacy than war.[43]

After returning to his home in Olympia, Hale wrote his official report dated June 30, 1863, to which several references have already been made. Regarding the reduced size of the new reservation, he wrote: "The boundaries . . . as fixed in the Treaty embrace within them about three fourths of the whole tribe and at least two thirds of the disaffected bands." According to this estimate, if the tribe numbered 3,000, then about 700 Nez Perces were excluded from the new boundaries, but this number included some of the friendly bands as Timothy's at Alpowa. Hence the number in the disaffected bands under Joseph and White Bird could not have been more than 450.

Hale also wrote:

From the accompanying map will be seen at a glance the relative difference in size between the new and the old reservations, the latter having covered an area of ten thousand square miles . . . while the former is reduced to a little over twelve hundred square miles. The amount thus relinquished is very nearly six million acres, and at a cost not exceeding eight cents per acre, when all expenses present and prospective on the ratification of the treaty shall have been met.

Lacking a proper survey, Hale like his predecessor Stevens, had grossly underestimated the extent of the 1855 reservation. As has been stated, the best available estimate is that it contained 23,666 square miles.[44] Since the reduced reservation contained 1,188 square miles, this means that the Nez Perces relinquished about 14,386,000 acres

[43] Original letter in O.H.S.   [44] See Chap. v, fn. 36.

rather than the 6,000,000 of Hale's estimate. And on this revised estimate, the cost to the Government would have been .034 cents per acre
rather than eight cents. Of course, this went for administrative expenses
and was not considered to be a purchase price.

How did the white people react to the terms of the new treaty?
Perhaps a story which appeared in the June 10, 1863, issue of the
Oregon Statesman would correctly reflect the majority opinion. The
unidentified reporter, who was at Lapwai during the meeting of the
Council, noted:

> It looks as if every mother's son who can get within cannon-shot of
> this rude Indian-American Congress, votes himself a "special" and
> straightway gets off a page or two . . . concerning the same.
> . . Mr. Injun is represented by two diplomats, namely — Lawyer
> and Big Thunder. The former, as his title indicates, is a Greek,
> [i.e., a tricky fellow], of much tongue and cunning. He owes his
> position to the Whites. . . On the contrary, Big Thunder holds
> his rank by hereditary right and prowess in arms. . . With such
> rival influences at work among the natives, negotiations make slow
> progress. Besides, haste is no special object with the Indians. As
> they are doubtless averse to giving up their country under any
> circumstances, they naturally adopt the tactics of the weak and
> unwilling, and seek every protest for delay. . .
> The Indian must yield, and he might as well have been treated
> as a child and told to go at once, however it may clash with our
> abstract notions of justice and philanthropy. In the providence of
> God, the Indian's day of possession has passed, and there is noth-
> ing left for him but to die or get out of the way of the stronger
> race. From the time that Joshua led the tribes of Israel into the
> land of the Canaanites to the present day, it has ever been so in
> the history of the world, and, for aught we can tell, will always be
> — at least this side of the millenium.[45]

These blunt, harsh words were true. The Indian's day of possession
of large tracts of country had passed. The white man, with his vastly
superior numbers, his military might, and his technological skills was
destined to dominate the red man. In the history of the United States,
we find no just or equable solution of the so-called "Indian problem."
Divided into many tribes, some numbering only a few hundred speak-

---

[45] From o.h.s. Scrapbook, No. SB, 112, p. 41. Reference furnished by Paul
Hovey, Portland.

ing many different languages, and scattered over the expanse of the continent from the Atlantic to the Pacific, the Indians were either killed or forced onto reservations. The Nez Perces were meeting the common fate of their red brethren.

LAWYER, CRITICIZED AND DEFENDED

Opinions among the Nez Perces and some historians are sharply divided as to whether Lawyer should be censured or praised for his willingness to sign the 1863 Treaty, which excluded Joseph's band and others from the new reservation.

A prime example of the bitterness felt by the anti-treaty Nez Perces towards Lawyer is found in an article written by Duncan McDonald which appeared in the June 7, 1878, issue of the *New North West,* published in Deer Lodge, Montana. McDonald's mother, a Nez Perce, was a sister of Eagle-from-the-Light. He was also a relative of White Bird. This explains in part his anti-Lawyer and anti-treaty sympathies. It should be remembered that McDonald was writing about a year after Chief Joseph's surrender in August 1877, at Bear Paw Mountain in Montana. The memories of that disastrous event were fresh in his mind when he wrote.

McDonald made the claim, often repeated to this day, that Lawyer was selected by Governor Stevens in 1855 to be Head Chief of the Nez Perces because he was a pliable tool in the white man's hands. McDonald wrote:

Lawyer, recognized by the Indians as a tobacco cutter [a sort of under secretary] for the chiefs Looking Glass, Eagle-of-the-Light, Joseph and Red Owl, was the chosen man. In other words, for certain considerations he was prevailed upon to sign away the rights of his brethren — rights over which he had not the slightest authority — and, although he was a man of no influence with his tribe, the Government, as in duty bound on account of his great services, conferred upon him the title and granted him the emoluments of Head Chief of the Nez Perces. The feelings of the Indians were at that time aroused to such a pitch of indignation that they at first determined to hang their new superior, but, as with them, so often has been the case, milder counsels prevailed, and indifference and contempt took the place of revenge.

McDonald then told of a discussion which Young Looking Glass [46] had with some Crow chiefs in 1876, about a year before the Chief Joseph uprising took place. McDonald quoted Looking Glass as saying: "I, Looking Glass, Eagle-of-the-Light, and Joseph's father were the ones who wanted to hang Lawyer for signing treaties with Governor Stevens.

"What right had he, or authority, to sign treaties? He does not belong to the blood. He is the offspring of a foreigner.[47] We blame him in signing the [1855] treaty. But he was not half as bad as Stevens. What right had Stevens to put Lawyer at the head of a nation that really does not belong to him? . . . We don't want any treaties."

The criticisms and aspersions by McDonald and Looking Glass against Lawyer have been echoed by more recent critics. These critics have focused more on what they consider to be the injustices of the 1863 Treaty than on that of 1855. An example of this is found in a quotation ascribed to the late Sam Lott, also known as Many Wounds, who in a letter addressed to Senator Burton K. Wheeler, then Chairman of the Committee on Indian Affairs in the U.S. Senate, wrote: "This treaty of 1863 is false and without jurisdiction; it was made for all the Nez Perce people by the few who represented the Upper Tribesmen when no Lower people were represented." [48]

Slickpoo and Walker, in their *Noon Nee-Me-Poo (We, the Nez Perces)*, referred to the 1863 Treaty as the "sell out" treaty and Lawyer as the "Red Judas," [49] a traitor to his own people.

Josephy, in his *The Nez Perce Indians*, passed the same judgment: "The [1863] treaty was a fraudulant act on the part of both Lawyer and the Commissioners. On the one hand, Lawyer and his followers had no right to sign away the lands of other bands, and they knew it." Josephy claims that the Commissioners were following "a time-worn and deceitful procedure for extinguishing the title to Indian lands when the rightful owners refused to sell," and that "Joseph and the other consignatory bands outside of the new boundary lines literally had their lands sold from under them by Lawyer." [50]

---

[46] Following the death of Looking Glass, Senior, in 1863, the son took his father's name. Hereafter all references to Looking Glass will be to the son, who was one of Young Joseph's chief lieutenants. He was killed at Bear Paw Mountain just before Joseph surrendered in October 1877.

[47] Called a "foreigner" because Lawyer's mother was a Flathead Indian.

[48] Slickpoo and Walker, *Noon Nee-Me-Poo*, p. 149. No date was given for the letter. Actually some chiefs from the Lower Nez Perces were at the Lapwai Council but they did not sign the treaty.   [49] *Op. cit.*, p. 154.   [50] *Op. cit.*, p. 430.

In defense of Lawyer, it should be stated that he never claimed that he and his followers were signing for the non-treaty chiefs, even though the Commissioners and other Government officials may have assumed that this was the case. As far as Lawyer was concerned, persuading the dissenting chiefs and their bands to move onto the reduced reservation was the Government's problem, not his. Establishing the comparatively small 1863 Reservation was not Lawyer's idea and, as has been indicated, Lawyer repeatedly begged the Commissioners at the 1863 Council to give a larger area.

Dr. Merle Wells, Director of the Idaho Historical Society, Boise, has written in defense of Lawyer. Wells points out that the Nez Perces were divided into four main bands at the time of the 1863 Council. The bands at Lapwai and Kamiah constituted the Upper Nez Perces, while those along the Salmon River and in the Wallowa Valley were the Lower Nez Perces. When the United States Government decided that the 1855 Reservation had to be reduced drastically in size, action was taken without consulting with the Indians.

Wells wrote:

> . . . the Whites insisted that the Kamiah and Lapwai groups make room for the lower Snake and Salmon-Wallowa bands to move in with them on a smaller reservation. Lawyer, as head chief, was expected to work out the details and gain assent of the other Indian leaders. This he could not do, even if he had wanted to. . .
>
> Lawyer had no interest in bringing a lot of rival bands to his village areas, nor could he have gotten them to agree to come even if he had tried to convince them that they should. . . Under these awkward circumstances, no one could negotiate any longer for the entire set of four band groups.

Upon the refusal of Joseph and White Bird and their subchiefs to sign the 1863 Treaty, Lawyer remained as Head Chief only of the Treaty Indians.

> Although he has been criticized, [wrote Wells,] as having sold out lands of the non-treaty bands to the Whites, he knew that he could not do this, and pointed out in later years that he had done no such thing. . . After all the new treaty was something needed by the United States — not by the Indians. . . Nothing that Lawyer nor the other Indians could have done could have

changed the situation in any significant way.   .   .   So there is no point in blaming Lawyer or other treaty leaders for signing the new treaty.[51]

OLD JOSEPH'S CHOICE LED TO WAR

Who chose the wiser course — Joseph or Lawyer? Let the history of what happened during the following fourteen years, 1863 to 1877, pass the final judgment. The best criterion for making that judgment is to compare the fate of the non-treaty Indians with those led by Lawyer. The story of the Chief Joseph uprising of 1877 has been frequently and fully told. But, in order to appreciate the full disastrous consequences of the policies followed by both Old Joseph and Young Joseph, it is necessary to summarize the events leading up to the 1877 uprising and the war itself.

It is true that Old Joseph and the other chiefs, whose lands were not included within the new reservation, had a far more difficult decision to make than did Lawyer and his followers who lived within the new borders. However, the fact remains that by refusing to sign the 1863 Treaty, Old Joseph started a chain of events which led to the 1877 uprising which levied a tragic toll of property loss and human suffering on all who took part.

The 1863 Treaty was not ratified until April 17, 1867. For the next ten years the non-treaty Indians were denied all of the benefits promised in the 1863 Treaty such as annuities, schools, mills, clothing, farm utensils, and white assistants as teachers and craftsmen. As will be noted, many of these benefits were delayed in being paid to the treaty Indians but eventually the promises made by the Government were fulfilled.

Being assured by the terms of the 1863 Treaty that the Wallowa and Grande Ronde valleys were then in the public domain, the u.s. General Land Office sent in surveyors to open the land for white settlers. This came after the treaty had been ratified in 1869. Old Joseph then realized that serious trouble was brewing.

By 1869, Old Joseph was nearly blind. Before he died in August, 1871, he is reported to have told his eldest son, then about thirty-one years old, whose Indian name was Hin-mah-too-lat-kakht (Thunder Traveling to Loftier Mountain Heights): [52] "When I am gone, think

---

[51] *Reference Series, No. 462,* June 1968, Idaho Hist. Soc.
[52] Josephy, *The Nez Perces,* p. 447.

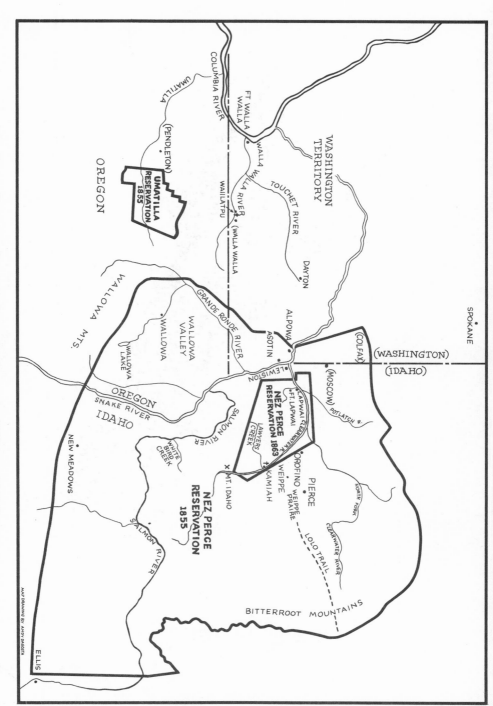

NEZ PERCE COUNTRY, SHOWING BOUNDARIES OF THE 1855 AND 1863 RESERVATIONS
Based on official records, and maps shown in Josephy's *The Nez Perce*

MAP DRAWING BY ANDY DAGOSTA

of your country. You are the chief of these people. They look to you to guide them. Always remember that your father never sold his country. You must stop your ears whenever you are asked to sign a treaty selling your home. A few years more, and white men will be all around you. They have their eyes on this land. My son, never forget my dying words, This country holds your father's body. Never sell the bones of your father and mother." [53]

Upon the death of Old Joseph, the son took his father's name and followed his father's policy of refusing to accept the terms of the 1863 Treaty. Young Joseph was fighting a losing battle, for the white settlers with their herds of cattle were moving into the Wallowa and Grande Ronde valleys in ever increasing numbers. Tensions between the Indians and the Whites sometimes climaxed in killings. As long as Young Joseph continued to resist white encroachments on land that he considered belonged to the Indians, conflicts and even bloodshed were inevitable.

General Oliver Otis Howard,[54] who had assumed command of the U.S. Army's Department of the Columbia with headquarters at Fort Vancouver in September, 1874, was under orders to force Young Joseph and his band to move onto the Lapwai Reservation. In a desperate effort to find a peaceful solution, Howard summoned Joseph and other non-treaty chiefs to meet with him and Indian Agent John B. Monteith at Lapwai during the first week of May 1877. Responding to the invitation were Joseph, his brother Ollokot, Young Chief of the Cayuses, White Bird, Looking Glass, and a chief who played an important role in the 1877 uprising, Toohoolhoolzote, a follower of the Dreamer religion, which had been preached by the Yakima prophet, Smohalla.

General Howard and Agent Monteith made their last appeal for the dissidents to move onto the 1863 Reservation. Faced with their adamant insistance that this be done, Joseph finally consented. Howard gave him only thirty days to move all of his people with their possessions and livestock onto the reservation. Before starting back to his home, Joseph inspected some sites along Lapwai Creek where his band might settle but he found nothing suitable. He then told Howard that perhaps he would settle on the upper Clearwater near where Looking Glass lived. The non-treaty chiefs left for their homes on May 15.

---

[53] *Ibid.,* p. 450.

[54] General Howard lost his right arm in the Civil War battle at Fair Oaks, Va.

The members of Joseph's band, especially the young warriors, were bitter when they heard that their chief had decided to move onto the reservation but, obeying orders, they began the trek to Lapwai. On June 13, while Joseph and his people were encamped on the Idaho side of the Snake River, still a few miles outside of the Reservation, one of Joseph's young warriors and two from White Bird's band slipped out of camp for the Salmon River country in order to wreak vengeance on some Indian-hating settlers. They killed three white men that day. The war had begun.

Joseph and his brother Ollokot happened to have been absent from the camp at the time of these killings. Upon their return, they were horrified to learn what had happened. In the meantime, some sixteen hot-headed young warriors of White Bird's band, roused by a desire to avenge reputed atrocities inflicted on Indians by the white settlers, set out on a rampage of lootings and killings. The orgy continued for two days during which time some fourteen or fifteen Whites were killed.

General Howard, then at Fort Lapwai, was stunned by the news of the Salmon River massacres. He immediately ordered two troops of cavalry to round up the hostiles and force them onto the reservation. The soldiers met the Indians in a skirmish in White Bird Canyon on June 17 and were roundly defeated. The troops suffered a loss of thirty-five officers and men killed, one-third of the command. The Indians had only three of their number wounded. An important effect of the conflict was the capture by the Indians of sixty-three rifles and a large supply of ammunition.

Joseph deplored the killings. Essentially, he was a man of peace but now forced by circumstances, he became a man of war. Following the skirmish in White Bird Canyon, the non-treaty Indians under the leadership of Joseph, Looking Glass, Ollokot, and Toohoolhoolzote began an amazing 1,500 [55] mile trek which took them over the Bitterroot Mountains, following the Lolo Trail, then down through the Bitterroot Valley, back and forth over the Continental Divide three times, through what is now Yellowstone National Park, then down Clark's Fork and across the Yellowstone River, across the Musselshell River and the Missouri River, and finally to Bear Paw Mountain where

[55] Estimates vary as to the length of the trek. This figure of 1,500 miles was given to me by my friend Jack Lincke, Pasadena, who made a horseback ride over the trail from White Bird Canyon to Bear Pay Mountain in 1928.

Joseph and the remnant of his band surrendered on October 5. The trek lasted about three and one-half months and has gone down as one of the greatest military achievements in American history. Joseph failed, by only a few days' march, to find refuge in Canada.

Accurate statistics are lacking as to the exact number of Nez Perces who made this astonishing journey. Estimates as to the number who left Idaho vary from 650 to 750 men, women, and children. The Indians had to abandon their herds of cattle when they started on their trek but took with them an estimated 3,000 horses nearly all of which were either killed or captured. The fleeing Nez Perces were pursued by General Howard, who was often several days behind them. Other units of the U.S. Army confronted the Indians in Montana, so that about 2,000 regular or volunteer soldiers were involved in the pursuit. During the retreat, Joseph's warriors fought a series of eight battles or skirmishes and won all but the last.

During these engagements, the Nez Perces suffered heavy casualties for, according to a reliable estimate, sixty-five men were killed and fifty-five women and children, making a total of 120 which was about 16% of their total number.[56] Among those killed were Ollokot, Looking Glass, Toohoolhoolzote, and Joseph's wife and infant daughter. White Bird escaped and fled to Canada. We have no figures to indicate how many of the Indians were wounded.

Following Joseph's surrender on October 5, 1877, the Government sent the captives, including 87 men, 184 women, and 147 children to Oklahoma, where most of them spent the next eight years in captivity. An unknown number of the Nez Perces succeeded in escaping to Canada. Contemporary records tell of the incredible sufferings endured by the captives while in Oklahoma. During captivity at least two hundred of them, especially children, died of malaria and other diseases.

The Government also paid a heavy price for the uprising. Losses among the U.S. troops included 180 killed and 150 wounded. The financial cost, including that of maintaining the remnants of Joseph's band in exile, ran into the millions of dollars.

Finally in May 1885, the Government permitted the survivors to return to Idaho. One hundred and eighteen went to Lapwai where they received a mixed welcome. Those who were followers of the

56 Joseph, *The Nez Perces*, pp. 632-3.

Dreamer cult were not welcomed. The larger group of the former exiles, numbering about 150, were sent to the Colville Reservation where some of their descendants remain to this day. Joseph went with this group. He died at Nespelem on September 21, 1904, being then about seventy-four years old.

Who chose the wiser course? Old and Young Joseph or Lawyer? The long chain of tragic events which followed the refusal of Old Joseph to move onto the 1863 Reservation, a decision which Young Joseph accepted for about six years, resulted in the surviving members of the Wallowa band being rendered destitute, having lost their great herds of cattle and horses. They suffered incredible sufferings and hardships while on their long trek into Montana. Hundreds of the band were killed, wounded, or died in captivity. In the end, the remnant was obliged to move onto reservations.

By contrast, the treaty Nez Perces, numbering about three-fourths of the tribe, remained under Lawyer's influence, even though he had passed away at the time of the uprising, and were at peace with the Government. With but few exceptions, none of the treaty Nez Perces joined in the rebellion. If we take as our standard of judgment the well-being of the people, then the conclusion is clear — Lawyer chose the wiser course.

CHAPTER EIGHT

Grievances of the Nez Perces

The eight years which elapsed between the close of the 1863 Lapwai Council and April 24, 1871, when John B. Monteith became Indian Agent at Lapwai, were marked by repeated Government failures to meet its treaty obligations. During the first two years of this period, the Government was involved in the Civil War, which may have accounted in part for the fact that no annuities were paid to the Nez Perces for about four years beginning in 1862. By May, 1866, the amount of arrears came to about $38,000.00.[1] This failure to receive his promised annual salary of $500.00 was especially hard on Lawyer who, because of his wounded hip and advanced age, was unable to cultivate the land which had been allotted to him.

Another complicating factor, which added to the frustrations experienced by the treaty Indians and especially by Lawyer, was the fact that during these years six different men served as Indian Agent at Lapwai. J. W. Anderson, who was Agent at the time of the 1863 Council, terminated his service at the end of that year and was succeeded by James O'Neill, who had been employed at the Agency as a tinsmith since 1861. According to one authority: "The beginning of O'Neill's regime marked the beginning of a period of miserable agents that would last until 1871. Most of them did as little as possible for the Indian and stole as much as they could get away with." [2]

Josephy wrote:

The cheating of the treaty bands continued year after year. Indian agents came and went at Lapwai. Each one complained about the

---

[1] A. L. Downer to Commissioner of Indian Affairs, May 9, 1866. O.I.B.

[2] Thompson, *Historic Resource Study*, p. 98.

irregularities and defalcations of his predecessors, and each one departed with Nez Perce money. James O'Neill, the agent from 1864-1868, absconded with $10,000. Lieutenant J. W. Wham, who served in 1869 was accused of scandalous frauds, and so was Wham's successor, Captain D. W. Sells.[3]

Even though Lawyer complained about the Government's failure to fulfill its treaty obligations, those to whom he complained could always blame others. Lawyer was often taunted by the non-treaty Indians, and there was nothing that he could do except to continue to protest to anyone who would listen.

Spalding Appointed Government Teacher

One of the immediate results of the 1863 Lapwai Council was the appointment of Henry Spalding as teacher for the Lapwai school by Commissioner Hale and Agent Anderson. Spalding's first wife, Eliza, had died at Brownsville, Oregon, on January 7, 1851. Besides her husband, she left four children ranging in ages from four to thirteen. On May 15, 1852, Spalding married Miss Rachel Smith, whose letters in the Oregon Historical Society show that she had had only a limited education. Rachel proved to be a devoted wife during the remaining twenty-one years of Spalding's life.

Reference has already been made to the comments expressed by Agent Anderson regarding the enthusiastic welcome given by the natives to Spalding when he returned to his old mission station to serve as an interpreter in the council. Regarding the reaction of the people when they heard that Spalding was to remain at Lapwai as a Government teacher, Anderson wrote: "They seemed most pleased at the prospect of having a school started amongst them & also of having a minister who could preach to them in their own language." [4]

Perrin Whitman was also employed at the Lapwai Agency following the closing of the council as interpreter. Friction developed between Spalding and Whitman which was a contributing factor in Spalding's dismissal in 1865. Spalding's school at Lapwai was not a success. This is not surprising in view of the fact that at that time there was no schoolhouse or suitable textbooks. Possibly Spalding conducted his

---

[3] Josephy, *The Nez Perces*, p. 437. Quotation used with permission.

[4] *Executive Document, No. 37, U.S. Senate, 41st Congress, 3rd Session,* 1871, p. 7.

classes in an Indian lodge or even in the out-of-doors. Due to lack of suitable housing for himself and his wife at Lapwai, the Spaldings found it necessary to live in Lewiston.

GOVERNOR CALEB LYON OF LYONSDALE

President Abraham Lincoln appointed Caleb Lyon, who usually signed his name with the additional words, "of Lyonsdale," [5] in 1864 as Governor of Idaho Territory. Lyon was a pompous, erratic man who curried favors with extravagant promises which he rarely was able to fulfill. Lyon was in Lewiston, then the capital of the Territory, in the summer of 1864 when the Legislature was in session. On Sunday, August 21, he attended a church service conducted by Spalding when some sixty Nez Perces, including Lawyer and Timothy, were present. Evidently the meeting was held in the largest available public hall, possibly the one then being used by the Legislature.

The San Francisco *Pacific* [6] for October 6, 1864, carried an account of the service from which the following has been taken:

> Services were opened with prayer, and then for want of hymn books, the Indians had to do the singing, although the house was crowded, not one of the white portion of the congregation had a hymn book, yet all of them educated and brought up under Christion influences.
>
> The highest officers of the Territory were present. His Excellancy, Gov. Lyon, the Hon. Judge Smith, Prosecuting Attorney of this District, Sheriff of this county, and Clerk of the 1st District Court, and a large portion of the citizens of the place, yet no hymn book. What a rebuke to you, to your Federal officials, to come here to be taught the true spirit of the Christian religion by the poor benighted Indians, with their hymn books printed in their own language, at Lapwai in 1841, by Mr. Spaulding's own hands. Through how many scenes have these books passed. Had they the power to speak, what could, what would they say to us? . . .
> He has educated them so that they can read and write . . .
> their women taught to weave by Mrs. Spaulding — the backs of the hymn books are made of cloth of her manufacture.

---

[5] Lyonsdale was probably a small community in Oneida County, N.Y., but is not now shown on any maps.

[6] The *Pacific* was a weekly Congregational-Presbyterian publication, San Francisco.

Surely this unknown reporter must have been writing with tongue in cheek, for what politician would carry his hymn book, if he had one, to a meeting of a legislature? If by some strange set of circumstances, this should be the case, which of the many denominational hymnals would be used?

The most significant reference in this quotation is to the Nez Perce hymnal which was printed on the mission press at Lapwai in 1843.[7] This consisted of thirty-two pages and contained both translations of familiar gospel hymns of that day and original Spalding compositions. Among the songs was the Lord's Prayer, put to the tune usually associated with "How Firm a Foundation." The reference to the little books being bound in cloth of Eliza Spalding's manufacture is most significant. Whitman and Spalding had imported sheep from Hawaii. The versatile Spalding made a spinning wheel in 1840 and had a loom in operation by August 1841. This was the only loom in the Mission.

Singing Christian songs became an essential part of the private devotions conducted by the Christian Nez Perces after the Spaldings were forced to leave their Lapwai home in December 1848. Reference has already been made in a previous chapter of this book to Kip's observations of how the Christian Nez Perces, who attended the 1855 Council, were singing the songs that Spalding had taught them.[8]

The reporter's eyewitness account continues:

> After Mr. Spaulding had concluded his sermon, the Indians sang, and Lawyer, the head chief, prayed; then Timothy, a subchief, spoke for some time in their own language; he spoke on the subject of breaking the Sabbath.[9] After singing another hymn and pronouncing the blessing, they were dismissed, when Lawyer asked permission to address Governor Lyon, which was granted, and the

---

[7] Although the imprint date on this item was 1842, yet Spalding in his diary entry for February 23, 1843, stated that he was then still at work on the hymnal. Drury, S. & S., p. 332.

[8] My interest in Nez Perce history began when, as pastor of the First Presbyterian Church of Moscow, Idaho, I attended a meeting of Walla Walla Presbytery at Walla Walla, where I heard a choir of these Indians sing from memory some of the songs in their native language which had been taught their forefathers by H. H. Spalding.

[9] The members of the Whitman-Spalding Mission laid great emphasis on the observance of Sunday, or the Sabbath as it was then called. According to the Puritan tradition, a Christian should refrain from all unnecessary work and travel on Sunday and spend extra time in worship. This was the outward sign of being a Christian.

accompanying remarks made by Lawyer and Timothy, as well as Governor Lyon's reply, which [follow].

LAWYER'S SPEECH, "GRIEVANCES OF THE NEZ PERCES"

As Lawyer sat in the audience in that crowded hall in Lewiston on that Sunday in August 1864, he realized that he had a golden opportunity to speak on the grievances of the Nez Perces to a select audience, such as he had never had before. The most important officials of the Territory, including Governor Lyon, members of the Legislature, and many of the county officials were present. Moreover he had with him about sixty of his most faithful followers who, according to Nez Perce custom, would voice their approval of what he had to say not by clapping hands, as did the white people, but by uttering a loud series of "aahs." It was a dramatic setting.

According to the newspaper account, Spalding acted as interpreter. Evidently someone who knew shorthand, possibly a court reporter, was present and took down the speeches of both Lawyer and Lyon, which were later published. Through the public press, Lawyer reached a larger audience than had ever before been possible. The first appearance of his speech was in the August 27 issue of Lewiston's *Golden Age* under the title: "Grievances of the Nez Perces. Speeches of Shadow of the Mountain [10] or Lawyer (Head Chief) and Gov. Lyon at Lewiston, Idaho, August 21st, 1864." This reappeared as a broadside, a copy of which is in the Beinecke Rare Book and Manuscript Library of Yale University; and, as stated above, in the October 6, 1864, issue of the *Pacific*. Finally, it appeared in the 1960 fall issue of *Idaho Yesterdays*.

In his introductory remarks, Lawyer referred to the four Nez Perces who visited General Clark in St. Louis in the fall of 1831 in quest of the white man's religion. He summarized the many times the Nez Perces had cooperated with the Government in the Indian wars of 1848-58. The main thrust of his speech was the faithfulness with which the Nez Perces had helped the Government, in sharp contrast to the failure of the Government to fulfill its treaty obligations.

Lawyer's speech, somewhat abbreviated, follows:

> This is the twenty-first day of August. Formerly myself and people were miserable, yet long ago my people sent to the East and in

---

[10] No other reference to Lawyer's name as meaning "Shadow of the Mountain" has been found and the use of it here is unexplainable. *See* Chapter i for a discussion of Lawyer's Indian name.

answer to that petition came Mr. Spalding and Dr. Whitman and from them we got an idea of the Holy Bible and the Testaments, and our people learned from them that the white man's religion was good. But those that were first instructed have about all passed away. Ellis was our head chief at the time of his death and when he was dying his instructions to us were to follow that religion.

Some years ago Governor Stevens and General Palmer met us in Council. Governor Stevens came . . . and what he said to us was understood to be the law. Many tribes and many people were in attendance and we were many weeks in Council. They addressed us as children of the Great Father. Governor Stevens said: "While I speak to you, the Great Spirit is watching over us, and knows what we say. I therefore want you to understand that. I dare not lie and what I say is the eternal truth."

Continuing to quote Governor Stevens, Lawyer said:

Therefore, we ask of you, Lawyer, as head chief of the Nez Perces, for a portion of unoccupied lands for the Whites to dwell upon and the first proposition we make you, as a compensation, we promise you a preacher, a schoolhouse for the benefit of all the children, a flouring mill, a saw mill, farmers, gunsmith, blacksmith, physician, teachers, and an agent and everything that is necessary to carry these on, and over the whole a Superintendent. This we pledge and it shall be faithfully fulfilled to the letter. There is a boundary for the reservation and the Americans shall never enter to settle.

At this point in the transcription, the secretary noted that Lawyer called upon his people to testify as to the truth of what he had said, and they responded with a chorus of "aahs."

Lawyer then stated that the Nez Perces had received the 1855 Treaty as "a sacred thing, and they laid hold of it as we would to life." He then quoted Stevens as saying:

We must hold on to this treaty as we would upon a firm foundation in time of flood and storms, and that if you do not accept our proposition, we must remind you that the Americans are like the rivulets of an oncoming flood that are increased by the melting snows; or the commencement of those black crickets that come in swarms and destroy the vegetation and blacken the whole earth. Nothing can stop the white people; therefore, it is of the greatest importance that you receive this treaty.

I stand here, as it were, naked so far as these promises are ful-filled. We fought with Major Haller,[11] with Colonel Wright, and Colonel Steptoe, and with the latter our blood was mingled with yours, and when defeated, had not Timothy and Levi conducted they out of the country, they would have all been killed.[12]

Upon the defeat of Colonel Steptoe, they [i.e., the Americans] called upon us for help. I furnished them warriors and their sub-sistance. I have spoken you my whole heart.

Lawyer then bluntly stated that if the Nez Perces had known that the provisions of the 1855 Treaty would never be fulfilled; "we would never have consented to the treaty."

Lawyer referred to the several killings which had taken place — Whites killing Indians and Indians killing Whites. "There have been several of our men killed by white men lately on the Salmon River," he said, "and our cattle and horses have been stolen by the Whites." Lawyer admitted: "I know of two of our men that have killed white men. There have been six of our men killed by the Whites and many wounded."

Lawyer concluded by saying: "I show both sides of the question." And again he called upon the Nez Perces present to give their approval, which they did. Then turning to Governor Lyon, Lawyer added: "You, as our Superintendent, I have now hopes of, may the Great Spirit keep you straight. I look to you for a church and schoolhouse and to supply the mills for our benefit for which myself and my people will express our gratitude."

In his closing remarks, Lawyer used the illustration of an elephant. "I have heard of an elephant," he said, "which, from the description, I suppose it to be a powerful animal. Doubtless if I take hold of his ears, he will not obey. I am confident that the master can lead the elephant. This Nez Perce Agency is that animal. I trust you can lead the elephant. I show you my heart. . . This is all I have to say."

Timothy then arose and said: "What our head chief has said, we all say Amen. You could not expect him to speak long, for he is very weak. There is but few of us here but what has been said, you can rest as-

[11] *See* Chap. vII, fn. 31.

[12] Some writers have cast doubt on Timothy's reported role in rescuing Colonel Steptoe and his men from their entrapment by hostile Indians at Rosalia in May 1858. Here, however, Lawyer, speaking only six years after the event, clearly indicates that Timothy and Levi did save the Steptoe command from annihilation.

sured, is the sentiment of all." Timothy then turned to the Nez Perces present for confirmation and they responded with their chorus of "aahs." Timothy continued: "As an apology for Lawyer, I will state that he had been wounded fighting for the Whites in the hip which has never gotten well, and is now very bad and it will probably cause his death."

GOVERNOR LYON'S REPLY

Governor Lyon, as the second Governor of Idaho Territory, was also Commissioner of Indian Affairs. His reaction to Lawyer's speech on the grievances of the Nez Perces was, therefore, awaited with considerable anticipation. What would he do to correct the injustices? Not being well informed as to the basic facts of the situation, Lyon spoke only in generalities.

He began by saying:

My ears have been open to what you have said. I am glad you have shown me your whole heart. The Great Father in Washington desires that you be hastily and honestly dealt with. . . I regret that you have not had the entire benefit of the grist and saw mills, a schoolhouse, and a doctor to reside among you to attend your sick, and other provisions of that treaty. These matters shall be attended to.

I regret that any of the Nez Perces have been killed by the early settlers and sorrier that any white men have been killed by the Nez Perces, but bad men on both sides breed bad blood.

Then turning to Lawyer, the Governor said:

Persuade your people to cultivate the soil for its cultivation, you shall not know hunger. The Government wants you to think it honorable to work with your hands. . . Idleness and a roving predatory life is the crooked trail that leads over the barren plains of want to the rocks of starvation, and ends in the fearful precipice of disease and death. Teach your young men to avoid whiskey drinking which is a great curse to the white men as well as to the red men.

Then addressing Lawyer with the rarely used name of "Aleiya," [13] Lyon continued: "I have seen with my eyes the still open wound that you have received thirty years ago while fighting against the Blackfeet

---

[13] *See* Chap. v, fn. 33 for comment on the name "Aleiya."

for the Boston [i.e., the American] men. Such services are never forgotten. The Great Spirit loves the brave. . . May you live to see
the Nez Perces a united, civilized, and industrious nation." Then, referring to the stenographer who was taking down all that was being
said, Lyon concluded his remarks: "The talk is in black and white and
the Great Father in Washington will hear what has been said this
day.[14] I have done."

Governor Lyon promised Lawyer and Spalding that he would visit
Lapwai the next day to make a personal inspection of the Agency.

GOVERNOR LYON'S INDICTMENT OF CONDITIONS AT LAPWAI

Upon Governor Lyon's arrival at Lapwai, he was given a petition
signed by Perrin Whitman and a few others, which begged the Governor to dismiss Spalding as teacher at Lapwai. It so happened that
Lyon came from Oneida County, New York, which was the home
county of the first Mrs. Spalding. This was one reason why Lyon became friendly with Spalding. No doubt, also, Lyon had been most
favorably impressed by Spalding's service at Lewiston the previous
day.

Regarding the fate of the Whitman petition, Spalding wrote: "[Lyon]
told the petitioners that he wanted no instruction about Mr. Spalding;
he knew him, and turning to me, he threw his arms around my neck
and exclaimed, 'You are the father of this country and the apostle of
this people, and you shall have a place here for life if you wish.'"

Lyon then demanded that Spalding be given the best quarters available on the grounds, that his orchard be fenced, that the schoolhouse
be restored, and then ordered the erection of a stone church on the
site of the meeting house that Spalding had built in 1843. The Governor declared that he would have inscribed over the entrance of the
church the names of Spalding and Whitman. "Truly," wrote the
exultant Spalding, "this great revolution in my favor is the work of
God. . . Lincoln [who had appointed Lyon] has redeemed himself
in my estimation."[15]

Following the Governor's assurances that funds would be made
available to pay for labor and materials, work was commenced on a
stone and adobe church with interior dimensions of 30 x 50 feet. The

---

14 The original report is in O.I.B., National Archives.
15 Drury, *Spalding*, p. 380. Original letter in Whitman College.

building was also to be used as a schoolhouse. A number of Indians labored for several months hauling large stones to the site and raising the walls, three feet thick at the base, to a height of sixteen feet.[16] Only adobe was used as mortar to hold the stones together.

The church was never finished. The erratic Governor fled the Territory in April 1866, taking with him over $46,400.00 in Agency funds. Agent O'Neill, in his report for 1865, stated that the Indian laborers, who were poor men, could not understand why they had never been paid the $1,185.00 due them. In time the adobe disintegrated or was washed away by the rains, and the walls gradually collapsed. Lacking an experienced stone mason and proper mortar, the ill-conceived project was doomed to failure from the very beginning. The ruin was long known as "Lyon's Folly." [17]

After inspecting the conditions at Lapwai on the Monday, August 22, 1864, following the church service mentioned above, Governor Lyon wrote a scathing indictment of the conditions as he found them at Lapwai. Lyon listed thirteen principal points for criticism. His first indictment was: "I find no schoolhouse, church, and no Indians under instruction." Here was a criticism of both Agent O'Neill and Spalding. A schoolhouse had been started in 1863 but was not finished by the time Lyon visited the site, yet Spalding was receiving a Government salary as a school teacher. In another reference to the lack of a school, Lyon wrote: "I find the wife of one of the Employees set down on the [payroll] papers as a Blacksmith, and the wife of another Employee stated to be an assistant Teacher who has never taught a single hour." These were but samples of the gross misappropriations of funds intended for the benefit of the natives.

Lyon was especially critical of the way the Whites had cut timber on the reservation without official permission, had the logs sawed into lumber at the Agency mill, and the lumber then sold to settlers at Lewiston who were in desperate need of building materials. In the days before barbed wire, the Indians needed boards for fences to protect their crops. Lacking boards, Lyon noted that the Indians had improvised fences out of brush.

Lyon accused the Agency employees, who had been hired to show

---

[16] Thompson, *Historic Resource Study*, p. 102.

[17] Some of the stones used in the building of the walls could still be seen a few years ago along the old highway, a couple of hundred yards south of the cemetery.

the Indians how to farm, of living in indolence, not even raising food for their own subsistence. "I find," he wrote, "there is neither a gunsmith nor wagon maker nor tin shop on the Reserve," although such had been promised in the 1855 and 1863 Treaties. Before James O'Neill was appointed Agent at Lapwai, he was listed on the payroll as a tinsmith, although he knew nothing of that occupation.

In concluding his report, Lyon wrote:

> I find nothing but criminal negligence and indifference as to the Treaty stipulations . . . by a majority of those at the Agency. I found great discontent among the Indians owing to such state of affairs and those of the tribe who did not sign the Treaty, it is observable that they are buying all the powder and lead they can find the means to pay for. . . Liquors are sold to the Indians in large quantities.

All of the grievances mentioned by Lawyer in his Lewiston speech were given confirmation by Governor Lyon. Moreover, Lyon in his report listed other instances of mismanagement, gross inefficiency, and misappropriations of funds not mentioned by Lawyer. How strange! He who castigated others for malfeasances in office himself a few months later became an embezzler of Nez Perce Agency funds.

Spalding Dismissed

In 1864 the Territorial Legislature passed an act which removed the capital from Lewiston to Boise. Being aware of the waning influence of Governor Lyon and knowing that his office had been moved to Boise, Agent O'Neill in September 1865 did what he had long wanted to do, he dismissed Spalding. For the second time, Spalding was obliged to leave his mission station. Nearly eighteen years earlier, he and his family had fled to Fort Walla Walla in fear of their lives because of the Whitman massacre. Now at the age of sixty-two, Spalding had to leave Lapwai for a double reason — the unfriendly attitude of Agent O'Neill and his own apparent failure to succeed as a teacher. In all fairness it should be noted that part of Spalding's difficulties as a teacher arose out of the lack of a schoolhouse and having no suitable textbooks.

Writing to Secretary S. B. Treat of the Mission Board in Boston on November 15, 1865, Spalding poured out the following account of his troubles: "I am starved and crowded out; every possible annoyance both by Whites and Indians. . . salary cut off and back salary not paid for two years. Only one little room for self and wife to live, to sleep, cook, eat. . .It is a shameful disgrace to the Black Republican party and to the Amer. Govt."

As soon as it became known that Spalding had left, a Catholic priest tried to establish himself at Lapwai. Of this he wrote to Treat: "The Priest told the Lawyer, head chief, 'As Mr. Spalding has not collected your children and taught them and has done you no good, you had better let us come as your missionaries.' The Lawyer made no reply. The P. urged him again and then a third time, when the Lawyer replied, 'Yes, I am the chief and it is for me to say, and I do say. . . You cannot come. I do not like your religion. We will not have it." [18]

Here is evidence that Lawyer retained the anti-Catholic attitude which had been implanted in him by the missionaries — Smith and Spalding in particular — during the early years of the mission period.[19] It was not until 1873 before the Catholics secured permission from the Department of Indian Affairs to erect a Catholic Church on the Nez Perce Reservation. Father I. M. Cataldo, a Jesuit, was in charge of this mission known as the Slickpoo Mission.

CONTEMPORARY REFERENCES TO LAWYER

Several contemporary references to Lawyer deserve to be included in this biography as they give fine appraisals of the chief in the prime years of his life. Thomas Donaldson, in his *Idaho of Yesterday*,[20] evidently drawing upon personal observations made sometime during the years 1865-70, wrote:

> Three other interesting men were Jason, Lawyer, and Timothy, leaders of the Nez Perce tribe and well-known to the Whites. Old Lawyer, tall and dignified, clad in broadcloth and an eternal silk hat, always attended the opening of each term of the territorial court at Lewiston. It was quite interesting to see Lawyer walk gravely in after the court was opened, bow to the bar, and extend his right hand to the judge. Then the judge would politely wave Lawyer to a seat of prominence. Lawyer's entrance and the courtesy always accorded him by the court, had good influence or effect

[18] American Board archives, Harvard Univ. has original letter.
[19] *See* Chap. II, under "Lawyer and the Roman Catholics."
[20] Caxton Press, Caldwell, Id., 1941, p. 23.

among his tribesmen; they considered him a part of the ceremonies and a man of authority with the palefaces.

Donaldson then referred to the fact that Lawyer was the son of the Nez Perce chief "with whom Lewis and Clark left their horses when they started toward the coast." The reference here is to Chief Twisted Hair, mentioned in Meriwether Lewis' Journal for May 4, 1806.

A second quotation from a contemporary writer worthy of inclusion comes from *An Illustrated History of North Idaho*.[21] The writer gives the following analysis of Lawyer's abilities and character:

> Another force in strengthening the friendship between Americans and Nez Perces was the commanding influence and rare ability of the Head Chief, Halhaltlosot, known among the Whites as Lawyer, on account of his ready wit and repartee. Wise, enlightened, and magnanimous, the head chief, yet one of the poorest of his tribe, stood head and shoulders above the other chiefs, whether in intellect, nobility of soul, or influence.
>
> His force of character and innate ability enabled him to overcome poverty and loneliness of birth and to achieve, while yet in middle life, the first place among his people. He used his influence for the amelioration of the tribe, directing his initial efforts against the two chief vices then obtaining — gambling and polygamy.
>
> *He has the distinction of having been the only western Indian possessed of sufficient statesmanship to discern that no resistance to the power of the Whites could avail anything, and that the wise course for his race to pursue was to adopt the white man's mode of life and live in amity with him.*[22]

Here is the finest contemporary statement of Lawyer's political philosophy that I have been able to discover.

In a letter addressed to the Commissioner of Indian Affairs dated January 24, 1866, Caleb Lyon reported: "In a letter from Agt. O'Neill, he states that he had paid Lawyer his salary for the year ending Dec. 31st, 1865, and that Lawyer was disappointed by not receiving Gold. He had purchased goods on credit and the amount in legal tender notes was not enough to liquidate such purchases." Lyon felt that Lawyer should be paid in gold or its equivalent, "considering the peaceful relations he and his people have sustained towards the Government." Because of the difficulties of exchange, legal tender notes were sometimes discounted as much as 50% in Idaho Territory.[23]

---

[21] Western Publishing Co. (n.p.), 1903.
[22] *Op. cit.*, p. 128. Italics the author's.   [23] O.I.B.

During the first week of May 1866, A. L. Downer, a special investigator for the Commissioner of Indian Affairs, visited Lapwai. Writing from the Agency on May 9, Downer reported: "The Head Chief Lawyer, being an aged man and not owning horses to do his farm work, is dependent upon the Agency to have his ten acres of land ploughed annually and prepared to raise crops, which is done for him by the farmers of the Agency."

Downer also reported: "There has not been any distribution of the yearly annuities . . . since 1862, making due them, including the present year, the appropriations for four years of about $38,000.00. This is a source of great dispute and inconvenience to them." Agent O'Neill, writing on July 20, 1866, a few weeks after Downer had written, stated that up to that date, Lawyer's pay was $625.00 in arrears and that his last quarterly payment received of $125.00 had to be discounted up to 50% because it had come in voucher form rather than in gold. "Yet," wrote O'Neill, "with all these things staring him in the face, his [i.e., Lawyer's] faith in the Government is as strong as ever, and not for him alone but for such chiefs as Ute-sin-male-cum, Spotted Eagles, Captain John, Three Feathers . . . and others." 24

AN APPEAL TO PRESIDENT LINCOLN

The eight-year period, following the ratification of the 1855 Treaty in 1859, was marked by so many failures of the Government to fulfill its promises that even Lawyer began to lose patience. Hearing that his friend, Dr. George H. Atkinson, pastor of the First Congregational Church of Portland, was planning to go East in the spring of 1865, Spalding suggested to Lawyer that he write a letter to President Lincoln and have Atkinson deliver it. We know that the Spaldings had taught Lawyer to read and write his own language. Two of his letters, written in 1867 and 1874, to which references will be made, have been located in the National Archives. These show that Lawyer was able to write in Nez Perce, printing out each letter much as a child would do today.

An account of Lawyer's appeal to President Lincoln is found on the front page of the San Francisco *Pacific* for June 14, 1866. The news item is signed with the letter "A", which was the way that Atkinson, then the Oregon correspondent of the *Pacific*, signed his articles. It reads:

On my visit to the East last year, I carried a long and well writ-

24 O.I.B.

ten letter from Lawyer, Head Chief to President Lincoln, with a translation by Mr. Spalding. But President Lincoln had been assassinated [April 14, 1865]. The letter was forwarded to President [Andrew] Johnson. Lawyer pleaded only for justice according to the promises of the treaties which had been made for them. A.

All efforts to locate this letter in the archives have failed.

LAPWAI COUNCIL OF JUNE, 1867

Following the ratification of the 1863 Treaty by the U.S. Senate on April 17, 1867, the Commissioner of Indian Affairs sent Special Agent, George C. Hough to Lapwai to notify the Nez Perces of the action of the Senate and to assure them that the Government intended to fulfill all of the treaty stipulations so long delayed. Hough went on a goodwill mission. He arrived at Lapwai on June 8. Lawyer at once sent out word to the chiefs, headmen, and others to assemble at Lapwai as soon as possible. By the 21st about 1,500 Nez Perces had gathered, including some of the non-treaty Indians. In his letter to the Commissioner of Indian Affairs in Washington dated June 27, 1867, Hough stated that forty-five of those who signed the 1863 Treaty were present.

Hough also reported:

The Nez Perces have for some years been divided [that is, Treaty and non-Treaty], about two-thirds of the tribe going with Lawyer, and the other third with Big Thunder (who died last January) and they being left without any Chief of sufficient intelligence and strength are gradually falling in with Lawyer. Red-Heart and Eagle-from-the-Light, and their bands numbered from three to four hundred souls, being now the principal ones to hold themselves aloof.

Hough made no mention of Young Joseph.

The Council opened on Friday, June 21, and continued until the following Tuesday, June 25. Perrin Whitman served as interpreter. Timothy was called upon to open each daily meeting with an invocation. This custom of opening council meetings with prayer was followed by the Nez Perces for years, often to the surprise and amazement of visiting Government officials.

According to the minutes of the meeting, which are on deposit in the National Archives, Judge Hough, in his opening remarks, paid the following tribute to Lawyer:

The President of the United States thinks a great deal of Lawyer. He believes him to be a good man, a very good man, and while he has always maintained friendly relations towards the United States, he invariably looks out for his people, and the President says he will take care of Lawyer and all other Indians who keep the treaty and the laws.

Nothing was accomplished at this Council except for an exchange of views and a deeper awareness on the part of Government officials as to the growing discontent among even the treaty Indians because of the continued failure of the Government to fulfill its promises. Judge Hough took note of this and said that one reason for the Government's failure was its necessity to give its attention and its resources to winning the Civil War. Regarding the misappropriation of funds by former Governor Lyon, Hough said: "The Government has sued Governor Lyon and he will be punished for not doing his duty." The Government was never able to recover the stolen funds.

Spotted Eagle, who had led a company of thirty Nez Perces in support of Colonel Steptoe, and who had lost a son in that engagement, told Judge Hough how the Treaty Indians had been taunted by the non-Treaty because of the Government's failures to fulfill the treaty obligations. Spotted Eagle claimed that the non-Treaty Indians had enticed some members of his band to join them.

Lawyer, at the Monday meeting, expressed his fears that the Reservation would be encroached upon by the Whites. Characteristic of the way he referred to himself with personal pronouns, I or me, he said: "Me, the old man looked upon the treaty as being broken by the Whites, which was made by the President. Me, the old man, notwithstanding everything, feel inclined to live by treaties." Lawyer repeated his fears that the 1863 Reservation was too small. "I, myself, the old man," he said, "would like to restrain the country as large as it was. . . The reservation is too small for us to settle." Referring to the unpaid annuities and also to the unpaid claims for horses supplied to the troops, Lawyer said: "When we hear the jingle of that money, we shall know it is here."

In reply, Judge Hough said: "In 1855 your country was too large, altogether out of proportion to your requirements." The Judge insisted that the 1863 Reservation was ample for all their needs. He said: "With the farms that each will have according to the Treaty of 1863, you will be able to raise ten times as much as you do at present." And the Judge insisted: "You are mistaken in reference to there not being land enough. There is not more than 600 of you that would work farms if you had them, and there is abundance of country for 1,000 farms. In fact, I feel assured that there is enough ground for every man to have two farms." It should be remembered that Hough was referring to the twenty-acre farms stipulated in the 1863 Treaty.

Lawyer remained skeptical and in his closing speech said: "The Treaty of 1855 has not been lived up to, and we have no faith that this [the Treaty of 1863] will be lived up to." These were disturbing words for Judge Hough to hear for if Lawyer, the Government's staunchest friend among the Nez Perces, felt that way, what would be the attitude of the non-Treaty Indians?

In his closing remarks, Lawyer looked into the future and wondered what future generations would say about him. He remarked: "I sometimes wonder what the future generations . . . will say in reference as to how I conducted my chieftainship. But after the years have gone by . . . a retrospective view of the past can be taken and [then some can] say how I, the Lawyer, did and . . . what kind of a law Lawyer kept when he was living." At this point, the secretary, who was keeping the minutes, noted: "Ah! ah! ah! ah! from the masses."

FOLLOWERS OF THE DREAMER CULT AMONG THE NEZ PERCES

The recorded proceedings of the June 1867 Council throw some interesting sidelights on the practices of the followers of the Yakima prophet, Smohalla, who were known as Dreamers. Just before the Council closed its sessions on Saturday afternoon, June 22, Ute-sin-male-cum, addressing his remarks to Judge Hough, referred to the fact that the next day would be Sunday and then, pointing to some Nez Perce Dreamers present, said: "Tomorrow . . . these people will fix themselves up in their feathers and trappings and sit around in squads. What makes them do it? Some of my people take an interest in their mode of doing and whether they are right or wrong, I wish you would tell me. I am a God fearing man."

Judge Hough had already taken note of the presence of some Dreamers and evidently disapproved of their practices. In his opening remarks before the Council on the following Monday morning, the Judge said: "Chiefs and Head Men of the Nez Perces, I understand that some of you are in the habit of conjuring and dancing around for religious rites on Sunday. Now this mummery does not amount to anything but is in truth sacrilegious. The sooner you abandon this the better for you. Do as your elders and chiefs advise and worship God in a proper spirit and reverent manner."

Smohalla, the founder of the Dreamer cult, was born about 1815, a member of the Wanapun band of Indians who lived along the Columbia River at Priest Rapids. He has been described as having been short, bald-headed, and a hunchback. He was known to be an eloquent speaker, having the power of self-hypnosis. He claimed to have had visions and from such mystical experiences to have received his messages. Hence the name Dreamer. During the Dreamer worship services, drumming was kept up almost continuously. Smohalla called on his followers to abandon the customs of the white man and return to the ways of their Indian ancestors. He exercised such a hypnotic effect on his hearers that he is reported to have had some 2,000 followers by 1872.

According to Josephy, all members of Joseph's band in the Wallowa were considered to be followers of the Dreamer cult.[25] This religious difference became another divisive force which widened the rift already existing within the Nez Perce nation. In addition to the treaty and non-treaty and the Lawyer and anti-Lawyer parties, which in reality were but two designations for the same factions, there now was the Christian and anti-Christian groups, the latter of whom were often called "heathens." [26] In reality the three "anti" parties coalesced into the anti-Lawyer faction.

HOUGH'S FINAL REPORT AND RECOMMENDATIONS

Writing from Lapwai on June 27, 1867, two days after the council had closed, Judge Hough passed on to N. G. Taylor, Commissioner of Indian Affairs in Washington, some pertinent observations regarding the explosive situation then existing within the Nez Perce nation together with his recommendations.

Hough had the following to say about Lawyer:

---

25 Josephy, *The Nez Perces*, p. 436.

26 The use of the term "heathen" to designate the non-Christians was introduced by the missionaries but it passed into common usage. The term is even found in some official documents emanating from the Lapwai Agency. I recall hearing the word used without any special opprobrium by some Nez Perces themselves when I lived in Idaho, 1928-38. It was just a synonym for a non-Christian.

Lawyer is getting old, being sixty-six years of age,[27] but he is a man of no little intelligence, a little education, and a consummate diplomat. He is now, and ever has been, a fast friend to the Government, but he informed me that his patience is getting worn out. He says every officer of the Government comes here with his mouth full of promises, but the promises are seldom fulfilled, and the annuities have not been paid for years. Yet the Government expects him to keep a wild and turbulent people at peace and on good terms with the Whites. . . I regret to say that even Lawyer, Capt. John, and Spotted Eagle have lost nearly all of their faith in the Government fulfilling the Treaty stipulations of 1855 and 1863.

Hough noted that among those who supported Lawyer's policy of cooperation with the Government were "those who have large droves of cattle and horses." The capitalist system had penetrated into the Nez Perce tribe and, for a few who were relatively rich, the acculturation was complete. They wanted to maintain the status quo. They would have nothing to do with the Dreamers or with the non-treaty party who often threatened to go to war against the Government.

Hough warned the Government officials:

I do not hesitate to say that in the event of an outbreak among the Nez Perces, they will take all of the adjacent tribes with them. I feel assured that Lawyer, Capt. John, Spotted Eagle, Ute-sin-male-cum, and many others of the older men who own large droves of cattle and horses, will do all in their power to prevent it. But of course, you with your knowledge of Indians know that however popular a chief may be with his people, he cannot always restrain them, particularly when they can throw it up to him that the Whites have not kept their word. . . And I again urge upon the Department the absolute necessity of immediately sending Agent O'Neill the necessary funds to pay the back annuities under the Treaty of 1855.

LAWYER VISITS WASHINGTON, D.C.

Frustrated by his repeated failures to induce the Government to live up to its treaty obligations, Lawyer decided to appeal directly to the President of the United States. Mention has already been made of the

---

27 If we accept Monteith's statement that Lawyer was born in 1796, then he would have been seventy-one in 1867 instead of sixty-six. Lawyer carried his years well in spite of the unhealed wound in his hip.

THE 1868 NEZ PERCE DELEGATION TO WASHINGTON WITH THEIR WHITE ADVISORS
Seated: Timothy, Lawyer and Jason. Standing: unknown, Robert Newell,
Perrin Whitman, unknown. One of the unknowns is Indian Agent James O'Neill.

NEZ PERCE CHIEF TIMOTHY
A signer of the 1868 treaty.
An 1868 photo by A. Z. Shindler, Wash., D.C.
Courtesy of the Smithsonian Institution.

Novembr 20 1867

1 ...

2 ...

3 1855 Cov Stevens ...

4 ...

Lapwai, November 20th 1867

To the President of the United States and others of the Government — I look upon you as being my Great Fathers. You my fathers who have the control of myself & people, listen to the few words I write to you. Have pity on me, the Lawyer. I show up to you that long ago Lewis & Clarke passed through our Country. Since that time we have ever had a strong friendship for the Whites. And in 1855 Gov. Stevens & Genl Palmer made a treaty with us. Myself the Lawyer will never put at naught laws or treaties. Myself the Lawyer am anxious to visit Washington with an Interpreter & one or more of my Chiefs. Have pity on me and give me permission to do so at the expense of the Government. These are words from Hd's Chief Lawyer

Lapwai Idaho Teritory

LAWYER'S LETTER TO PRESIDENT ANDREW JOHNSON, NOVEMBER 20, 1867
From the original in the National Archives, Washington, D.C. See text p. 247.

Office Nez Perces Ind Agency
Lapwai Nov 20 1867

Sir

For several months Lawyer has expressed a desire to visit the States, I have told him to try & get some of his people to sell a few horses enough to pay his expenses & that of some of his chiefs, but they refused to do so, the influence the Nez Perces have over the surrounding tribes is very great, they are looked up to by the Spokans Cœur d'Alenes Cayuses Umatillas & Flatheads and a visit of Lawyer & some few of the other leading chiefs would be very beneficial, the expense in going, to leave here next Spring via Fort Benton & down the Missouri would be but little, the return would probably be heavy, trusting I may be able to lay your answer before them soon

I have the honor to be Respectfully
Very Respectfully
Your obt St Sant
James O'Neill
U S Ind Agt

Hon N G Taylor
Commissioner of Ind Affs
Washington DC

INDIAN AGENT O'NEILL'S ENDORSEMENT OF LAWYER'S LETTER

letter he sent to President Lincoln written in the spring of 1865. Since this letter reached Washington after Lincoln's assassination, it was turned over to President Johnson but, so far as is known, there was no response. At that time President Johnson had other more important matters on his mind — that of pursuing what he believed would have been Lincoln's policies of reconstruction following the Civil War.

Following the unsatisfactory Council of June 1867, Lawyer decided that, if his expenses could be covered, he would go to Washington and make a personal appeal to the President and other officials concerned, in behalf of the Nez Perces. He approached Agent O'Neill with his proposal. According to O'Neill's letter of November 21, 1867, (*see* illustration) Lawyer was told "to try and get some of his people to sell a few horses, enough to pay his expenses and that of some of his chiefs, but they refused."

Lawyer then felt moved to write to the President and ask for expense money. This he did in a letter dated November 20, 1867, written in the schoolboy style of printed letters taught him by the Spaldings. (*See* illustration) The translated text follows:

Lapwai, November 20, 1867

To the President of the United States and others of the Government.

I look upon you as being my Great fathers. You, my fathers, who have the control of myself & people. Listen to the few words I write to you. Have pity on me, the Lawyer. I show up to you that long ago Lewis & Clark passed through our Country. Since that time we have ever had a strong friendship for the Whites. And in 1855 Gov. Stevens and Gen. Palmer made a treaty with us. Myself, the Lawyer, will never put at naught laws or treaties. Myself, the Lawyer, am anxious to visit Washington with an interpreter & one or more of my Chiefs. Have pity on me and give me permission to do so at the expense of the Government. These few words from Head Chief Lawyer.[28]

Lawyer's appeal brought favorable results. No doubt Judge Hough's warning about the growing resentment among the Treaty Nez Perces aroused some apprehension in Washington. The officials there did not want another Indian war on their hands. They still had vivid memories of the terrible Sioux uprising of 1862 when more than 800 settlers and

[28] O.I.B.

soldiers were killed in Minnesota. Word was sent to Agent O'Neill inviting him, Lawyer, and several of his chiefs to go to Washington in the spring of 1868 with all expenses paid by the Government.

Lawyer chose three of his closest friends — Timothy, Jason, and Ute-sin-male-cum — to accompany him. There was a difference of opinion regarding the choice of an interpreter. O'Neill wanted Perrin Whitman; Lawyer preferred Robert Newell. It was finally decided to take both. Fortunately for our story, Newell's unpublished diary, which he kept on this journey, is extant. From it we get a day-by-day account of their experiences while traveling and while in Washington.[29]

Since it was not practical to travel east by the overland route, the O'Neill party found it necessary to go by sea. According to Newell's diary, he boarded a river steamer at Lewiston on March 27, 1868, and arrived in Portland on the evening of the 31st. O'Neill, Whitman, and the four Indians took a later steamer for they did not reach Portland until April 2. The presence of the four Nez Perces attracted the attention of a reporter from the *Daily Oregon,* who wrote the following account of their visit for the April 3 issue of that paper:

> Yesterday afternoon, Messrs. James O'Neill and Perrin B. Whitman, with a delegation of Nez Perce chiefs, arrived here en route to Washington City. The names of the chiefs are Lawyer, Ute-sin-male-cum, Timothy, and Jason. Lawyer is the chief of all the Nez Perces and is a man of great shrewdness and influence. The delegation are going to Washington in compliance with instructions . . . to consult in relation to the pending unsettled affairs . . . growing out of the treaties of 1861 [*sic*] and 1863. . . We predict for the party a continual sensational ovation from the moment of landing in New York.

The party sailed from Portland for San Francisco on April 12. They arrived on the 16th. Newell noted in his diary on the 14th that Ute-sin-male-cum and Jason got seasick. While in San Francisco, Newell called on a number of old friends including Dr. Elijah White, who in 1842 had persuaded the Nez Perces to adopt a code of laws. The party left San Francisco on the 22nd and arrived at Panama City, May 6. The Isthmus was crossed in one day, and on the 7th they set sail for New York City where they arrived on the 14th. The voyage, including the lay-overs, had taken four and one-half weeks.

---

[29] See reference to this diary in "Sources and Abbreviations."

Newell, pushing on ahead of the others, arrived in Washington on May 15. O'Neill and the four Indians spent a day sightseeing in New York, so did not reach Washington until the 16th. As predicted by the Portland reporter, the four Nez Perces did create a sensation wherever they went. Newell, writing in his diary on May 19, noted: "The people stare at the Indians." Also, on that same day, he wrote: "Went to market with Timothy and Jason who were surprised to see the throng of people & vegetables." The sights and wonders of three sea voyages, of the trip through the jungle across the Isthmus, and then the marvels of such great cities as New York and Washington were tremendous experiences for these four chiefs who came from the wilderness of Idaho.

On May 22, Newell wrote in his diary: "Ute-sin-male-cum, the Indian, quite sick." On the 25th, he added: "Ute-sin-male-cum died today of Tyfoid fever." By a strange twisting of facts, McWhorter in his *Hear Me My Chiefs* wrote that Ute-sin-male-cum incurred the wrath of Nathaniel Taylor, the Commissioner of Indian Affairs, because he refused to sign the new treaty which Taylor had drawn up for the Nez Perces. This is false, as we learn from Newell's diary that during the ten-day interval between the arrival of the Indians in Washington until the death of Ute-sin-male-cum, the Nez Perces had had no opportunity to discuss the terms of the new treaty with any Government official.

McWhorter also wrote that because Ute-sin-male-cum had refused to sign the treaty and had spoken strongly against it, "he was shoved from a high window and killed." McWhorter claimed that he got that story from Timothy after he had returned to his home.[30] Attributing the story to Timothy gives further evidence of McWhorter's anti-Lawyer and anti-Timothy bias.

Newell, in his diary entry for May 26, noted: "Ute-sin-male-cum buried at the Congressional Ground. Four carriages attended by Friends." The Congressional Cemetery is located east of the Capitol on the bank of the Anacosta River. It served as the Government's national cemetery before Arlington Cemetery was opened during the Civil War.

While serving as a Navy chaplain in Washington following World War II, I visited the cemetery and located the grave of the Nez Perce

[30] *Op. cit.*, p. 113.

chief who had died far from his home in Kamiah, Idaho. The small headstone bore the inscription:[31]

UTESINMALECUM

McWhorter, in his comments about Ute-sin-male-cum, makes one statement which seems to be correct. He writes: "Nathaniel Taylor, or his agent, gave Lawyer, Timothy, and Jason whiskey. Ute-sin-male-cum would not drink." Newell in his diary, June 18, wrote: "Lawyer got a little tight." And again for August 11: "Lawyer, Timothy, and Jason got tight last night." Since the officials in the Indian Department were exasperatingly slow in working out the details regarding the desired amendments to the 1863 Treaty, the three Nez Perces had lots of idle time on their hands. The weather was miserably hot and humid for weeks. They were in a strange city with no friends. Consequently it is easy to imagine how some of the members of the Indian Department would try to entertain their guests by taking them to a bar. The temptations of the capital city were just too much for the uninitiated chiefs who, in their Idaho homes, were known for their strict views on temperance.

Newell was an Episcopalian, which he listed in his diary entry for June 20 as "my favorite denomination." His diary shows that he was most faithful in attending an Episcopal Church whenever he could. On June 7, while in Washington, he wrote: "Went to Trinity Church in forenoon. . . [took] Lawyer and Timothy. After the service was over, each spoke to the congregation." On Sunday, August 9, he wrote: "In the evening, took a walk with Lawyer. A beautiful evening. The Indians had worship in my room. We all went to bed about nine o'clock."

The Lawyer party happened to be in Washington at the time of the impeachment trial of President Andrew Johnson by the U.S. Senate. On May 26, Newell noted in his diary: "The result was acquittal." On June 1, Newell and the Nez Perces called on the President. "We had a good time," Newell wrote, "and proud of our visit." In a number of diary entries, Newell made mention of Senator H. E. Corbett of Oregon. For instance, on June 8, he wrote: "Saw Mr. Corbett with O'Neill and the Indians. Quite a talk about our mission and the non-compliance

---

[31] Audrey W. Jones, Superintendent of this Cemetery, in a note to me dated May 20, 1977, stated that the "Utesinmalecum" grave is in Range 221; site 75. He lies buried next to a Sioux Indian, named Scarlet Crow.

of Treaty stipulations." Lawyer was so impressed with the Senator that when a grandson was born to his son James, Lawyer persuaded the parents to call him Corbett.[32]

Newell showed the Indians the sights of the city. On June 17, he wrote: "Went with Lawyer to the Senate Chamber; went to the Department of the Interior; visited about generally. Many strangers were in town. It is wonderful how people do come and go to Washington City." On June 29, Newell and his Indian friends called on General Grant, whom Newell described as being "a quiet, reserved man, and looked well for a man who is to be run for President." As will be noted, after Grant became President he instituted what came to be known as the "peace policy" which dealt with the administration of the various Indian Reservations by church denominations. This greatly affected the Nez Perces.

Sometime while in the capital city, the three Nez Perces, and their white friends, Newell, O'Neill, Taylor, and Whitman visited a photographic studio and had their pictures taken as a group.[33] (See illustration) Both Timothy and Jason had their pictures taken wearing native dress, and each with a peace pipe. Timothy had another taken in ordinary civilian dress.

O'Neill, who had served as Indian Agent at Lapwai since January 1, 1864, had come under criticism by the spring of 1868 for inefficiency and even for misappropriation of funds.[34] While in Washington, Newell learned that the Department of Indian Affairs was planning a replacement for O'Neill, so he decided to seek the appointment. Newell induced the three Nez Perce chiefs to sign a petition asking the President to appoint him. President Johnson accepted the recommendation and on July 22 forwarded his name to the U.S. Senate for confirmation. The Senate approved. Newell assumed his duties when he returned to Lapwai on October 1, 1868. For the first time in the history of the Lapwai Agency, the Nez Perces had an agent who could speak their language.

Progress with the Department of Indian Affairs regarding the supplemental treaty to that of 1863 was exasperatingly slow. Newell wrote in his diary on August 10 that the Department was "the slowest place

[32] See Chap. vii, fn. 42.

[33] Photos taken by A. E. Shindler Studio, Washington, D.C.

[34] Josephy, The Nez Perces, p. 457: "James O'Neill . . . absconded with $10,000."

in the world to do business." Finally on the 13th, the treaty was ready for signatures. Nathaniel G. Taylor, as Commissioner of Indian Affairs, signed first, followed by Lawyer, Timothy, and Jason and then by two members of the Department and Robert Newell. This was the fourth treaty that Lawyer had signed as Head Chief. In each case, he signed first. Two of the treaties were of major importance — 1855 when fifty-eight chiefs and headmen signed, and 1863 when forty-seven signed with Lawyer. The two treaties of lesser importance came in 1861 when fifty-one signed with Lawyer, and then the Washington treaty of 1868 when only Lawyer and two others signed.

The Washington Treaty was short, consisting of only three Articles. The first dealt with the survey of certain lands within the 1863 Reservation which were then not under cultivation. Article II dealt with timber rights on the Reservation. Article III stated: "It is further hereby stipulated and agreed that the amount due said tribe for school purposes and for the support of teachers that has not been expended for that purpose since the year 1864, but has been used for other purposes, shall be ascertained and the same shall be reimbursed to said tribe by appropriation by Congress." [35]

The 1868 Treaty was ratified on February 16, 1869. In addition to the provisions above noted, the Nez Perces, through their personal intercession with high Government officials, let it be known that the stipulations in the treaties of 1855 and 1863 would have to be honored or there would be serious trouble even with the Treaty Indians. Subsequent events proved that the Government heeded the warning. The back annuities were paid and other provisions were fulfilled.

THE RETURN TRIP

Newell and the three chiefs decided to return to Lapwai by the overland route. They boarded a train in New York on August 26. After taking some stop-overs along the way, they arrived in Chicago on September 1. They were in Omaha by the next morning. Since Newell made no mention in his expense accounts of the four using a "sleeping car," it seems evident that they sat up each night while traveling.

After leaving Omaha, the Union Pacific railroad roughly followed the old Oregon Trail to the Rockies. Gone were the great herds of

---

[35] Charles Kepler (ed.), *Indian Affairs, Laws and Treaties* (Washington, 1904), Vol. II, p. 1025.

buffalo, the fur company's caravans, the emigrants' covered wagons, and even the pony express. A new day had dawned with the coming of the railroad. The train, in which the Newell party was riding, crossed the Continental Divide on September 6 and deposited its passengers at Bitter Creek, about sixty miles east of Green River, which was the end of the line at that time. The rest of the journey to Walla Walla had to be made by stage coach.

When Newell saw the mountains and streams which he knew so well when engaged in trapping beaver in his younger years, he noted in his diary: "Saw Wind River Mountains and such of the old country of former days which brought to mind many incidents of my former life." Lawyer and his fellow chiefs must also have had memories awakened when they too gazed on familiar landmarks and remembered how in earlier years they had joined the trappers and traders at the annual Rendezvous, often held on Green River.

The Newell party arrived at Walla Walla on September 19. There they parted for the time being. Newell noted in his diary that the Indians secured some horses for the remaining section of their never-to-be-forgotten journey. Within two or three more days, the three Nez Perces were back in their respective homes.

CHAPTER NINE

Lawyer's Closing Years

Lawyer returned to his home at Lapwai in September 1868, deeply pleased with the results of his memorable journey to Washington. The sea voyages first to Panama and then from Panama to New York were in themselves unforgettable experiences. The sights of such great cities as New York and Washington, followed by the amazing rail journey across the vastness of the country to the end of the railroad in western Wyoming, imprinted vivid memories on his mind which were beyond his ability to describe to his fellow tribesmen. But he tried. Indeed he must have talked about his adventures so much during the more than seven years before he died that even members of his family came to believe that he had made the journey twice for they inscribed on his tombstone: "He made two trips to Wash."

According to Newell's diary, he and his Nez Perce friends called on General Grant twice while they were in Washington. The first time was on May 18, on which occasion Newell mentioned a "Gen. Dent" who evidently was present at the time of the interview. General Grant was elected President of the United States in the November 1868 election and was inaugurated on March 4 of the following year.

Among the many administrative problems which President Grant faced were those of finding jobs for the surplus Army officers left over from the Civil War and also the necessity of introducing reforms in the administration of the many Indian Agencies. Grant decided that he could solve both problems, in part at least, by appointing Army officers as Indian Agents. Word of these contemplated changes reached Lawyer's ears and he was troubled, for it meant that his friend Robert Newell would be replaced by some Army officer. Lawyer decided that he would send an appeal to General Dent urging him to use his influence to keep Newell at Lapwai. Lawyer called on a friend, Judge Milton Kelly in Lewiston, on June 26, 1869, and dictated the following letter which Kelly wrote:

When I was in Washington last year, I told the President I had come to tell him how things were going on, on this Reservation. I was promised a good many things we didn't have. We had a saw mill but when a log was sawed, the lumber was sold. We had no lumber, no fences, no schools. The Agents we had, had promised us many things, but they put it off by telling — next year, they would do so and so. I told the President next year, next year, wouldn't do. I was getting old. I wanted those things done. My people were poor. The President showed me four men, the Commissioners. He said whatever agreement the Commissioners should make should be good. I had a long talk with the Commissioners. I remember all that was said.

The Commissioners found out all about the Agent. [i.e., James O'Neill] . . . They found out about the interpreter, [i.e., Perrin Whitman]. They told me I should have another Agent. They asked me which man I would have for the Agent. I told the Commissioners, I had brought along Mr. Newell. I wanted he should be our Agent. Mr. Newell was appointed. He came back with me. He has been with us ever since.

Since Mr. Newell has come here as the Agent, he has built a good many fences for us. He has a good many children at school, and he has plowed up ground for us and we got lumber from the saw mill, and many other things that we have never had. This is the only year we have had an Agent here.

We have never had a Doctor before that would go away from his place or among the people to see the sick. The Commissioners told me if Mr. Newell didn't do any thing for my people, they would find it out. It would be but a very few days when it will be ten months that we have had Mr. Newell as our Agent.

I have heard lately that there was going to be Government officers [i.e., Army] to take charge of all the Agencies and one I hear is coming here to take Mr. Newell's place. Mr. Newell has done a great deal of work for my people, and I would like to have him kept on doing for us. If we hadn't had these things done for us by Mr. Newell, I would have reported it to the President. I want General Dent to remember the talk we had in Washington City. I would like to have this explained to the President by General Dent.

I have talked this to your Judge Kelly and want you to let the President know what I have said.

In a postscript, Judge Kelly certified that "the foregoing talk or speech" was Lawyer's and that "the same was interpreted to me at the time the same was made and taken down in writing."

Lawyer's plea in Newell's behalf was in vain for on June 10, more than two weeks before Lawyer dictated his letter, the Government had appointed Lieutenant J. W. Wham to be Indian Agent at Lapwai. Wham arrived at Lapwai on July 14, 1869. Newell died at Lapwai during the following November.

In his first and only report to Washington, Wham had the following comment to make regarding the non-Treaty Indians:

I found that at first there were comparatively few of them and they said . . . that the Government never meant to fulfill its stipulations; that the white men had no good hearts. And as time passed on, these assertions were verified to some extent by the failure of the Government to build the churches, school-houses, mills at Kamiah, and fence and plow their lands as provided by the treaties of 1855 and 1863, until many of the Indians on the treaty side are beginning to feel sore on account of such failure.

The implication of this criticism lies in the fact that although the Government had made improvements at Lapwai, it had failed to do so at Kamiah.

Wham also reported that the boundary lines of the 1863 Reservation had not then been surveyed as provided by the treaty. "This is the cause of much trouble," he wrote, "from the fact that there are many white men living near where the line is supposed to be, who abuse the Indians and treat them badly. The Indians then come to me and make complaint, and ask me to make the white man leave their country. I cannot decide as to whether these white men are on or off this reservation." Wham added: "These Indians boast with great pride that they, as a nation, never shed a white man's blood, but the Government has, through its agents, been so dilatory in fulfilling the treaty stipulations . . . that they do not believe that any agent can or will tell the truth."

Lieutenant Wham was succeeded by Captain D. M. Sells on February 10, 1870. In the one and only report submitted to the Commissioner of Indian Affairs, dated September 10, 1870, Sells stated that the

Nez Perces then numbered 3,200 and that: "The survey of the Reservation was commenced this spring. . . The saw and grist mills at Kamia are in complete running order." After years of frustrating delays, the promised mills at Kamiah were finally built.

Sells also noted in this letter that there was some dissatisfaction with Lawyer. He wrote: "The chiefs were called together [i.e., during the spring of 1870] for the purpose of electing a new chief, but very few came to the Agency. There not being a sufficient number to justify their making a choice, the selection was postponed until fall, in case a change should then be desired."

Sells explained: "There is no possible objection to the present head chief, [Lawyer]. The reason for the hostility to him by the Indians is in consequence of his alleged misrepresentations of the additional treaty stipulations." This seems to indicate that some of the non-Treaty chiefs had objected to the supplemental Treaty of 1868. Sells added: "I have invariably informed both the treaties and the non-treaties that they must inevitably move on the reservation and, as far as the present indications go, quite a number will come in the spring, in addition to those already living here."

Perhaps the main reason for the growing disatisfaction with Lawyer was the fact that he was getting old. Assuming that Monteith's estimate of Lawyer being born in 1796 is correct, then the chief would have been in his 75th year in 1870. Since there is no record of any council being held in the fall of 1870, it appears that this issue of electing another Head Chief was held over to be settled by Sell's successor, John B. Monteith.

John B. Monteith

President Grant's plan to use Army officers as Indian Agents was not a success. There was widespread criticism of inefficiency, injustices, and financial corruption among those who had been appointed. As a result, the President in 1870, adopted his "peace policy" by which the administration of Indian Agencies was assigned to various religious denominations. These denominations were given the right to select the Agent and certain other employees as teachers. In theory the denominations would be more selective in the choice of personnel than had previously been the case and more conscientious in the expenditure of Government funds. The Presbyterians were assigned to the Nez Perces.

A new agent was needed at Lapwai as Captain Sells, at his own request, was discharged from the Army on December 31, 1870. It has been alleged that he, too, was guilty of absconding with a large amount of Agency funds. The Presbyterian Church was then asked to nominate the next Agent.

The Presbyterian Church, U.S.A., turned the responsibility of selecting a man for the Lapwai Agency and a teacher for the tribal school over to its Board of Foreign Missions.[1] Dr. Walter Lowrie, Secretary of the Board, wrote to Dr. Edward R. Geary in Oregon asking for his recommendations. After consulting with his colleagues, Geary nominated John B. Monteith, son of another pioneer Presbyterian minister to Oregon, the Rev. William J. Monteith, to be the Agent and Henry H. Spalding, the teacher.[2]

The Government accepted the nominations. The salaries of both men were to be paid by the Government. Monteith began his duties on February 10, 1871, and served with distinction through eight years, when he resigned on account of ill health on April 22, 1879. He died on the following August 7.

LAWYER REPLACED AS HEAD CHIEF

Shortly after taking over the duties of his office, Monteith became aware of the necessity of having Lawyer replaced by a younger man. Although others in the tribe shared the same feeling, there was no unanimity on the subject. The basic problem was who should succeed him. There was a dearth of qualified leadership. There was no one of Lawyer's stature to whom they could turn.

A council of the chiefs and headmen was held at Lapwai in the fall of 1871 at which time Lawyer was deposed as Head Chief, although no agreement could be reached as to who should replace him. During the following year, when there was no Head Chief, Monteith continued to consult with Lawyer, whose judgments he greatly respected.

The loss of his chieftainship was a serious blow to Lawyer, for it meant that the Government would stop paying his annual stipend of $500.00 which was his chief source of income. Lawyer, faced with the realities of the situation, decided that if he were not to be Head Chief,

---

[1] The Presbyterian Board of Foreign Missions, organized in 1837, absorbed some of the activities of the American Board in 1869. Thus Spalding, who had gone out to Oregon under the auspices of the American Board, now came under the jurisdiction of the Presbyterians.

[2] Drury, *Tepee*, pp. 35-6, gives Geary's letter of recommendation of Jan. 7, 1871.

there was no longer any need for him to continue living at Lapwai. He would return to his native village at Kamiah. Lawyer then asked Monteith if the Government would not build him a house at Kamiah. As a result of this request, Monteith wrote the following to the Commissioner of Indian Affairs in Washington, under date of February 17, 1872. Since it contains so much pertinent information, it is here given in full.

Sir, I have the honor to report the following in regard to Lawyer, former Head Chief. Lawyer is now about 78 years old [3] and having been wounded several times during his younger days is unable to do any hard work. During the time he was head chief and drawing a salary from the Government, he could lay up nothing for his old age for the reason that all looked upon him as under obligation to entertain any and all who visited him. Consequently it took all his salary to meet his expenses. He now lives in Kamiah, where he has selected a piece of land about 15 acres and has asked me if the Govt. would not be willing to build and furnish him a comfortable house. A suitable house could be built — the lumber being sawed at the Kamiah Mill — with little expense to the Government. The furnishings would cost the most.

I estimate the cost of a house 16 x 24 feet, furnished, at $350.00. The lumber being sawed at the Kamiah Mill and the house one story high and would recommend that the above amount, or as much thereof as may be necessary, be taken from the fund, viz — "Incidental and Contingent Expenses, Indian Service, Idaho."

The reasons I would give are — Lawyer's well known friendship for the Whites from the time they first made their appearance in this country and by his influence here. [He] always kept the Nez Perces from joining any of the hostile tribes who lived on all sides of them, thereby helping the Govt. by keeping this powerful Tribe peaceable while all the rest were at war. He has several times told me of the first appearance of the Whites among them [Lewis and Clark] when he was about 12 years of age and also of the assistance rendered under Cols. Steptoe and Wright, as well as Gov. Stevens, during the expeditions organized against the Spokanes and Crows.[4]

For these reasons and others that might be mentioned, I would

---

[3] Another error in dates. If Lawyer had been born in 1796, as Monteith later indicated, then he would have been 76 in 1872 rather than 78.

[4] A reference to the fact that some Nez Perces were with Gov. Stevens when he visited the Flathead and Crow country in western Montana in the summer of 1855.

recommend that the amount asked for be appropriated for the purpose mentioned.

Very respectfully. You Obd. Servant, Jon. B. Monteith, U.S. Indian Agent.

The request was granted and a house was built for Lawyer in 1871-72 on the right bank of the Clearwater River, above the place where the First Presbyterian (Indian) Church stood.[5]

SPALDING RETURNS TO LAPWAI AS A GOVERNMENT TEACHER

The Commissioner of Indian Affairs sent J. Ross Browne to Oregon in 1857 to investigate the causes of the Indian wars which plagued the Pacific Northwest following the Whitman massacre. Browne submitted his official report in January 1858, to which he had attached a pamphlet, written by Father J. B. A. Brouillet who was answering some of the charges that Spalding had made against the Catholics. Browne's report, with the Brouillet article, appeared in 1858 as *Executive Document, No. 38, House of Representatives, 35th Congress, 1st Session.*

As could be expected, neither Spalding nor any of his close friends were readers of Government publications. About ten years passed before Spalding's attention was drawn to the publication of Brouillet's pamphlet as a part of an official Government document. Spalding was immediately aroused. He became possessed with a consuming desire to obtain a vindication through some official Congressional publication.

Carrying a hodge-podge collection of documents, including copies of his anti-Catholic lectures, affidavits, and testimonials from friends, Spalding left for Washington from Portland on October 28, 1870. He sailed to San Francisco where he boarded a train for the East. This was the first time he had returned since he had gone out to Oregon in 1836.

After spending some time visiting relatives and friends in western New York, Spalding went to Boston where he called on the Secretaries of the American Board. While in Boston, Spalding learned about President Grant's peace policy and that the Presbyterian Board of Foreign Missions, with its headquarters in New York City, had been given the responsibility of nominating both the Indian Agent and the school teacher for the Nez Perces. To him, this was exciting news.

---

[5] Information from a letter written to me by a Nez Perce, Mrs. Lydia A. Corbett, on January 20, 1960. Original now in Idaho Hist. Soc., Boise.

Spalding hastened to New York to call on Dr. Walter Lowrie, Secretary of the Foreign Board from whom he was delighted to learn that Dr. Edward Geary had nominated him to be the teacher at Lapwai along with Monteith as Indian Agent. His salary would be $1,200.00 a year. In addition he would be provided with a house and a cow. Moreover, Dr. Lowrie told Spalding that a provision had been made for a second teacher, who would receive $1,000.00 a year, plus a house and a cow, and asked Spalding to make a nomination. Again Spalding was delighted with this turn of events.

While in New York, Spalding induced the American Bible Society to reprint his Gospel of Matthew in Nez Perce, which first appeared from the Lapwai press in 1845. Evidently Spalding was then planning to use this as a textbook in the Lapwai school to help the natives master their own language. The Bible Society printed 1,000 copies which were delivered at Lapwai during November, 1871.

Spalding arrived in Washington on January 5, 1871, where he spent two months. Through the influence of Senator H. W. Corbett of Oregon, Spalding succeeded in having his documents published by the U.S. Senate under the title *Executive Document, No. 37, U.S. Senate, 41st Congress, 3rd Session,* in an edition of 1,500 copies. The pamphlet contained eighty-one pages. Spalding had added reason to be jubilant. He felt that he had been completely vindicated.

HENRY T. COWLEY

Mindful of Lowrie's request that he find someone to be associated with him in his educational work with the Nez Perces, Spalding succeeded in recruiting Henry T. Cowley. Cowley, thirty-seven years old, was a senior in Auburn Theological Seminary, a Presbyterian institution. He was married and had three children. The Presbyterian Board accepted Spalding's nomination and Cowley was notified of his appointment on June 7.

Following his ordination on July 6, Cowley left with his family for Lapwai. They arrived at their destination on August 12, after spending more than five weeks on their journey. Since their home at Kamiah was still under construction, the Cowleys were temporarily housed at Lapwai in a dwelling which had been built for the Spaldings.

There was no one at Lapwai who gave the Cowleys a more enthusiastic welcome than Lawyer. Also at Lapwai to welcome the Cowleys was the Rev. W. J. Monteith, father of the Indian Agent, who in a letter to Secretary Lowrie dated July 18, 1871, had written that Lawyer "was highly delighted" when he heard that a teacher was coming to open a school at Kamiah.[6] A solemn promise which had been made by the Government in its 1855 Treaty was at long last about to be fulfilled.

During Cowley's six-week sojourn at Lapwai, waiting for his house at Kamiah to be made ready, he discovered to his surprise that several at the Agency were openly critical, even hostile, of Spalding. Monteith, who had had nothing to say about Spalding's appointment, was disturbed because of his long delay in arriving. Whitman, the interpreter, harbored a deep dislike of Spalding and was quick to express it whenever opportunity afforded. Cowley was pained by hearing these criticisms of Spalding and felt that they were "utterly inconsistent" with his impressions of the man. Cowley optimistically felt that Spalding would quickly dispell all such criticisms as soon as he was able to assume his teaching duties.

As the weeks passed, Cowley became increasingly impatient to begin his work at Kamiah. Even though he knew that his house was not ready for occupancy, he and his family left for Kamiah on September 25. When they arrived, they found that only the frame of the house had been erected. The Cowley family had to find temporary shelter in a log cabin, already occupied by six of the Agency employees, where they were obliged to live for two weeks. They then moved into one room of their new home which had just been completed. Cowley opened his school on October 2 with twelve pupils. By the end of December the number had increased to fifty-nine.

BACKGROUND OF THE GREAT REVIVAL

Spalding's return to Lapwai was delayed for a variety of reasons, one being the serious illness of a daughter at Brownsville, Oregon. It was not until October 26, 1871, that he and his second wife, Rachel, arrived at Lapwai. This was more than eight months after Monteith had assumed his duties.

Friction between Spalding and Monteith became immediately evident as soon as Spalding arrived. During Spalding's long absence, Monteith had found it necessary to hire the Rev. R. N. Fee and his daughter, Mary, who happened to be relatives, to teach the Lapwai school. Thus when Spalding reported for duty, he was denied any

---

[6] Drury, *Tepee*, p. 51.

responsibility for the school. Spalding was further disturbed when Monteith refused to approve the use of his Nez Perce *Gospel of Matthew* as a textbook in the school to help the children learn their mother tongue. Monteith insisted that the standard school texts be used so that the pupils could learn English.

Monteith was faced with a problem. How could Spalding best be used since he held a Government appointment as a teacher? Writing to the Commissioner of Indian Affairs on December 22, 1871, Monteith explained:

> As Mr. Spalding came here in the special character of a Missionary, I thought his duties in that relation would fully occupy his time. He has permission to visit the schools and address the pupils when he pleases, and on Saturdays he is at liberty to gather them together and give them religious instruction, but I keep the control of the schools in my own hands.

Indian Commissioner Walker replied on January 26, 1872, demanding an explanation as to why Spalding, who was listed on the Government payroll as Superintendent of Instruction, was not to have charge of the schools. "The appointment is all the more inexplicable," wrote Walker, "from the fact that there was evidence that he would not be acceptable or successful in that capacity. . . If the design was in this manner to pay the salary of a missionary, not appointed by the Government, you will understand that such a proceeding will not be permitted." [7] Walker asked for an investigation, the results of which will be given in a following section of this chapter.

Not being permitted to teach school, Spalding turned his attention to preaching. There followed during the next two years a great revival, which resulted in the conversion and baptism of over 1000 Nez Perces, Spokanes, and Cayuses, and the establishment of two Nez Perce Presbyterian churches on the Reservation, one at Lapwai and one at Kamiah. As will be noted, Lawyer played a prominent role in this revival.

The revival which Spalding initiated in November 1871, did not come spontaneously. There had been a long period of preparation. Among the negative factors which prepared the way for a spiritual revival was the spread of the white man's customs and vices through-

---

[7] From a copy of Walker's letter, Spokane Public Library. *See also,* Drury, *Spalding,* p. 400.

out the tribe. During the years of the Rocky Mountain fur trade, the great holiday for the trappers and traders was the Fourth of July. Whenever this day came during the annual Rendezvous, it was commemorated with excessive drinking, gambling, and immoralities. Later, these excesses were followed in the frontier communities which sprang up in the Indian country. Thus it became easy for the Nez Perces to emulate the practices of the Whites during the Independence Day commemoration.

The Americans, not the Hudson's Bay men, introduced intoxicating liquors to the Indians and this trade was further promoted by unscrupulous white men who moved into the Indian country. Even though the Treaties of 1855 and 1863 specifically forbade the introduction and sale of intoxicating liquors on the Reservations, yet there was little that the Indian Agents or the chiefs or the law enforcement officers could do to stop the traffic. Excessive drinking became a curse among the Nez Perces. Lawyer, who was strongly opposed to drinking, did what he could to stop the traffic but his efforts were ineffectual.

The Presbyterian missionary to the Nez Perces, Kate McBeth, in her *The Nez Perces Since Lewis and Clark*, describes how both the Whites and the Indians during the early 1870s would extend the Independence Day celebrations at Lewiston and on the Reservation over a two-week period. She wrote:

> Drinking and fighting were common. The white men's methods of gambling were added to their own. Gambling was always a favorite pastime with them. Such a mix-up of heathenism, white men's vices, and religion [8] was perhaps never known before. And how they all did enjoy it! Especially at their great annual July camp for drinking, racing, and "swapping wives." [9]

Then, in the summer of 1870, an amazing event took place at Weippe prairie, about twenty miles northeast of Kamiah, where a large number of Nez Perces had encamped on their favorite camas root grounds. Kate McBeth tells the story: "Now, right into such a wild degraded camp as this, in June 1870, came four young Yakimas from Father Wilbur's Methodist mission on the Yakima reserve. The leader was George Waters."

In 1860, two years after Colonel Wright had completely crushed the

---

[8] A reference to the Dreamer religion. *See* Chap. viii, "Followers of the Dreamer cult."   [9] *Op. cit.*, p. 77.

coalition of rebellious Indian tribes in a battle at Spokane Plains, the Rev. James Wilbur, a Methodist missionary, and often called Father Wilbur, opened his mission among the Yakimas. The tribe was still reeling from the crushing defeat administered by Colonel Wright. Their militant chiefs as Owhi and Qualchen had been killed; Kam-i-ah-kan had fled to Canada; hundreds of their horses had been captured and slaughtered, and they were a defeated people. Into this vacuum came Father Wilbur, preaching his Christian gospel. The response was immediate and favorable. Many were converted among whom was George Waters, who had married into the family of Chief Timothy and who became a licensed Methodist preacher in 1868. Another was the Head Chief of the tribe, Thomas Stevier.

During the troubled years, 1855-58, the Yakimas, under the aggressive leadership of the militant Kam-i-ah-kan, had been sending agitators to the Nez Perces trying to stir them up to go to war against the Whites. Now there was a complete reversal of policy. Instead of advocating war, the Yakimas had sent a delegation to the Nez Perces to preach the gospel of Jesus Christ.

The Yakima preacher, George Waters, was another John the Baptist, for he came preaching repentance. He called upon the Nez Perces to throw away their whiskey bottles, to give up polygamy, and to discard their Dreamer and Wy-ya-kin fetishes. The emotional preaching of Waters and his companions struck home, and many wept for their sins.[10] Waters preached a gospel of forgiveness which is found in placing faith in Jesus Christ.

Kate McBeth's account continues:

> The spirit was so manifestly present that the camp became a "Bockim," and the place is still called "The Place of Weeping" [11] . . . At the time of the spiritual awakening, there was no Mr. Spalding there, and no white missionary. Just God and their guilty souls. Then and there, they threw away their bottles, their pipes, the feathers and tails of animals, and their wives. The wives were not easily thrown away. The men had many councils and much discussion as to which one to retain, and whom to cast away. . .
> The feathers and tails which were thrown away were emblems of their attending spirit, the "Wy-ya-kin" and when these were discarded, it was confessing, "I trust in you no longer." [12]

---

[10] *Ibid.*, p. 78.

[11] A reference to Psalm 84:6 (K.J. version): "Who passing through the valley of Baca, make it a well." The Hebrew word "Baca" means "weeping."

[12] McBeth, *Nez Perces*, p. 78.

According to McBeth, Waters held evangelistic services at Kamiah, Lapwai, and Alpowa during the months following his first visit to the Nez Perces. In doing so, Waters was unwittingly preparing the way for Spalding.

THE GREAT REVIVAL, 1871-1873

Spalding was given an enthusiastic welcome, especially by the older Nez Perces, when he returned to Lapwai in the latter part of October 1871. The fact that he was able to preach to them in their own language drew large crowds to his services. Old age and gray hairs, together with the memories of his eleven-year residence with them, 1836-48, gave him a prestige which exceeded that which he had ever before enjoyed.

Two important developments had taken place which prepared the way for Spalding's return. The first was the spiritual revival initiated by the preaching of the Yakima evangelist, George Waters. The second was the political situation which had developed within the tribe which had resulted in the rejection of Lawyer as Head Chief. The majority of chiefs, who had assembled in council shortly before Spalding's return, agreed that Lawyer was too old to continue as Head Chief. Even Monteith, who was friendly to Lawyer, gave his reluctant approval for a change. Lawyer was unhappy, not only because he had been deposed, but also because a small group within the council had tried to elect one called Jacob, a non-Christian, to take his place. The council closed without a final decision being made. Those present agreed to meet in the fall of 1872 when a definite choice would be made.

On the basis of this evidence, it seems clear that Lawyer felt that it would be advantageous for him, as well as for the whole tribe, if the Christian party could be increased. Without disparaging the sincerity of his Christian convictions, still it is reasonable to believe that, under the circumstances, Lawyer was willing to mix tribal politics with religion. He therefore enthusiastically endorsed Spalding's preaching and joined him in seeking converts.

When Spalding returned to Lapwai in the fall of 1871, he carried with him the original record book of the First Presbyterian Church of Oregon, the Mission Church which had been organized at Waiilatpu on August 18, 1838. On November 12, Spalding noted in this volume the fact that he had found "18 of the old church alive." Although the church was called Presbyterian, actually it had never been attached to a Presbytery. Although Spalding had noted in the record of its organization that it was to be attached to the Presbytery of Bath in New York State, this ecclesiastical connection was never made, perhaps due to the difficulties of communication at that time. In polity, the church was Congregational. Upon his return to Lapwai, Spalding arbitrarily selected two of the most faithful of the original membership, Timothy and Jude, to serve as elders in his unofficial session.

After only two Sundays of preaching, Spalding felt that the time had come for him to baptise and welcome his converts into the membership of the old Mission Church. On Sunday, November 12, 1871, the ingathering began when Spalding baptized twenty-one men and twenty-three women. Heading the list, as recorded by Spalding in the minute book, was Lawyer, whom Spalding listed as "Head Chief." Although Spalding followed the custom of bestowing Biblical names upon his converts, a practice then widely followed by both the Roman Catholic and Protestant missionaries, he made no effort to name Lawyer after an Old Testament king or prophet, or after one of the New Testament disciples. The chief had been called Lawyer for over forty years, and this honored name was to be kept.

The second in the list of males baptized, as recorded by Spalding, was Tack-en-sua-tis, once known by the mountain men as Rotten Belly, who with Lawyer had welcomed the members of the Whitman-Spalding party at the Rendezvous in July 1836. Spalding bestowed on him the name of the Old Testament prophet, Samuel.[13] Then followed other Biblical names — Enoch, Daniel, Thomas, Moses, Paul, and Noah. With the passing of the years, many of these Christian names became family surnames, which continue to this day. Mixed with the Biblical names were some which were non-Biblical.

Among the men baptized that day were the two sons of Lawyer who were already known as James and Archie. These names remained. After being tutored for several years by Miss Sue McBeth, a Presbyterian missionary who arrived on the Nez Perce field in 1873, Archie Lawyer was ordained to the Presbyterian ministry in 1891.[14] Spalding bestowed

---

[13] Drury, *Spalding*, p. 402. Identification of Samuel with Tack-en-sua-tis was given to me by Nez Perce friends in 1935. Yet, the name of Tack-en-sua-tis does not appear as one who signed either of the 1855 or 1863 Treaties. He might have been known by another name, or the identification could be in error.

[14] *See* Mary Crawford, *The Nez Perces Since Spalding* (privately printed, 1936), for picture of Archie Lawyer, p. 66. The first Nez Perce to receive Presbyterian ordination was Robert Williams, 1879. Archie was the second.

on one couple the baptismal names of himself and his first wife — Henry and Eliza Spalding. The list of baptized men included the name of William, who probably was the Billy mentioned in the proceedings of the Councils of 1855 and 1863.

Even as most of the men were given Biblical names, likewise the list of the women — Martha, Lydia, Sarah, Mary, etc. Among them, no doubt, was the wife of Lawyer although the name given to her is not known. The name of Lawyer's wife as found on her tombstone in the cemetery of the Second (Indian) Presbyterian Church of Kamiah is Tillie.

Spalding was jubilant, as is evident in the following notation which he wrote after listing the names of his converts: "This is a glorious day. Bless the Lord, oh my soul. That I am permitted to return after so long expulsion in my old age but once to witness the wonderful work of God upon the hearts of this people."

During the early mission period, 1836 and following, Spalding was severely criticized by his fellow missionary, Asa B. Smith, for what Smith considered to be irregularities in receiving natives into the Mission Church.[15] Now there was no one to object. All inhibitions were removed. Spalding felt free to baptize all who requested it. There was no formal indoctrination in Christian teachings beyond Spalding's eloquent and at times emotional preaching. Now, following Lawyer's example and encouragement, joining the church was the thing to do.

The record book shows that on Monday, November 13, Spalding baptized nineteen; on the 14th, fourteen more; on the 20th, another twenty. Altogether 108 were baptized before the end of the year. And this was but the beginning of the revival.

Lawyer, First Elder of the Kamiah Church

Hearing of the success of the revival at Lapwai, Cowley made a trip from Kamiah in mid-December to see for himself. After his return, he wrote to Secretary Lowrie on January 5, 1872, saying:

> Notwithstanding the reports that the natives would not receive Bro. S., the schoolhouse on that bitter cold sabbath on which I was favored for the first time in hearing Bro. S. preach to the Indians in their own language, was filled and the tears rolled down on many a brown cheek, as the preacher told them in his touching & forcible manner of the Savior who was lifted up that He might

---

[15] *See* Drury, S. & S., pp. 157 ff., for an account of Smith's criticisms of Spalding.

draw all men unto him. After the discourse were fearful and agonizing confessions, and three were received to fellowship by baptism. . .

My visit to Bro. S. was most refreshing, & strengthened spiritually, I returned to Kamia with a spark of his zeal. Here it needed but to thrust in the sickle & reap. The harvest was already white.[16]

Inspired by what he had heard and seen at Lapwai, Cowley began a series of evangelistic meetings at Kamiah before Christmas which continued until after New Year's day. Cowley was obliged to use two interpreters. He spoke first to a young Flathead Indian woman who translated the English into Flathead to Lawyer who then spoke in Nez Perce.

Cowley, in his January letter to Lowrie, described the Christmas Day, 1871, meeting. It was held in a communal lodge which measured about 100 by 20 feet. Into this about 300 people had crowded around several fires which burned in the center. The meeting began at 10:00 a.m. and lasted until 3:30 p.m. "Without any artificial excitement," wrote Cowley, "but with a deep & subdued earnestness we prayed and sung together, and I explained the mystery of the Gospel. As a result, 25 came forward for baptism."

According to information given to me personally by some of the older members of the First Presbyterian (Indian) Church of Kamiah, when I lived at Moscow, Idaho, during the 1930s, their church was organized on Christmas Day with Lawyer being elected as its first elder.[17] Although no longer Head Chief of the Nez Perces, he then became the leading elder of the Presbyterian Church at Kamiah. Lawyer was proud of his new office. Inscribed on his tombstone at Kamiah are the words: "He was the first elder of the 1st. Presby. Church of Kamiah." Monteith, in his obituary of Lawyer, wrote: "Lawyer made a profession of religion in 1871, and ever after maintained a consistent Christian character . . . and manifested a deep interest in the progress of religion among his people."

Cowley, in his letter to Lowrie, gave the following description of how the newly baptized Christians at Kamiah celebrated New Year's Day, 1872:

---

16 Original Cowley letter is in the Presbyterian Hist. Soc., Philadelphia.

17 The late John Frank, an elder of First Church, Kamiah, told me that the original session book of the church was lost about 1889 when it fell out of the saddlebags of an elder returning from a Presbytery meeting.

Original

LAWYER'S LETTER TO WASHINGTON, JANUARY 11, 1874
The original letter, here somewhat abbreviated, is in the files of the
Old Indian Bureau, National Archives, Washington, D.C. See text page 284.
The transcription shown on the following page is complete.

June 30th 1863 - been silent & kept silence by the will of our father - and of the government at Washington made I am that no whites should live on the Reserve. If whites settled on it, they should be removed by the Agents.

June 5th 1863 Mr. Hale for all of the government made another law, and it was the same, that no whiteman should live in the middle of the Reservation, but the Agent should put off such white person quickly.

August 13th 1865 Mr. ... and Mr. ... told me one of the law of all the government, I the Lawyer, that which was not forgotten, that which was told me about law by one desire in Washington and New York City, the amount of which was that no white man could live in the middle of the Reservation, but the Agent remove and them that from the Reservation of law, Paul, Joe - Since the and Baird to Sawin & Hamlin that shall the Indians what come on the Reservation, when it is filled up ...

there remaining on the outside shall be entitled each to a field of twenty acres and watched over by the Agent.

Our first Agent was Mr. Miller, next Mr. Craig, next Mr. Cain and ... and Mr. Anderson and Wm. O'Neil or ... Russell, and ... Blain, and Captain Silke and ... John ... if he slowly removing the ... he would remain the same ... white man should live in the midst of the Reservation.

Jan. 14th 1874 The Lawyer do not forget what I heard in Washington to New York City. I the Lawyer wish my children have ... of my ... and this to- you my ... Peace chiefs, children. South (...)

If trouble should arise with the Indians do not think my children will do not class them with bad Indians.

This much I say to you.
Yours, the Lawyer

A meeting for watching and praying had been held through the previous night, and about 10 o'clock in the morning, a procession of all who had been baptized by Bro. Spalding and those baptized here, was formed with Lawyer at their head, and a large American flag waving over them, and with a cheerful greeting of "Happy New Year," they marched into one door of our cramful kitchen & out the opposite door into the larger unfinished sitting room where Lawyer addressed them briefly in a stirring & eloquent manner.

I joined the procession & we marched to the lodge singing some of their favorite hymns. In front of the lodge were gathered in single file almost every man, woman, & child not in the procession & then occurred a most affecting scene; shaking hands and expressing cordial good wishes. So infectious was the spirit of goodwill that I noticed many shedding silent tears. . . Inside the lodge, which was crowded to its utmost capacity, the Holy Spirit seemed present with great power. 4 came forward confessing their sins.

The revival continued unabated in fervor throughout the Nez Perce nation during the spring and summer of 1872. During the first week of May, a delegation of Yakima Indians, headed by Chief Stevier and the licensed preacher, George Waters, paid another visit to Kamiah. Cowley's vivid description of their arrival at Kamiah is found in his letter of May 11 to Lowrie. He wrote:

Nearly every man, woman & child of the church & many others turned out to meet & welcome them. Many brethren from Alpowa, Lewiston, & Lapwai joined the delegation at these places, and the whole company numbered about sixty-five on their arrival here. They approached us over the hills singing beautifully a hymn of greeting. As they came in sight, we greeted them with a hymn of welcome. At a signal, they halted about fifty yards from us & Lawyer, [still the Head Chief in the hearts of the people], stepped forward and in a brief address bade them welcome to Kamiah. Then the two chiefs joined in prayer.[18]

Since the Yakimas spoke the Flathead language, Lawyer could have served as the interpreter on this occasion.

The Fifth Article of the 1863 Treaty stated: "A further sum of $2,500 shall be paid within one year after the ratification hereof to enable the Indians to build two churches, one of which is to be located at some suitable point on the Kamia and the other on the Lapwai." Although

---

[18] Drury, *Tepee,* p. 72.

the 1863 Treaty was ratified on April 17, 1867, the two churches were not erected until 1873. The Kamiah church was dedicated that summer and it may be assumed that the Lapwai church was also dedicated then. Several years later, because the Lapwai congregation needed a larger building, the treaty church was moved to a new site and used as a warehouse. This was later destroyed by fire.[19] The Lapwai Christians erected a new building in 1885-86 which was given a brick veneer in 1936, the centennial of the arrival of the Spaldings at Lapwai.

The church at Kamiah is reported to be the oldest Protestant church in continuous use in Idaho.[20] The graves of Lawyer, the McBeth sisters, and several of the early Nez Perce ministers are in the cemetery adjacent to the church.

Lawyer's Plea in Defense of Spalding

The closing three years of Spalding's life were filled with controversies, frustrations, and disappointments, relieved intermittently by some joys and triumphs. As a follow-up to Indian Commissioner Walker's demand for an investigation of Spalding's status, the Presbyterian Board of Foreign Missions appointed Dr. E. R. Geary to visit Lapwai and appraise the situation. Geary visited Lapwai during the latter part of March 1872, and in a twenty-four page report[21] exonerated both Whitman and Geary from all charges made against them by Spalding. Geary claimed that Spalding was a trouble-maker.

Lowrie wrote to Spalding on June 5 saying that the Board had accepted Geary's recommendations. This led to Spalding's dismissal by Monteith as of July 1, 1872, and Spalding was ordered to leave Lapwai and move to Kamiah. Thus for the third time, Spalding was forced to leave his old mission station. The first time was after the Whitman massacre in 1847, the second in 1865. This third time came as a bitter experience for Spalding. To ameliorate the situation, the Presbyterian Church assumed responsibility for his salary and appointed him as a missionary to the Nez Perces for the rest of his life.

Since Cowley had signed an endorsement of many of Spalding's unfounded charges against Monteith, without investigating their merit

---

19 McBeth, *Nez Perces*, p. 149.

20 St. Michael's Episcopal Church, Boise, Idaho, now called Christ Chapel, has an older building but this has not been in continuous use for religious services.

21 A copy of this report was published in the *Journal of Presbyterian History,* March, June, Sept., 1942, pp. 104 ff.

but merely relying on Spalding's word, he too was involved. Monteith notified Cowley that his Government pay would cease as of October 1, and that he was to vacate his house at Kamiah so that the Spaldings could occupy it. Cowley accepted a teacher's position in a school at Mt. Idaho, which was outside the bounds of the reservation.

Spalding's dismissal prompted Lawyer to give a spirited defense of his old friend. More than twenty years ago, my attention was directed to a four-page manuscript in the files of the Oregon Historical Society which was written from Lapwai, September 18, 1872. It bore the notation: "Memorial from Lawyer, head chief of the Nez Perce nation, an Elder in the native church known as the 1st Presbyterian Church in Oregon, to Rev. H. K. Hines, P[residing] E[lder] of the Walla Walla District of the M[ethodist] E[piscopal] Church." A note on the index card in the Society states that the document was incomplete. The text ends abruptly and it is evident that at least one page is missing.

Since the Memorial was written in fluent English, the question arises — Who was the scribe and who the interpreter? Spalding noted in the church's record book that he had baptized nine converts at Wild Horse Creek, a stream which empties into the Umatilla River, on Friday, September 27, 1872, and that the Rev. H. K. Hines was present. It is possible that Hines was present at Lapwai on the 18th, previous to Spalding's going to Wild Horse Creek, and that it was then that Lawyer and Spalding dictated the Memorial which Hines wrote, addressing it for some reason to himself.

After having had a copy of this document in my files for over twenty years without making use of it, I can now appreciate its significance. Beneath the fluent English used by the scribe, we see revealed Lawyer's deep appreciation of Spalding as his old teacher and friend. The Memorial carries a protest against the way Spalding had been treated and asserts that Spalding was more needed then than ever before because of the hundreds of new converts who needed instruction in God's word. The Memorial contains so many of Spalding's repeated complaints and so much of his terminology that we are obliged to assume that he was present when it was written.

The text of that part of the Memorial which is extant follows *en toto:*

Dear Brother. My prayer is to you for help and fellowship. The Presbyterian agent for my nation has informed me that the Presbyterian Board has appointed two missionaries to displace Mr. Cowley, who arrived last year with his family to spend their lives with my people, to teach & do them good, and Mr. Spalding, an old missionary & father. To be deprived of these teachers would be a loss to my nation, which could not be made up.

Father Spalding is the only man who can preach to us & translate the Bible in our language. He has been our teacher and pastor since the year 1836. He came to our country with Dr. Whitman & their wives at the call of our nation who sent a delegation to the rising sun to get the book from heaven [22] and men to teach it. Their wives were the first white women to cross the Rocky Mountains, and the whole distance was full of war, starvation, and death. Father Spalding translated the Word of God into our language and collected our people twice a day to teach them that Word.

He brought wheat, corn, and plows, & taught us to cultivate the land. Mrs. Spalding taught our women to spin & weave & had a large school, sometimes of five hundred.[23] But the war which was undertaken to break up the American settlements when Dr. Whitman and many Americans were killed, made it necessary for us to take Mr. Spalding & family out of the country to save their lives. And then darkness settled down upon our land. But we continued to worship God & read his Word as Mr. Spalding had taught us and to raise cattle and cultivate the soil.

But Mr. Spalding has been returned to us and our people rejoice to receive him as one from the dead. Indeed it is like bringing back to us from the dead our fathers who met him a thousand miles distant on the divide of the Rocky Mountains, and conducted him & Mrs. Spalding to our country, and gave them a home here for life, & where all their children were born. The Great Shepherd, the Lord Jesus, immediately crowned Father Spalding's labors with great blessings. Multitudes of my people listened to the heavenly message and gladly received pardon at the hands of our glorious Prince.

I, myself, was made to taste the Word of Life, and with 44

---

[22] The phrase, "book of heaven," appears in the fanciful speech which Spalding attributed to one of the four Nez Perces who visited St. Louis in the fall of 1831 when meeting with General Wm. Clark. *See* Drury, *M. & N.W.*, Vol. II, p. 380. Possibly Spalding had used the phrase so often that it had been accepted by Lawyer.

[23] The "five hundred" figure is an evident exaggeration which can be attributed to Spalding. Spalding, in a letter written on January 27, 1837, reported that 100 were then enrolled in the school. This marked the peak of the school attendance. Drury, *Spalding*, p. 172. In 1842, Spalding reported that the average attendance in the Lapwai school was 85. *Ibid.*, p. 272.

others, the second sabbath after our pastor arrived, received holy
baptism, & entered the fold of Christ. The next day 14, the next
day 18, and on two others days 66 & 33 were received into the
church. In all up to this time, Mr. Spalding & Mr. Cowley have
received into the fold, 463 since they arrived last fall & the good
work still goes on.[24]

These young converts are but babes in Christ and will need constant instruction from God's Word, as the new born babe needs the
milk of its mother, and there is no other man but Mr. Spalding
who can preach to us & translate the Word of God into our language & his labors are indispensable in training native helpers
needed at once to labor in this great church scattered over a large
territory.

But the Presbyterian Board of Missions, it seems, have appointed
other missionaries who cannot speak our language and sent them
forward to displace Mr. Spalding & Mr. Cowley. The Agent has
also sent to Washington to ask liberty for Catholic priests to labor
on the Reservation & use the church at Lapwai. The Mission Board
has instructed the Agent to turn Mr. Spalding & wife out of the
teacher's house & the work of education, & he has done so, and he
does not allow Mr. Spalding in the school, nor to collect the converts every night & morning in Bible classes, as he did daily when
here before, and he has put the building & the converts into the
hands of those who cannot speak our language, and who cannot
teach us the Word of God, nor pray with us as Mr. Spalding can.
Some of them smoke, drink whiskey, & break God's holy sabbath.
Many of my people have taken their children from the school. The
Agent ordered Mr. Spalding onto the horse to ride, from camp to
camp over the mountains. . .

The last sentence of this incomplete document refers to an order
which Monteith had given Spalding: "You are to travel among & preach
to the people, to have nothing to do with the schools." [25] Spalding's
replacement at Lapwai was the Rev. George Ainslie, who arrived in
the fall of 1872 and who remained for three years.[26]

---

[24] The statistics as given in Lawyer's Memorial are approximately the same as
those to be found in Spalding's record book.   [25] Drury, *Tepee*, p. 80.

[26] Ainslie acquired sufficient knowledge of the Nez Perce language to enable
him, with Perrin Whitman's help, to translate the Gospel of John into Nez Perce.
This was published by the Presbyterian Board of Publication in 1876, along with
a short catechism in Nez Perce.

LAWYER AGAIN LOSES TRIBAL ELECTION

As has been stated, Lawyer lost his chieftainship by action of the 1871 Council of Nez Perce chiefs held at Lapwai. Since the Council failed to select his successor, Lawyer still served in an unofficial capacity as Head Chief for another year, according to a statement made by Monteith in his obituary of Lawyer. When the chiefs met again in council in the fall of 1872, Jacob, the unsuccessful candidate for the office of Head Chief in 1871, was this time elected. Even though the revival had brought more than 460 new Nez Perce converts into the church, thus strengthening the Christian party within the tribe, Lawyer failed to be reelected. It is evident that even his many friends felt that at seventy-six, he was too old for that office.

For some unknown reason, Jacob disliked Monteith. Jacob, who belonged to the non-Christian party, started a movement to have Monteith dismissed. In May 1874, Thomas Newell, a half-breed son of the late Robert Newell, circulated a petition addressed to the President of the United States which called for the removal of Monteith as Indian Agent at Lapwai. The first among the sixty-seven who signed was "Jacob, Head Chief." [27] Several of the signers were half-breeds. Lawyer was asked to sign but he refused to do so. The petition failed to accomplish its purpose.

There was so much dissatisfaction with Jacob by Monteith and the majority of the chiefs that he was deposed at a council held in the fall of 1874. But again the council could not agree as to who should have the office, so Lawyer was again asked by Monteith to continue as Head Chief for the time being. Another council was held on April 5, 1875, at which time, Reuben, a Christian, was elected. Reporting to Washington on April 30, Monteith stated: "I am sorry that Lawyer was defeated as Head Chief as the Indians said he was too old and wished for a younger man. Lawyer got 23 votes; Reuben, 58; Timothy Jr., 25; Felix 6." A total of 112 votes was cast.

Thus Lawyer's distinguished service of nearly twenty-five years as Head Chief of the Nez Perces came to an end. Even though his wife was a sister of Young Joseph, Reuben strongly disagreed with his brother-in-law. For the most part, Reuben followed Lawyer's policies. He believed that all of the non-treaty Indians, including Joseph's band, should move onto the Reservation.

---

27 Original in O.I.B.

Closing Years of Spalding's Life: His Death

Spalding was indefatigable in his old age in pursuing his evangelistic labors. During the summer of 1872, in his sixty-ninth year, Spalding made a horseback trip of several hundred miles in order to visit the Yakimas on their reservation. He took with him, to Monteith's great displeasure, some thirty of his Nez Perce followers, just at the time when the men should have been harvesting their crops. Spalding felt that a more important harvest was at hand.

Lawyer joined Spalding in some of his travels. Monteith, in his obituary of Lawyer, wrote that after Lawyer was defeated in the last election for Head Chief, "he spent most of his time visiting among the Indians, exhorting them to abandon their heathenism practices, and embrace the Christian religion."

Neither Spalding nor Cowley was satisfied with Geary's investigation and report of March 1872. Spalding decided to appeal to the Presbytery of Oregon for a reappraisal of the situation. He, therefore, traveled to Albany, Oregon, where he made a personal appeal before the November meeting of the Presbytery. As a result of his intercession, the Presbytery agreed to hold its May 1873 meeting at Lapwai in order to make a first-hand investigation.

The Presbytery met according to its promise at Lapwai on May 10 with eight members present, all of them ministers. Sensing the importance of presenting their cause to the Presbytery in as favorable a light as possible, both Spalding and Lawyer agreed that some dramatic display of the strength and vitality of the revival was timely. So it was decided to send a delegation of Christians from Kamiah to join those at Lapwai in order to impress the members of Presbytery with their numbers. The opening events of the Presbytery are described in the official minutes from which the following has been taken:

> With unfeigned thankfulness to the Great Head of the Church, we refer to the work of grace which is going on among the Nez Perces. Over 600 Indians have been gathered into the church, though many of these, it is asserted, give no satisfactory evidence of conversion. The greatest results have been attained at Kamia, and as Presbytery was unable to visit that field, it being 60 miles distant from Lapwai, a delegation of 200 rode over to greet us.

The clerk's description of the arrival of the Kamiah Indians, headed by Lawyer who, without a doubt, would have been carrying his prized flag, follows:

We shall not soon forget the effect produced on our minds as we met these brethren in Christ. As we approached them, their whole company joined in singing the missionary hymn, "From Greenland's icy mountains,"[28] after which ex-Chief Lawyer offered prayer in the Nez Perce tongue and was followed by prayer in English by our Moderator. The whole band then dismounted and a general hand shaking took place.

In the afternoon a conference was held, made intelligible to all by an interpreter. The whole congregation engaged with vigor in the singing, of which the natives appear to be very fond. The prayers were solemn and apparently very earnest, and all the exercises of this and other meetings, evinced a heartiness on the part of the converts which impressed us very favorably.

Three services were held on Sunday in the open air, no building on the Reservation being large enough to contain the company of worshippers. At all these services, the people were addressed through interpreters, by members of the Presbytery and at the last of them, the Lord's Supper was administered. We shall long remember our feelings as we stood in the light of the blazing campfire in the solemn stillness of that sabbath evening and together with our Indian brethren partook of that holy communion feast. [29]

According to Presbyterian polity, ordained elders assist the ministers in serving communion. Thus at this service, Lawyer, Timothy, and Jude would have taken part. It should be noted that in addition to the 200 visitors from Kamiah, more than that number of Nez Perce Christians living at Lapwai or in neighboring places would also have been present, so the combined number could well have been over 500.

The members of Presbytery were deeply impressed with all that they had seen and heard. A resolution was passed commending Spalding to the Presbyterian Board of Foreign Missions. Action was taken to divide the First Presbyterian Church of Oregon, founded at Waiilatpu on August 18, 1838, into two parishes, Lapwai and Kamiah. Spalding, Lawyer, and Ainslie were appointed a committee to formalize the organization of the Kamiah church according to Presbyterian polity. Monteith and Spalding composed their differences and each agreed to refrain in the future from mutual incriminations.

---

[28] This is one of the hymns which Spalding translated into Nez Perce during the mission period, 1836-47.   [29] Drury, *Tepee*, p. 93.

During the summer of 1873, before the meeting of the Presbytery, Spalding made a trip to the Spokane country, at Spokane Garry's request,[30] where his preaching met with spectacular success. He noted in the record book that during the summer, he baptized "among Spokanes, 112 males; females 141; and infants, 81," making a total of 334.[31]

On November 26, 1873, which was Spalding's seventieth birthday, he wrote in the church's record book, with evident pride: "Received males — 278; females 372 — 650 from the Nez Perces & infants 212. This brought the total Nez Perce baptisms to 862. These totals must have included some of the baptisms performed by Cowley at Kamiah. When the Spokane totals are added to those of the Nez Perces, the grand total is increased to 1,194. The statistics listed in the *Minutes of the Presbyterian General Assembly* for 1876, about two years after Spalding had died, show that the number of native church members at Kamiah, Lapwai, and among the Spokanes was 1,054.[32]

Spalding received an injury while cutting wood at his home in Kamiah in November 1873. His health declined during the following winter and spring. Sometime during the week following July 4, 1874, Cowley visited Spalding at Kamiah and found his old friend very weak. It was then decided that he should be moved to Lapwai where he could be placed under the care of the Agency's physician, Dr. George Alexander. Spalding was taken to Lapwai lying on a cot which had been placed in the bed of a farm wagon. There he was given a room in one

---

[30] Garry wrote to Spalding, March 27, 1873, inviting him to visit the Spokanes and "baptize and marry" his people. Original in Washington State Univ., Pullman.

[31] During the summer of 1949, while visiting some of the Spokane Indians, I met Levi, then 97 years old, who said that he was baptized by Spalding during the summer of 1873 at a spring near present-day Cheney, Washington. He may have been the last living Spokane convert who had been baptized by Spalding.

[32] Presbyterian membership among the Nez Perces is now at a low ebb due in part to the fact that there were in July 1977 only 1,714 Nez Perces living on the Reservation, with 33% of the total enrollment of 2,583 living off the Reservation. Those on the Tribal Rolls include all who have at least one-fourth tribal blood. These figures do not include Nez Perces living on the Colville Reservation. Information by kindness of Robert L. Morris, Superintendent of the Nez Perce National Park. This means that the tribe today numbers a little more than one-half of what it was in Spalding's day. The Nez Perce Presbyterian Churches reflect the problems of modern conditions which adversely affect the membership of Presbyterian churches throughout the nation.

of the Government houses. Miss Sue McBeth, who had arrived as a Presbyterian missionary at Lapwai the previous autumn, assisted Mrs. Spalding in ministering to the needs of the dying man.

The two women were at his bedside when the end came on August 3. No detailed account of the Spalding funeral has been found. Since Spalding often had congregations numbering into the hundreds at Lapwai, we can well believe that the funeral service would have drawn far more people than ever could have been accommodated in the treaty church. Perhaps the service was held on the council grounds just to the west of the original Spalding cabin. Surely such chiefs as Timothy, Jason, and Lawyer would have been present. The Rev. George Ainslie, the resident Presbyterian missionary, would have been in charge of the service. They laid his body in a grove of locust trees,[33] a few hundred yards south of the old Spalding home, where it still lies. The remains of Eliza Spalding were moved from Brownsville, Oregon in 1913 and placed beside those of her husband. In the summer of 1925, the Presbyterian Synod of Washington erected an imposing monument over the two graves.

Thus ended the career of one of the most colorful and controversial characters ever to move across the pages of the history of the Pacific Northwest. No missionary of any branch of the Protestant church which sent workers into the Old Oregon country was as effective in his endeavors to civilize and Christianize the natives as was Henry Harmon Spalding.

Spalding's obituary, which appeared in the August 22, 1874, issue of the *Portland Oregonian*, included the following appraisal: "He has been a noble, self-sacrificing, faithful laborer for the elevation of the Indians. . . Perhaps it is to his influence more than to any other single cause, that the Nez Perces are indebted for the distinction they enjoy of being regarded as the most intelligent, and the least savage of all our Indian tribes."

LAWYER CONFRONTS THE NON-TREATY CHIEFS

Trouble began brewing in the Wallowa Valley early in 1871. White settlers began moving into the valley, which Young Joseph claimed for

---

[33] Both Whitman and Spalding took seeds of the locust tree from their homes in New York State to Oregon and planted them on their respective mission sites. This tree is not native to the Northwest. Locust trees are still growing on the mission sites at Waiilatpu and Lapwai.

his band. Tensions grew as the Government laid increasing pressure on the Indians to move onto the 1863 Reservation. In his report to Washington, dated November 22, 1873, Monteith told of the meeting of the Nez Perce Council held at Lapwai beginning November 3.

"Many of the Non Treaties were present," wrote Monteith, "including Tip-Con-a-pune [34] (Eagle-from-the-Light) and the two sons of Old Joseph (Young Joseph and Ollokot) who claim the Wallowa Valley." Here at this Council, these three non-Treaty chiefs met Lawyer, head of the Treaty party, in open confrontation.

Monteith's report to Washington is revealing as it highlights the fundamental positions taken by the two parties within the Nez Perce nation. He wrote:

The controversialists were very bitter in their remarks towards Lawyer and other Treaty chiefs, accusing them of selling their country to the Whites and bringing all kinds of trouble among them. Eagle-from-the-Light said he had never made any treaty and never would, that he lived on the Salmon River in his own country, that the trails over the mountains and across the country were made by his forefathers, that he traveled them, and would travel them again.   .   .

Lawyer and other Treaty Chiefs replied to him. Lawyer [pointing to Eagle-from-the-Light] said: "You are responsible for the Cayuse War in 1856 and also the war with the Yakimas and that you are always trying to make trouble and had it not been for me [i.e. Lawyer], our people would have been swept from this country by the Whites; that by making the treaties of 1855 and 1863, we have secured to us this Reservation; the Government has built us churches, schoolhouses, mills, and shops and are rendering us great assistance for which I am very thankful and that you (Eagle-from-the-Light) ought to be thankful for these benefits and not try to make any more trouble."

Monteith then summarized the continued discussion:

Lawyer said he could see that the law from Washington was for their benefit and would recommend that all his brothers obey the same. The Government was their friend. Jacob (Head Chief) agreed with Lawyer and told the non-Treaties to abandon their roaming habits and drumming religion and settle down as the rest were doing. Eagle-from-the-Light said: "I have heard the law, but

[34] Josephy, *Nez Perces*, p. 323, spells the name Tipyahlanah Ka-oo-pu.

my law does not come from Washington but from the earth. The earth tells me what to do and I keep it. I will go where I please. . ." 35

After the Council had adjourned, Joseph approached Monteith and said that he would like to go to Washington "to visit the Great Chief." At first Monteith thought that he spoke in jest but when Joseph repeated the request, Monteith decided to write to Washington and recommend that this be done. Monteith also suggested in his letter that Joseph be joined by Head Chief Jacob, two other non-Treaty chiefs, and two Treaty chiefs. Unfortunately, the Government failed to act on this recommendation.

The last known letter that Lawyer wrote is dated January 11, 1874. It was forwarded to Washington by Monteith. Following his confrontation with Joseph and Eagle-from-the-Light during the preceding November, Lawyer sadly realized that an armed conflict between the non-Treaty Indians and Government forces was almost inevitable. The stage was being set for the uprising which came about a year and a half after Lawyer had died. He would never have consented to such a rebellion. Lawyer wrote:

> I, the Lawyer, do not forget what I heard in Washington & New York City. I, the Lawyer, with my children have repented of my sins and pray. I say to you, my Seniors . . . if trouble should arise with the Indians [i.e., with the non-treaty], do not think my children are in it. Do not class them with the bad Indians. This much, I say to you. I, the Lawyer.36

When Lawyer used the term, "children," he was not referring to his immediate family but rather to all of his followers. The treaty Indians were his children. When the 1877 rebellion broke out, Lawyer's prophecy came true. The uprising divided the tribe more sharply than ever before between the Christian and the non-Christian. Joseph's band and the other non-treaty bands seemed to have been entirely untouched by the Spalding revival. Kate McBeth, in her *The Nez Perces Since Lewis and Clark*, wrote that there were no Christians in the uprising and that not many followed Joseph from either the Kamiah or Lapwai communities, "although great efforts had been made to get the peace-loving Nez Perces to join them." 37 Monteith, in his report of the upris-

35 O.I.B.   36 O.I.B.   37 *Op. cit.*, p. 95.

ing to the Commissioner of Indian Affairs, gave the same testimony.

J. F. Santee, writing in 1934 for the *Washington Historical Quarterly*, asked the question: "What is the greatest name on the roster of Nez Perce chiefs?" Then answering his own question, Santee wrote: "Some would say Young Joseph, but Joseph rashly began a war which was foredoomed to failure and which brought only misery in its train." As has been stated in a previous chapter, Joseph did not actually begin hostilities. He had reluctantly bowed to the adamant demands of the Government to move onto the Reservation when some of his hot-headed young warriors precipitated the uprising by killing some white settlers in White Bird Canyon in June 1877. Joseph was then drawn into the conflict, reluctantly.

Santee, in contrasting Joseph with Lawyer, wrote: "Lawyer was wiser. He followed the way of peace, patiently assisting the induction of his people into the white man's cultural heritage." [38] Herein lies Lawyer's greatest contribution to his people. He believed that peaceful cooperation with the Government was better than resorting to war.

DEATH OF LAWYER

Chief Hol-lol-sote-tote, better known as Lawyer, died at his home in Kamiah on Monday, January 3, 1876. According to Monteith, Lawyer was eighty years old when he died.

In 1962, when Dr. and Mrs. Gordon D. Alcorn, now of Tacoma, Washington, were visiting some Nez Perce friends at Stites, Idaho, they were given the following account of the death of Lawyer by Harry Wheeler, an elder in the Indian Presbyterian Church of Ahsahka, Idaho. It was Lawyer's custom to fly his American flag [39] from a pole in front of his lodge or house. On the day that he died, knowing that his end was near, he instructed some member to gradually pull down the flag. The flag would be lowered a bit and then Lawyer, after a time, would say: "Pull it down a little more." So the flag was lowered a little more. This was repeated several times and when the flag touched the ground, Lawyer died.

The funeral service was conducted by the Rev. Warren Norton, a Presbyterian missionary who had but shortly before arrived at Kamiah.

---

[38] *Washington Hist. Qtly.*, Vol. xxv (1934), pp. 48 ff.

[39] *See* illustration showing Corbett Lawyer, a grandson, holding his grandfather's flag. This has 34 stars which indicates that it was not the flag given to him in 1848 but rather one presented at the time of the 1863 Council.

Just where the service was held is not known, probably in one of their long communal lodges. Cowley mentions holding a service in such a lodge when 300 were crowded in. Norton made the following notation on a page of the church's record book under the heading of "Deaths:"[40]

Chief Lawyer, the noblest man
in the Nez Perce tribe, died Jan. 6, 1876
He was an old man and ripe for glory.

Monteith in his obituary stated that Lawyer died on January 7. Thus we have three different dates given for Lawyer's death — the 3rd on the tombstone, the 6th in the record book, and the 7th in Monteith's account. The difference probably lies in the fact that both Norton and Monteith were referring to the date of burial and Monteith, who wrote his obituary several days, perhaps several weeks, after the funeral could easily have been mistaken regarding the date of the funeral by one day.

An interval of three days between Lawyer's death and the funeral would have given time for Timothy, Monteith and others in their vicinities to travel to Kamiah. It is easy to believe that among those who gave tributes to Lawyer's eventful life were such men as Timothy and Monteith.

Lawyer's modest granite tombstone which stands in the cemetery adjacent to the First Presbyterian Church of Kamiah bears the following inscription:

CHIEF LAWYER

Died January 3, 1876, about 74 yrs. of age. In 1855 & 1863, he was present at the Gov. treaties at Walla Walla, rep. the Nez Perce Indians and was elected Spokesman for the Indians residing on the reservation. He was the first elder of the Presby. Church at Kamiah. He made two trips to Wash. D.C. This monument was erected by his direct descendants.[41]

Lawyer's eighty years stretched from the time before Lewis and Clark arrived in 1805 to the eve of the Chief Joseph uprising in 1877. The story of the people he knew and the events in which he took a leading part give us a panoramic view of the first seventy-five years of

---

40 Original record book in the Presbyterian Hist. Soc., Philadelphia.

41 The lettering on the monument has been so eroded that the inscription is difficult to read.

the history, not only of the Nez Perce nation, but also of the whole Pacific Northwest.

Lawyer was well qualified to serve, as he did, as Head Chief of the Nez Perce nation for about twenty-five years. He spoke two Indian languages, the Flathead and the Nez Perce, and had a fair command of English. He was the best educated Nez Perce of his generation, being able to read and write his native tongue. Wiser than most of his contemporaries, Lawyer realized that the white man with his superior skills, material resources, and overwhelming numbers was destined to rule over all of the Indian tribes of the Northwest. For him, armed resistance was folly. Lawyer consistently and continuously advocated cooperation with the Government. He laid great emphasis on obeying the law. During his chieftainship, Lawyer led in the negotiations with the Government of two major treaties, 1855 and 1863, and two of lesser importance, 1861 and 1868.

Because of his qualifications and his achievements, Lawyer towered above all of his Nez Perce contemporaries.

What an array of names, famous in the history of the Old Oregon country, dot the pages of this biography. As the son of Chief Twisted Hair, Lawyer as a boy remembered Lewis and Clark. Others whose life paths crossed his included Benjamin L. E. Bonneville, Jim Bridger, Robert Newell, William Craig, and Joe Meek. He welcomed the first Protestant missionaries who arrived in Oregon — Jason Lee, Samuel Parker, Marcus and Narcissa Whitman, Henry and Eliza Spalding, the Walkers, the Eells, and the Smiths. He met Father Pierre DeSmet, the pioneer Catholic missionary to the Northwest. And he knew the latest company of Presbyterian missionaries, the Cowleys, Sue McBeth, and George Ainslie.

He was a welcomed guest in the homes of some of the most distinguished residents of the lower Columbia River country — Dr. John McLoughlin, Governor George Abernethy, Governor Joseph Lane, and the U.S. Army officers at Fort Vancouver. He knew Dr. Elijah White, Governor Isaac I. Stevens, General Joel Palmer, Lawrence Kip, Colonels Cornelius Gilliam, E. J. Steptoe, and George Wright. He knew Governor Caleb Lyon, Perrin B. Whitman, Frances E. Fuller, the historian, and all of the Indian Agents at Lapwai up to 1876, including especially John B. Monteith. While in Washington, D.C., in the summer of 1868, he met General U.S. Grant, later to become President and other high Government officials.

Lawyer knew all of the important chiefs of the Nez Perce tribe active during his lifetime including Ellis, Timothy, Jason, Old and Young Joseph, Old and Young Looking Glass, Big Thunder, White Bird, Eagle-from-the-Light, Speaking Eagle, Jacob, Reuben, and Ute-sin-male-cum. He knew also the leading chiefs of his generation from neighboring tribes — Spokane Garry, Kam-i-ah-kan, Owhi, Qualchen, Peu-peu-mox-mox, Young Chief, and the Yakima chiefs, Thomas Stevier and George Waters.

In this biography of Lawyer's life, we can read the catalog of "Who was Who," both among the Whites and the Indians, during the mid-fifty years of the last century in the Old Oregon country.

When the Rev. Warren Norton, a comparative newcomer to the Nez Perces, recorded the passing of Lawyer in the original record book of the First Presbyterian Church of Oregon, he reflected the common sentiment of that day when he wrote: "Chief Lawyer, the noblest man in the Nez Perce tribe."

APPENDIX

Monteith's Obituary of Lawyer

The most revealing contemporary account of the life of Chief Lawyer was written by John B. Monteith, Indian Agent at Lapwai, 1871-78. Since Lawyer died on January 3, 1876, this means that Monteith's services at Lapwai overlapped the last five years of Lawyer's life. During these years, Monteith became well acquainted with Lawyer and was able to gather facts about his life not found elsewhere.

A typewritten copy of Monteith's obituary of Lawyer was located in the archives in the Smithsonian Institution, Washington, D.C., with the notation that the original had been sent to the editor of the Portland *Oregonian*. At my request, the Rev. E. Paul Hovey, made search of the files of the *Oregonian* in the Oregon Historical Society and found that it had appeared in the February 6, 1876, issue of that paper. The obituary is of such importance that it is here given *en toto*.

LAWYER, THE NEZ PERCE HEAD CHIEF

To the Readers of the Oregonian:

Thinking it may be of interest to some of your readers at this time, I give some of the incidents connected with the life of Lawyer, or La-La-Chol-Sote (the meaning of which is, "The bat that flies in the day time,") late head chief of the Nez Perce tribe of Indians, who died on the 7th inst. at the age of eighty years.

Lawyer was the son of an Indian of some prominence living on the south fork of the Clearwater river, and is the last of the tribe who remembers Lewis and Clark and their journey through this section of the country.[1] At the time he must have been eight or nine years old,

---

[1] Monteith overlooked Timothy whose dates on his monument in Beachview Park, Clarkston, Wash., are 1800-1891. Timothy may have been too young when Lewis and Clark passed through the Nez Perce country to have remembered them, whereas Lawyer did.

and the impression made upon his mind remained until the day of his death.

When a young man, Lawyer spent much of his time among the Flat Head Indians, and while in that country became acquainted with many of the traders of the American Fur Company, and trappers, and was frequently employed by them to assist in trapping and trading with other tribes of Indians. Owing to his shrewdness, he received from them the name of Lawyer. Lawyer continued to spend most of his time East of the mountains until 1836 when Mr. Spalding came among this people as a missionary. When Mr. Spalding opened his school, Lawyer was among the first to give assistance, and attended himself, learning to read and write the Nez Perce language, and in fact, was the only one who could do so with any degree of correctness.

Up to 1840, the Nez Perces were divided into thirty or forty bands,[2] living along the Snake and Clearwater Rivers and their tributaries, each band having its chief and head man. But there was no head chief recognized as such by the whole tribe.

When excursions were made to the buffalo country, representatives would come together from the different bands and before starting, would select a leader, and the party so selected would, generally, remain in that capacity until their return. Lawyer was generally the selected one,[3] when he accompanied the parties, whether for the purpose of making war on some adjoining tribe or hunting.

In 1840, Dr. White was sent out as agent for all the tribes living in what was Oregon Territory at that time. He made a visit to this tribe and called them together in council. He found them without a recognized head chief and appointed an Indian named Ellis as such and gave the Indians a code of laws to be governed by. Ellis, with an Indian from the Cayuse and two from the Spokane tribe, had been taken by a party of Hudson Bay traders to the Selkirk settlement [4] and placed in school, where they remained about five years, and when Ellis re-

---

[2] According to other estimates, there were between forty and fifty bands.

[3] Here is evidence that Lawyer, years before the Whites recognized him as Head Chief, was being accepted by his people in a leadership role.

[4] The Selkirk Settlement was at Red River, at the present-day site of Winnipeg, Canada. Here the Anglicans had established a mission school for the education of Indian youth. See Drury, M. & N.W., Vol. I, pp. 30 ff. for a detailed account of the seven Oregon Indians sent by the Hudson's Bay Company to this school.

turned, he could read and write.[5] For this reason he was selected as head chief by Dr. White.

Ellis remained chief for a short time only, when he became restless, and the Indians not liking the new order of things, he left with a party for the buffalo country, where he spent most of his time and died there in 1847. In 1847, the Cayuse Indians murdered Dr. Whitman and wife. The Nez Perces took no part in this lamentable affair, but held some of their young men back from joining the Cayuses. They assisted Mr. Spalding, the missionary at Lapwai, in getting out of this country, sending a guard to protect him and his family in reaching the boat, sent by the Hudson Bay Company to Wallua [i.e., Fort Walla Walla] to take all of the whites out of the country. They also rescued some of the women and children taken prisoners by the Cayuses.

Among those who attended Mr. Spalding's school with Lawyer was Old Joseph. He made a profession of religion and had his eldest son, now the leader of the Wallowa band of Indians, and daughter baptized.[6] None of Old Joseph's children attended school, except his daughter, who lived in Mr. Spalding's family a number of years. She is now the wife of Tip-u-lai-lu [Reuben], an Indian farmer at Kamiah. Neither of his sons ever learned to read or write.[7]

From the date of the death of Ellis up till 1855, there was no head chief among these Indians.[8] In 1855 Gov. Stevens and Hon. Joel Palmer were commissioned by the Government to make a treaty with this tribe.

---

[5] Ellis was nineteen or twenty years old when he entered the school, the eldest of the group sent. He stayed at least four years at the school.

[6] *Minutes of the Presbyterian Synod of Washington,* 1936, contain a copy of the records of the First Presbyterian Church of Oregon. The records show (p. 307), that Spalding baptized on Nov. 24, 1839, the following children of Old Joseph and his wife: Mary, "about eleven years old"; Abigail, "about 7"; Hannah, "about 5"; Manassa, "son . . . about 2." On April 12, 1840, Spalding baptized "Ephriam, son of Joseph & Aseneth," who is believed to have been Young Joseph. What happened to the older son is not known.

[7] Old Joseph and his wife had three other children born after Young Joseph. One was Ollokot, who played a leading role in the uprising of 1877. He was killed at Bear Paw Mountain. Young Joseph did not speak English.

[8] Monteith overlooked the fact that American officials who were trying to apprehend the Whitman murderers in the spring of 1848 appointed Richard to service as Head Chief. He was ineffective and, as has been noted, the Government officials turned to Lawyer even though there is no record of any Nez Perce Council being held before 1855 to elect him to this office.

Finding no head chief, Gov. Stevens appointed Lawyer as such, giving him a commission (I saw this commission about a year ago),[9] signed by him as Superintendent of Indian Affairs. The treaty of 1855 was made; Lawyer signing it as head chief, Old Joseph and Looking Glass being the first to recognize him, signed next to him; then all the chiefs and head men signed the treaty, excepting Eagle-from-the-Light and Big Thunder,[10] as will be seen by consulting the United States statutes of 1855 and 1856.

There was no division among these Indians until the discovery of the mines on Salmon River,[11] which drew many whites there, a portion of the tribe objected to the miners crossing the reservation. E. R. Geary, D.D., the Superintendent of Indian Affairs, visited the tribe and held a council with the Indians, the result being an agreement made by which the miners were permitted to cross the reservation en route for the mines. Lawyer again leading the Indians and by his influence induced them to sign the agreement.[12]

The real cause of the division of the tribe into treaty and anti-treaty was the treaty of 1863. Lawyer and the prominent chiefs were in favor of making this treaty. Big Thunder, Eagle-from-the-light, and Old Joseph opposed the same. Big Thunder and Old Joseph then tried to break up the convention, and it was Lawyer's influence over the leading men of the tribe that accomplished the end sought, i.e., making the treaty of 1863. All the prominent chiefs signed said treaty, including the head men under Big Thunder, Eagle-from-the-Light, Old Joseph, and Looking Glass. The object of the 1863 treaty was to contract the boundaries of the reserve on the south and east so as to throw out of the reserve that section that was supposed to be rich in mineral wealth.

[9] According to the wording of the commission (see illustration), Stevens did not appoint Lawyer to be Head Chief but rather "recognized" a status already existing.

[10] Monteith was mistaken for both of these chiefs were present at the 1855 Council and both signed the Treaty. Evidently Monteith failed to recognize the way the secretary at this Council spelled their names. The tenth to sign after Lawyer was "Tippelanecbuposh" or Eagle-from-the-Light. The forty-second to sign after Lawyer was Big Thunder, also known as Old James. His name was spelled "In-mat-tute-kah-ky." Josephy, in the index of his Nez Perces, spelled their names "Tipyahlanah" and "Hin-mah-tute-ke-kaikt."

[11] Another error. Elias D. Pierce is reported to have discovered gold in 1860 near Orofino within the eastern boundary of the Reservation.

[12] See account of Geary's visit to Lapwai in April 1861 in Chap. vii. Check index.

Lawyer made a profession of religion in 1871, and ever after maintained a consistent Christian character.[13] He was an elder in the Presbyterian Church at Kamiah, and manifested a deep interest in the progress of religion among his people.

The Wallowa Valley was held in common by all the Indians of this tribe as a fishing and hunting ground, and for many years after the treaty of 1863, no one of the chiefs claimed it over another. The first dispute in regard to the valley took place about in 1871, at which time white settlers began to move into said valley, and Young Joseph laid claim to it. The spring of 1873, Supt. Odeneal [14] was sent here to have a talk with Young Joseph and his people. The council was held in the school house at Lapwai.

Joseph's complaints were heard and a report made and forwarded to the Commissioner of Indian Affairs. The executive order reserving the valley to the Indians was based on said report.[15] I united with Supt. Odeneal in the recommendations contained in the report in question. Last year [i.e., in 1875] the order was rescinded and the valley opened to settlement. Upon receipt of the order, I sent for Young Joseph and imparted to him the contents of the order. He was very angry and abused Lawyer and all the chiefs who made treaties with the government.

Old Joseph was half brother of Five Crows, chief of the Cayuses, and his wife — mother of Young Joseph — was a woman from the lower Snake river, and part Cayuse. The Nez Perces often tell Young Joseph to go home, to his own country, meaning the Umatilla Reserve.

Looking Glass was not a chief, but a "Tewat" or medicine man, and by his jugglery performances made the Indians believe that he could cause their death by merely wishing it, hence the Indians on the Ashotin [16] where he lived made him their chief.

---

[13] *See* Kip's account of Lawyer holding devotional services in his lodge, according to Christian practices, at the 1855 Council. Check index. Lawyer was known to be a Christian long before he was baptized by Spalding in November 1871.

[14] T. B. Odeneal, Superintendent of Indian Affairs in Oregon, met Young Joseph and other chiefs at Lapwai in March 1873, at which time Odeneal became convinced that Joseph had a legal right to keep the Wallowa Valley and so recommended to Washington.

[15] A Presidential order, designed to prevent further settlement by Whites in the Wallowa Valley, was signed April 30, 1873. Josephy, *The Nez Perces*, p. 456.

[16] Present-day Asotin, Washington.

In the fall of 1872, the Indians held an election for head chief and Lawyer was defeated by one Jacob who lives on the Lapwai. Jacob held said position until 1874 when at the general election, Lawyer was again elected, and filled the position until April 1875, when an election was held and Reuben was elected.

Reuben, or Tip-u-lai-lu, is a brother-in-law of Young Joseph, and one of the best farmers on the reservation. He does not sympathize with Young Joseph.

After his defeat, Lawyer moved back to Kamiah, where he spent most of his time in visiting among the Indians, exhorting them to abandon their heathenish practices, and embrace the Christian religion.

The above facts I have received from the Indians. Messrs [Perrin] Whitman and Spalding and the records of the office.

Jno. B. Monteith
u.s. Indian Agent

Bibliography

See also "Sources and Abbreviations" at the beginning of this book. Bibliographic data about books not mentioned more than twice are given in footnotes with the author's name listed in the index. The following titles have been cited several times:

Annual Reports, Commissioner of Indian Affairs. Government Printing Office, Washington, D.C.

Bancroft, Hubert H. *History of Oregon.* 2 vols., San Francisco, 1886-8

Carey, Charles H. *A General History of Oregon.* 2 vols., Portland, Or., 1935-6

Fuller, George W. *A History of the Pacific Northwest,* N.Y., 1931

Gray, William Henry. *A History of Oregon.* Portland, Or., 1870

Josephy, Alvin M., Jr. *The Nez Perce Indians and the Opening of the Northwest.* New York, 1965

Kip, Lawrence. *Army Life on the Pacific.* New York, 1869

———. *The Indian Council in the Valley of the Walla Walla.* Tarryton, N.Y., 1915

McBeth, Kate C. *The Nez Perces since Lewis and Clark.* N.Y., 1908

McWhorter, Lucullus V. *Hear Me, My Chiefs.* Caldwell, Id., 1952

Ruby, Robert H. and Brown, John A. *The Cayuse Indians.* Norman, Ok., 1972

Slickpoo, Allen P., Sr., and Walker, Deward E., Jr. *Noon Nee-Me-Poo (We, the Nez Perces).* Boulder, Co., 1974

Splawn, Andrew Jackson. *Kam-mi-akin, the Last of the Yakimas.* Portland, Or., c. 1917

Stevens, Hazard. *The Life of Isaac Ingalls Stevens.* 2 vols., Boston, 1901

Synod of Washington Minutes, (Presbyterian). Seattle, 1903, reprinted in 1936, with "Records of the First Presbyterian Church, Territory of Oregon"

Thompson, Erwin N. *Historic Resource Study, Spalding Area.* National Park Service, U.S. Dept. of Interior, 1972

Victor, Frances Fuller. *Early Indians Wars of Oregon.* Salem, Or., 1894

Index

In addition to the abbreviations listed on p. 13, the following also are used in this index: ff. — and following; fn. — footnote; Ind. — Indian or Indians; illus. — illustration; N.P. — Nez Perce; Pby. — Presbyterian or Presbytery; Lap. — Lapwai; W.W. — Walla Walla.